W9-BOM-122

another DIRT sandwich

Some Rambling and Hilarious
Explots of Tbyrd Fearlessness

by
ray friesen

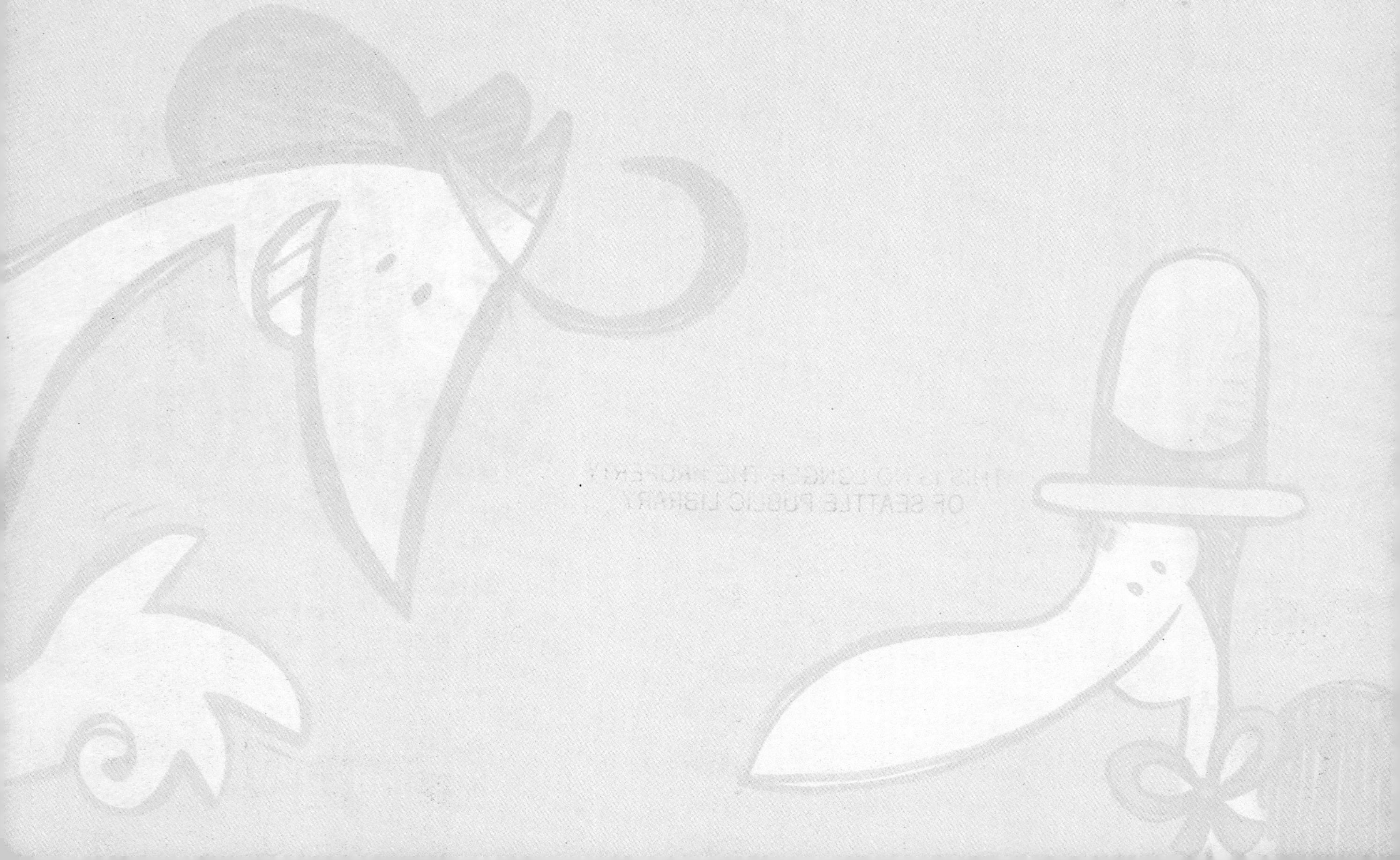

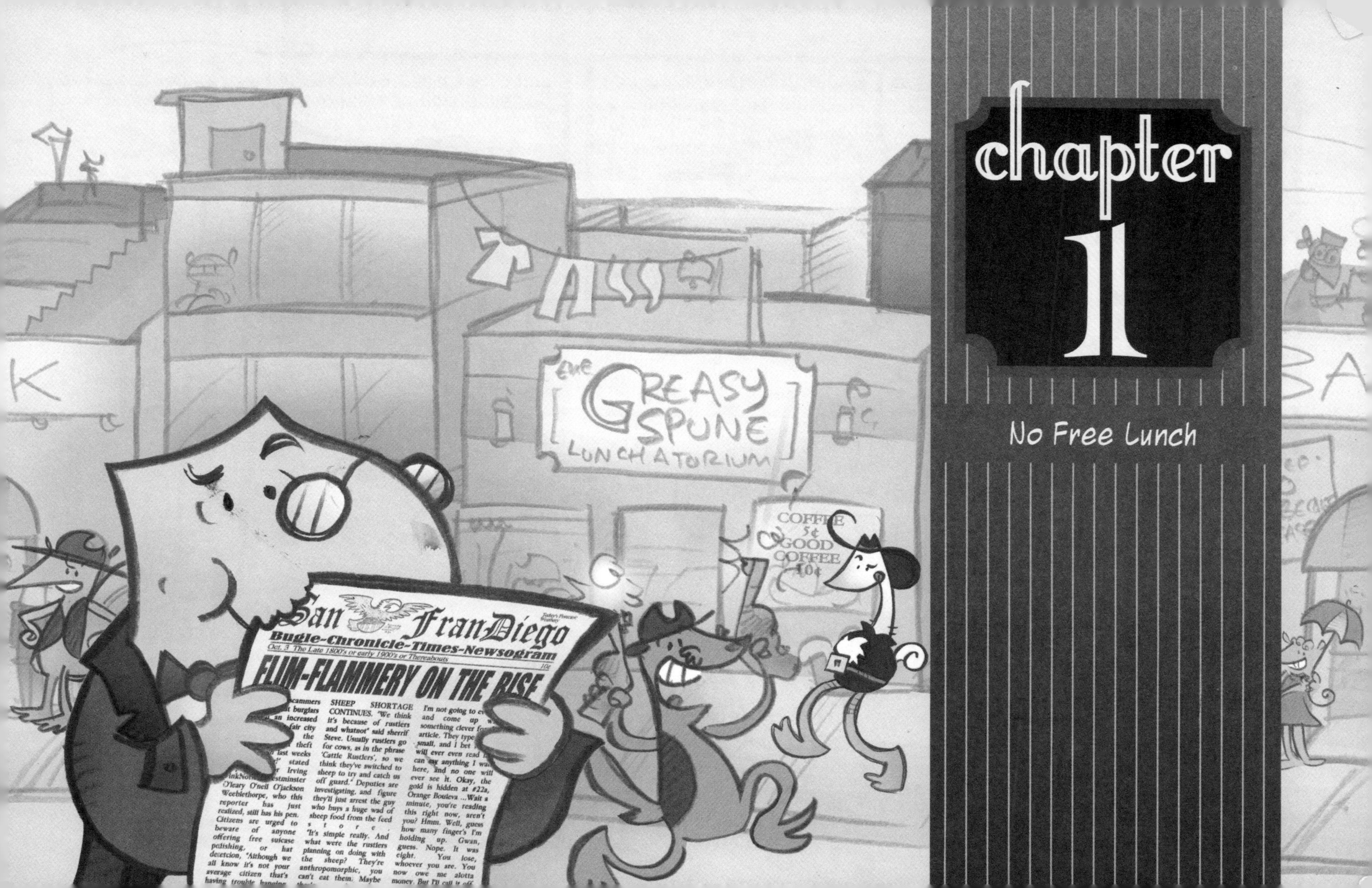
THE GREASY SPUNE
LUNCHATORIUM
COFFEE 5¢
GOOD COFFEE 10¢
San FranDiego
Bugle-Chronicle-Times-Newsogram
Oct. 3 The Late 1800's or early 1900's or Thereabouts
10¢
FLIM-FLAMMERY ON THE RISE
O'leary O'neil O'jackson Weeblethorpe, who this reporter has just realized, still has his pen. Citizens are urged to beware of anyone offering free suicase polishing, or hat detection, "Although we all know it's not your average citizen that's having trouble hanging
SHEEP SHORTAGE CONTINUES. "We think it's because of rustlers and whatnot" said sherrif Steve. Usually rustlers go for cows, as in the phrase 'Cattle Rustlers', so we think they've switched to sheep to try and catch us off guard." Deputies are investigating, and figure they'll just arrest the guy who buys a huge wad of sheep food from the feed store. "It's simple really. And what were the rustlers planning on doing with the sheep? They're anthropomorphic, you can't eat them. Maybe
here, and no one will ever see it. Okay, the gold is hidden at #22a, Orange Bouleva ...Wait a minute, you're reading this right now, aren't you? Hmm. Well, guess how many finger's I'm holding up. Gwan, guess. Nope. It was eight. You lose, whoever you are. You now owe me alotta money. But I'll call it off

chapter 1

No Free Lunch

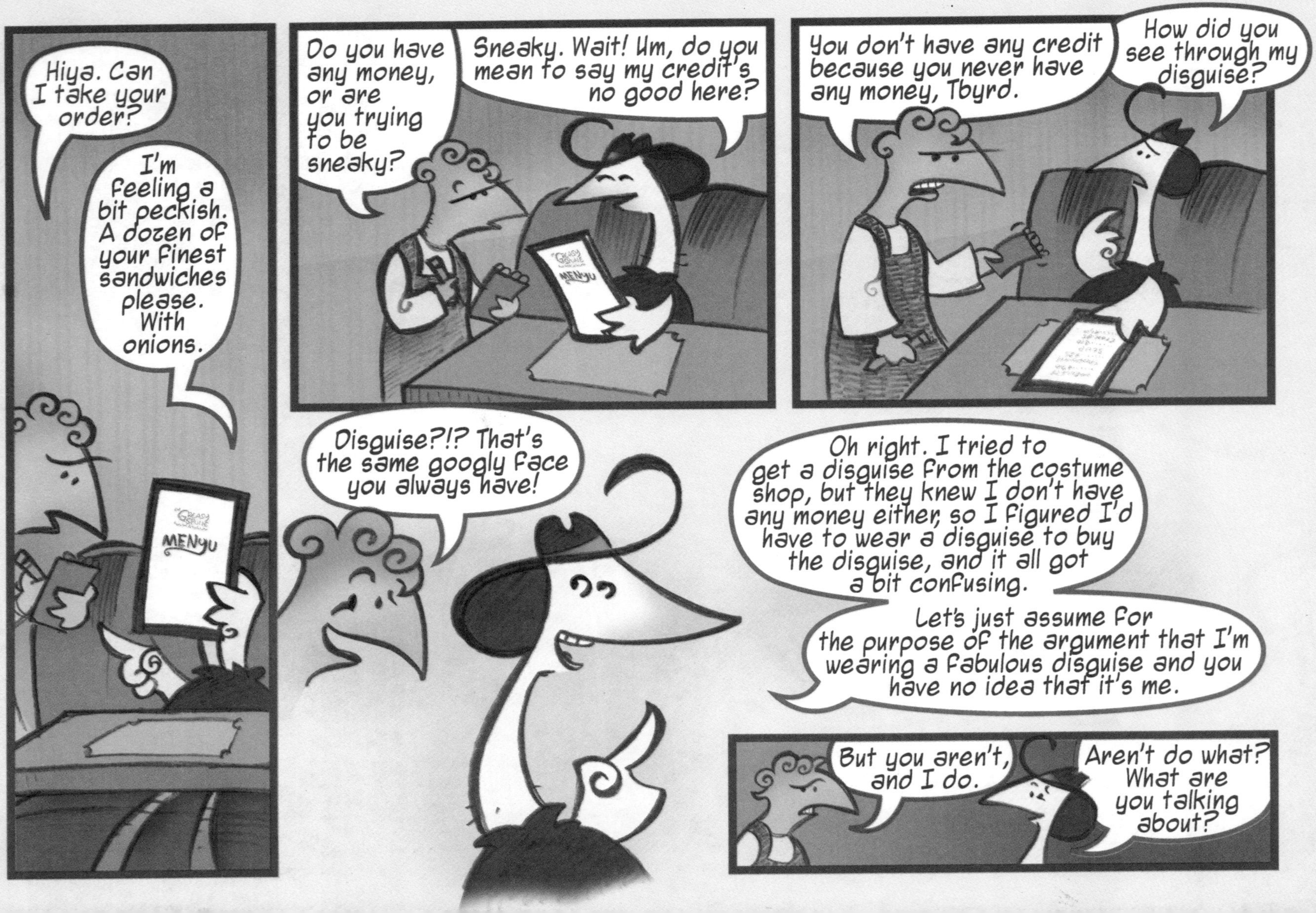

Hiya. Can I take your order?
I'm feeling a bit peckish. A dozen of your finest sandwiches please. With onions.
MENYU
Do you have any money, or are you trying to be sneaky?
Sneaky. Wait! Um, do you mean to say my credit's no good here?
MENYU
You don't have any credit because you never have any money, Tbyrd.
How did you see through my disguise?
Disguise?!? That's the same googly face you always have!
Oh right. I tried to get a disguise from the costume shop, but they knew I don't have any money either, so I figured I'd have to wear a disguise to buy the disguise, and it all got a bit confusing.
Let's just assume for the purpose of the argument that I'm wearing a fabulous disguise and you have no idea that it's me.
But you aren't, and I do.
Aren't do what? What are you talking about?

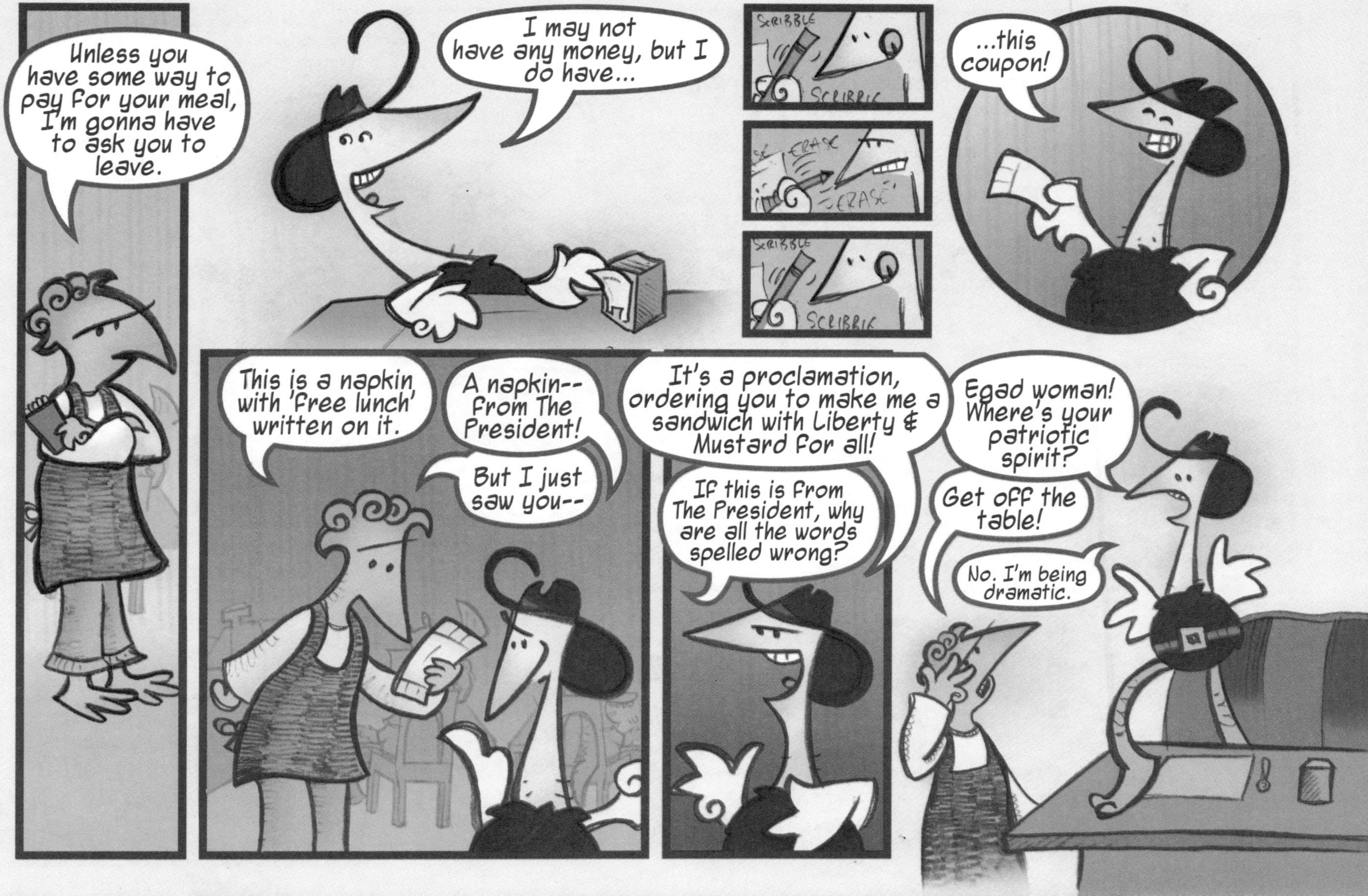
Unless you have some way to pay for your meal, I'm gonna have to ask you to leave.
I may not have any money, but I do have...
SCRIBBLE
ERASE
ERASE
SCRIBBLE
...this coupon!
This is a napkin with 'free lunch' written on it.
A napkin--from The President!
But I just saw you--
It's a proclamation, ordering you to make me a sandwich with Liberty & Mustard for all!
If this is from The President, why are all the words spelled wrong?
Egad woman! Where's your patriotic spirit?
Get off the table!
No. I'm being dramatic.

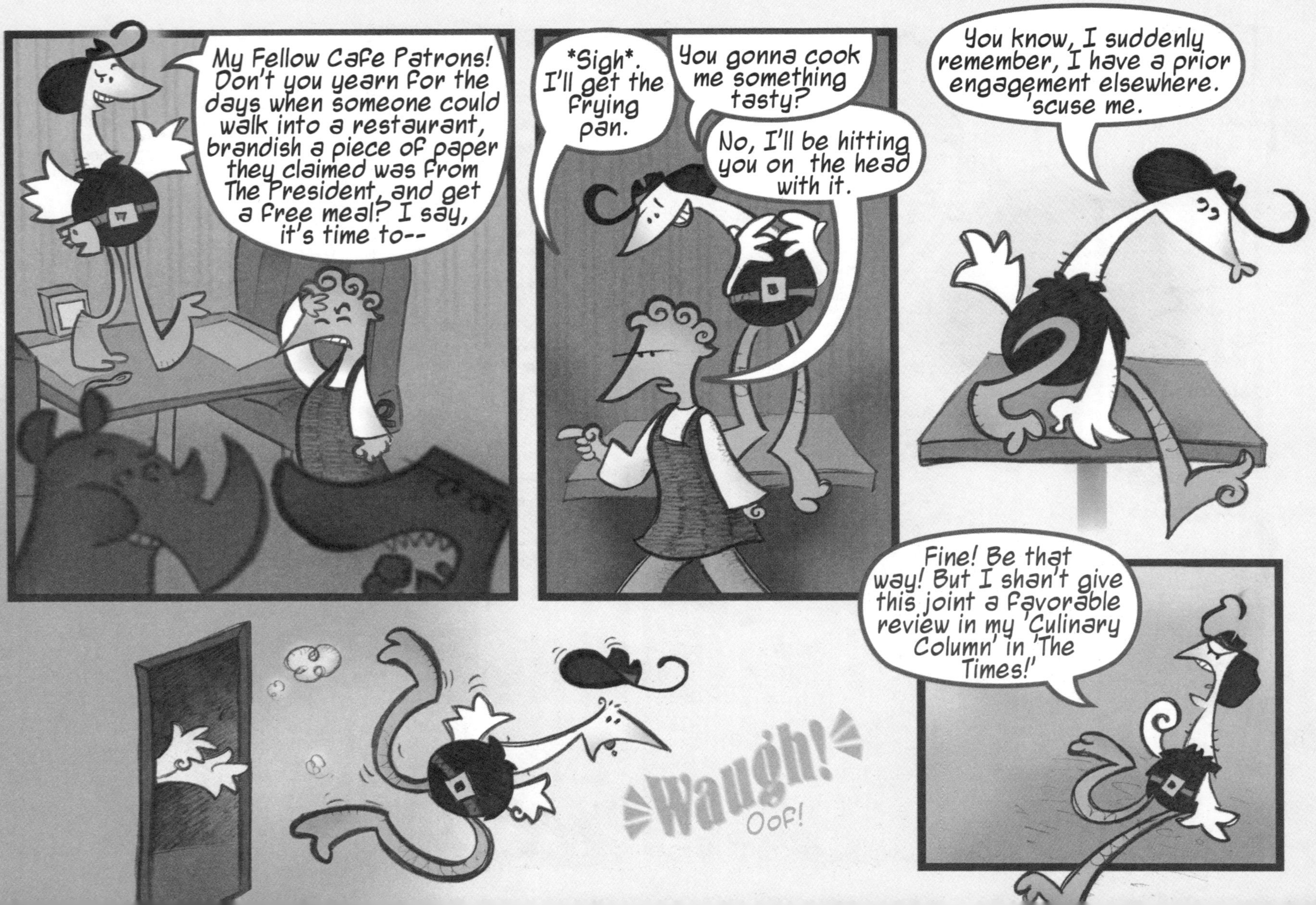

My Fellow Cafe Patrons! Don't you yearn for the days when someone could walk into a restaurant, brandish a piece of paper they claimed was from The President, and get a free meal? I say, it's time to--
Sigh. I'll get the frying pan.
You gonna cook me something tasty?
No, I'll be hitting you on the head with it.
You know, I suddenly remember, I have a prior engagement elsewhere. 'scuse me.
Waugh!
Oof!
Fine! Be that way! But I shan't give this joint a favorable review in my 'Culinary Column' in 'The Times!'

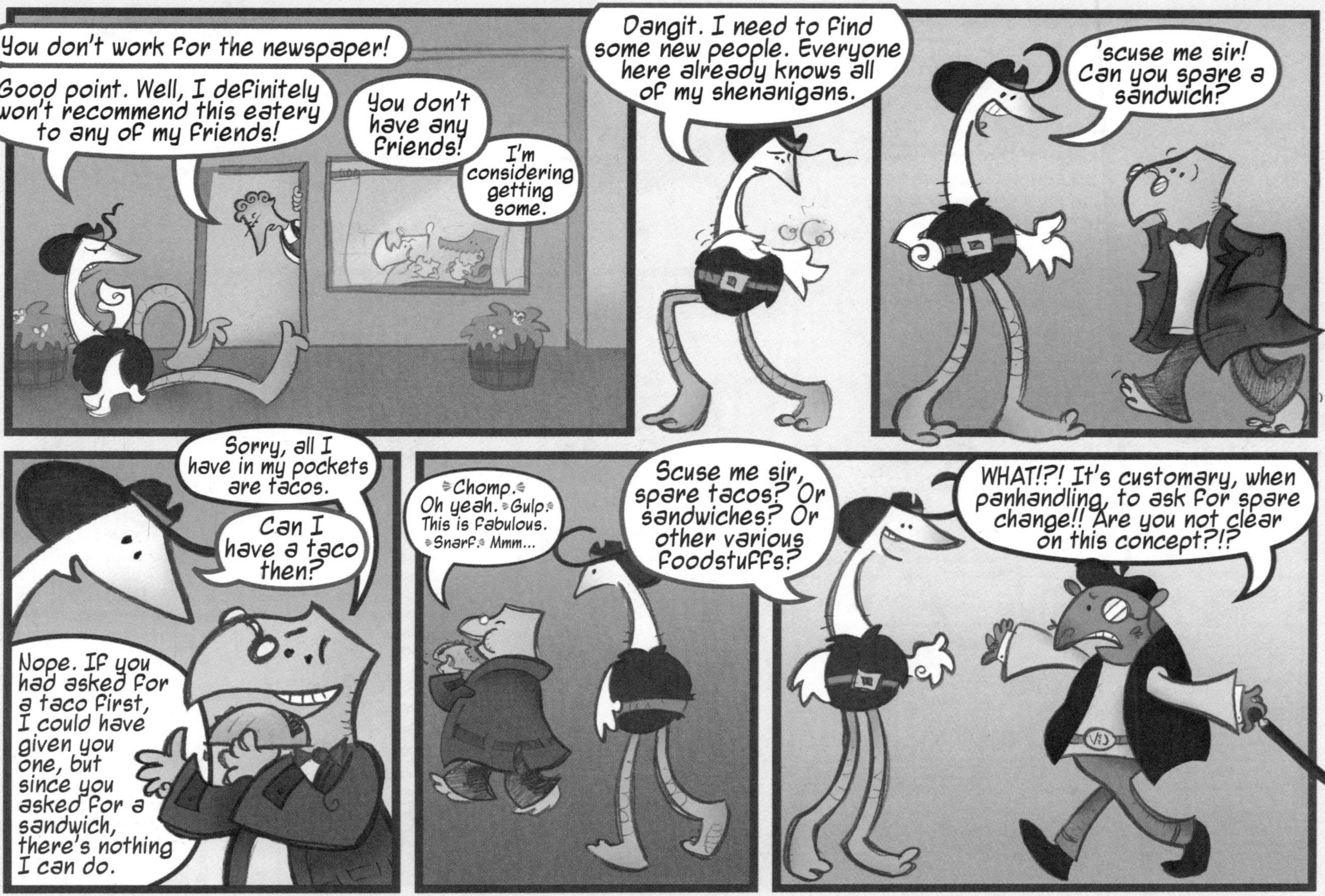
You don't work for the newspaper!
Good point. Well, I definitely won't recommend this eatery to any of my friends!
You don't have any friends!
I'm considering getting some.
Dangit. I need to find some new people. Everyone here already knows all of my shenanigans.
'scuse me sir! Can you spare a sandwich?
Sorry, all I have in my pockets are tacos.
Can I have a taco then?
Nope. If you had asked for a taco first, I could have given you one, but since you asked for a sandwich, there's nothing I can do.
Chomp. Oh yeah. Gulp. This is fabulous. Snarf. Mmm...
Scuse me sir, spare tacos? Or sandwiches? Or other various foodstuffs?
WHAT!?! It's customary, when panhandling, to ask for spare change!! Are you not clear on this concept?!?

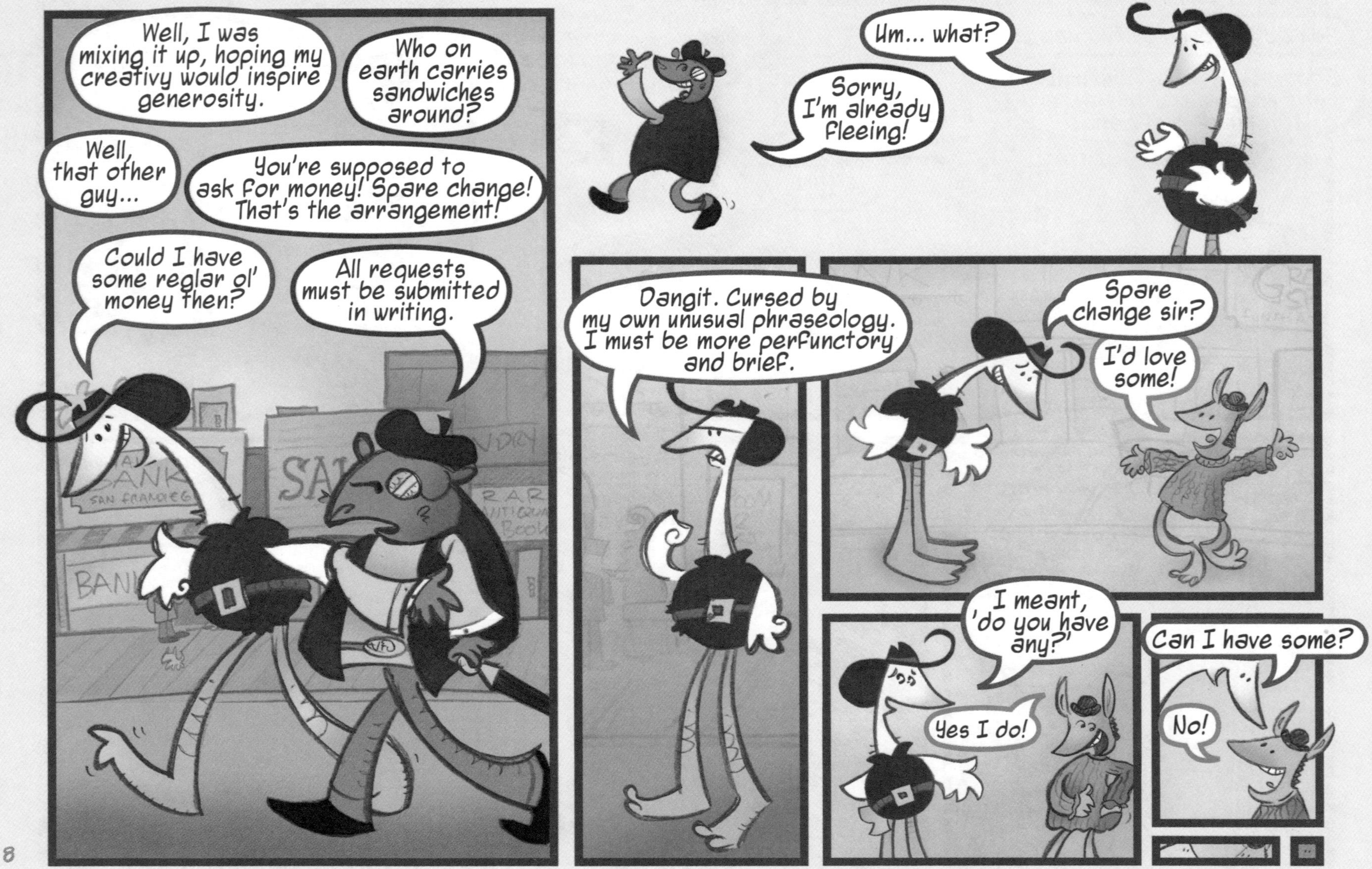

Well, I was mixing it up, hoping my creativy would inspire generosity.
Who on earth carries sandwiches around?
Well, that other guy...
You're supposed to ask for money! Spare change! That's the arrangement!
Could I have some reglar ol' money then?
All requests must be submitted in writing.
Um... what?
Sorry, I'm already fleeing!
Dangit. Cursed by my own unusual phraseology. I must be more perfunctory and brief.
Spare change sir?
I'd love some!
I meant, 'do you have any?'
Yes I do!
Can I have some?
No!

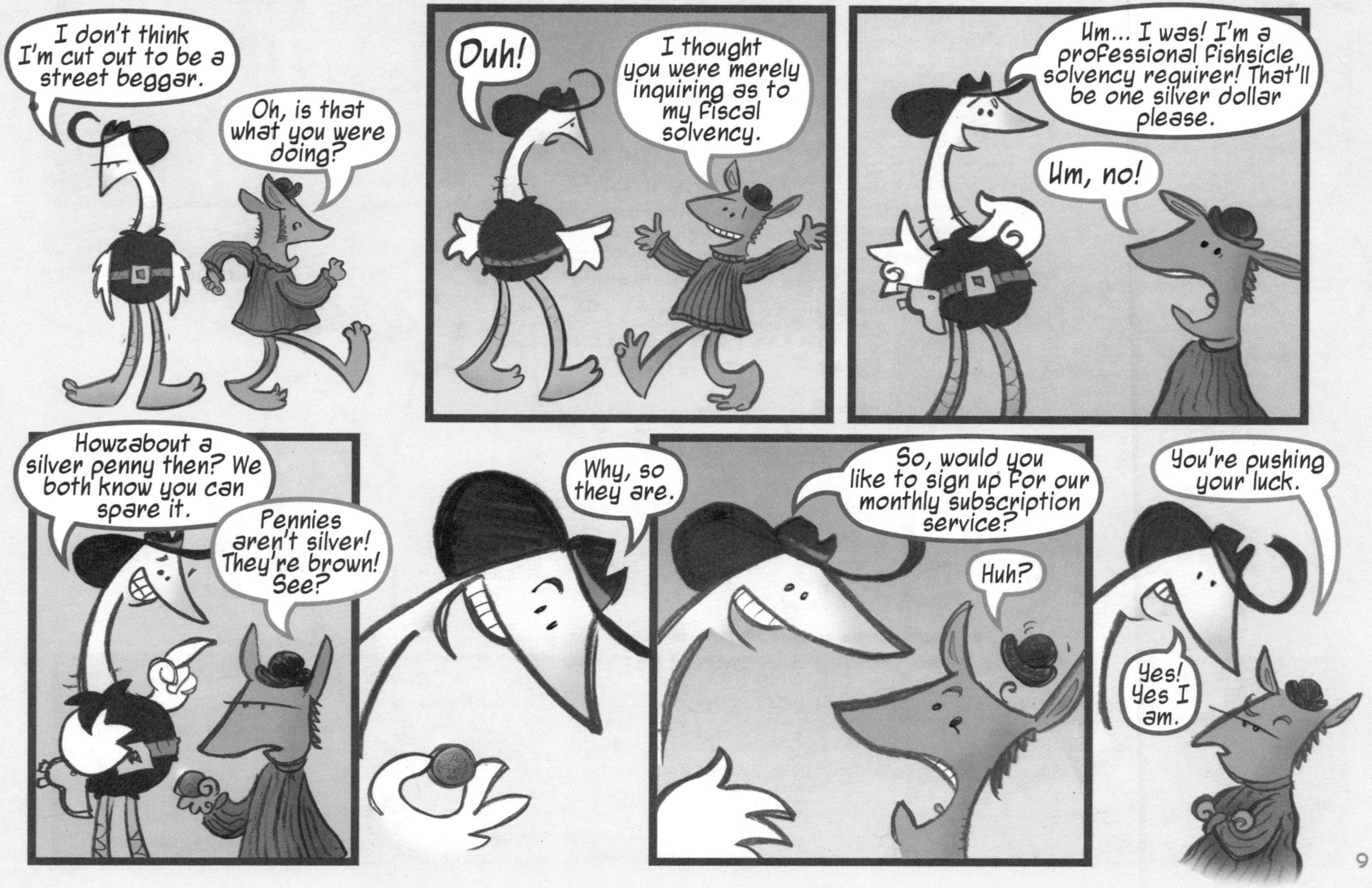
I don't think I'm cut out to be a street beggar.
Oh, is that what you were doing?
Ouh!
I thought you were merely inquiring as to my fiscal solvency.
Um... I was! I'm a professional fishsicle solvency requirer! That'll be one silver dollar please.
Um, no!
Howzabout a silver penny then? We both know you can spare it.
Pennies aren't silver! They're brown! See?
Why, so they are.
So, would you like to sign up for our monthly subscription service?
Huh?
You're pushing your luck.
Yes! Yes I am.

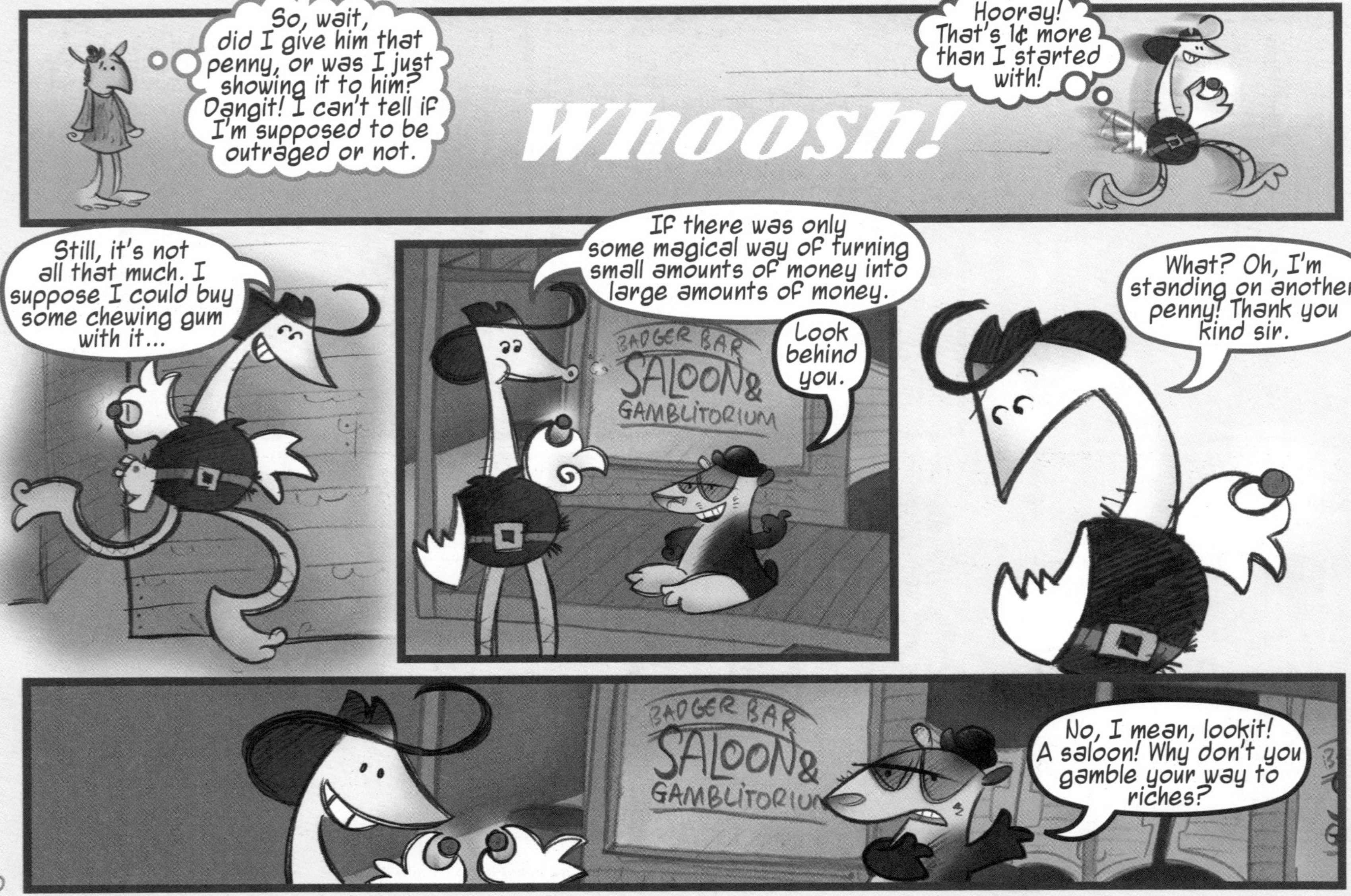

So, wait, did I give him that penny, or was I just showing it to him? Dangit! I can't tell if I'm supposed to be outraged or not.
Whoosh!
Hooray! That's 1¢ more than I started with!
Still, it's not all that much. I suppose I could buy some chewing gum with it...
If there was only some magical way of turning small amounts of money into large amounts of money.
BADGER BAR SALOON & GAMBLITORIUM
Look behind you.
What? Oh, I'm standing on another penny! Thank you kind sir.
BADGER BAR SALOON & GAMBLITORIUM
No, I mean, lookit! A saloon! Why don't you gamble your way to riches?

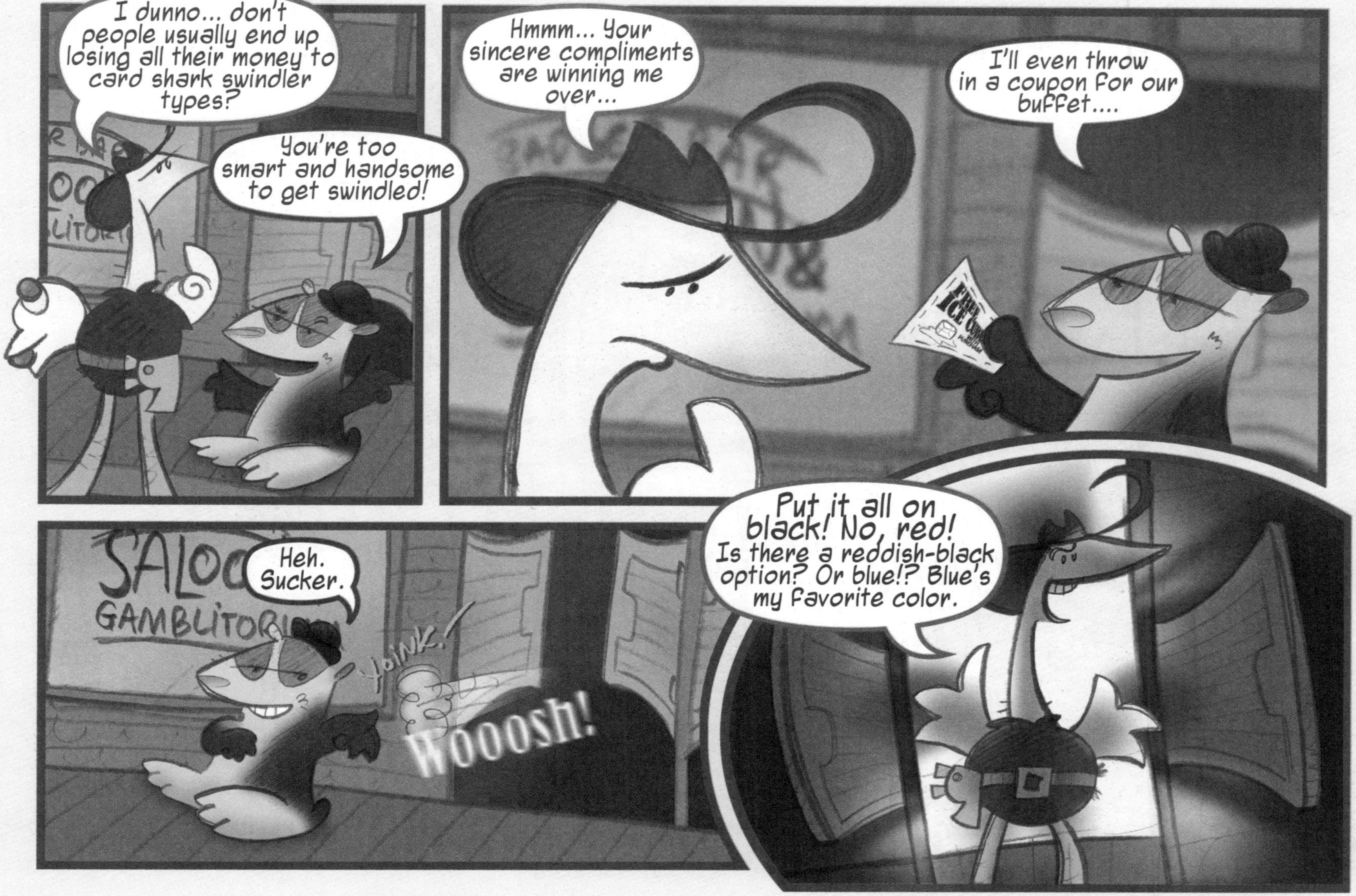
I dunno... don't people usually end up losing all their money to card shark swindler types?
You're too smart and handsome to get swindled!
Hmmm... Your sincere compliments are winning me over...
I'll even throw in a coupon for our buffet....
FREE ICE CUBE
SALOO
GAMBLITORI
Heh. Sucker.
YOINK!
WOOOSH!
Put it all on black! No, red! Is there a reddish-black option? Or blue!? Blue's my favorite color.

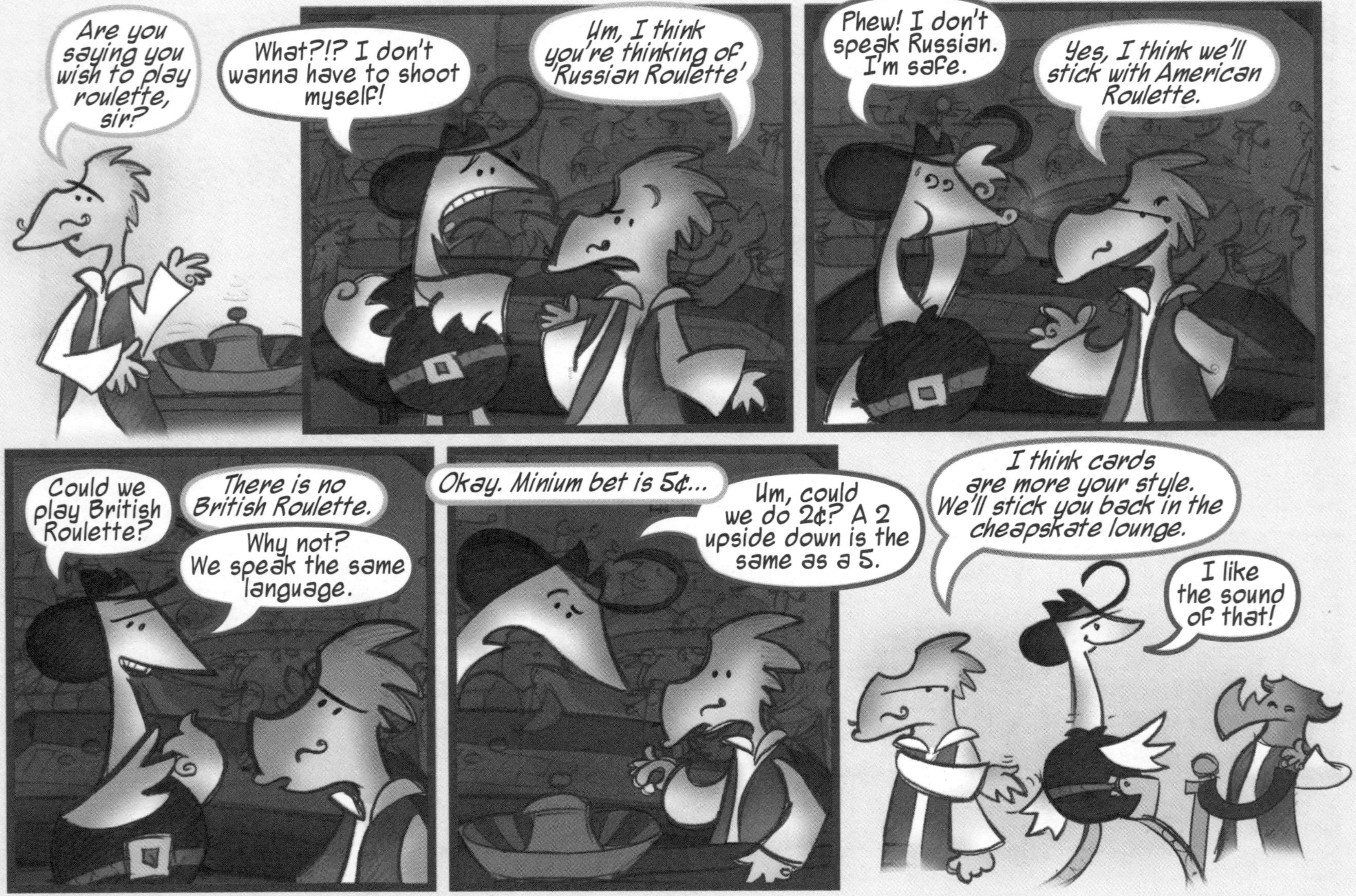
Are you saying you wish to play roulette, sir?
What?!? I don't wanna have to shoot myself!
Um, I think you're thinking of 'Russian Roulette'
Phew! I don't speak Russian. I'm safe.
Yes, I think we'll stick with American Roulette.
Could we play British Roulette?
There is no British Roulette.
Why not? We speak the same language.
Okay. Minium bet is 5¢...
Um, could we do 2¢? A 2 upside down is the same as a 5.
I think cards are more your style. We'll stick you back in the cheapskate lounge.
I like the sound of that!

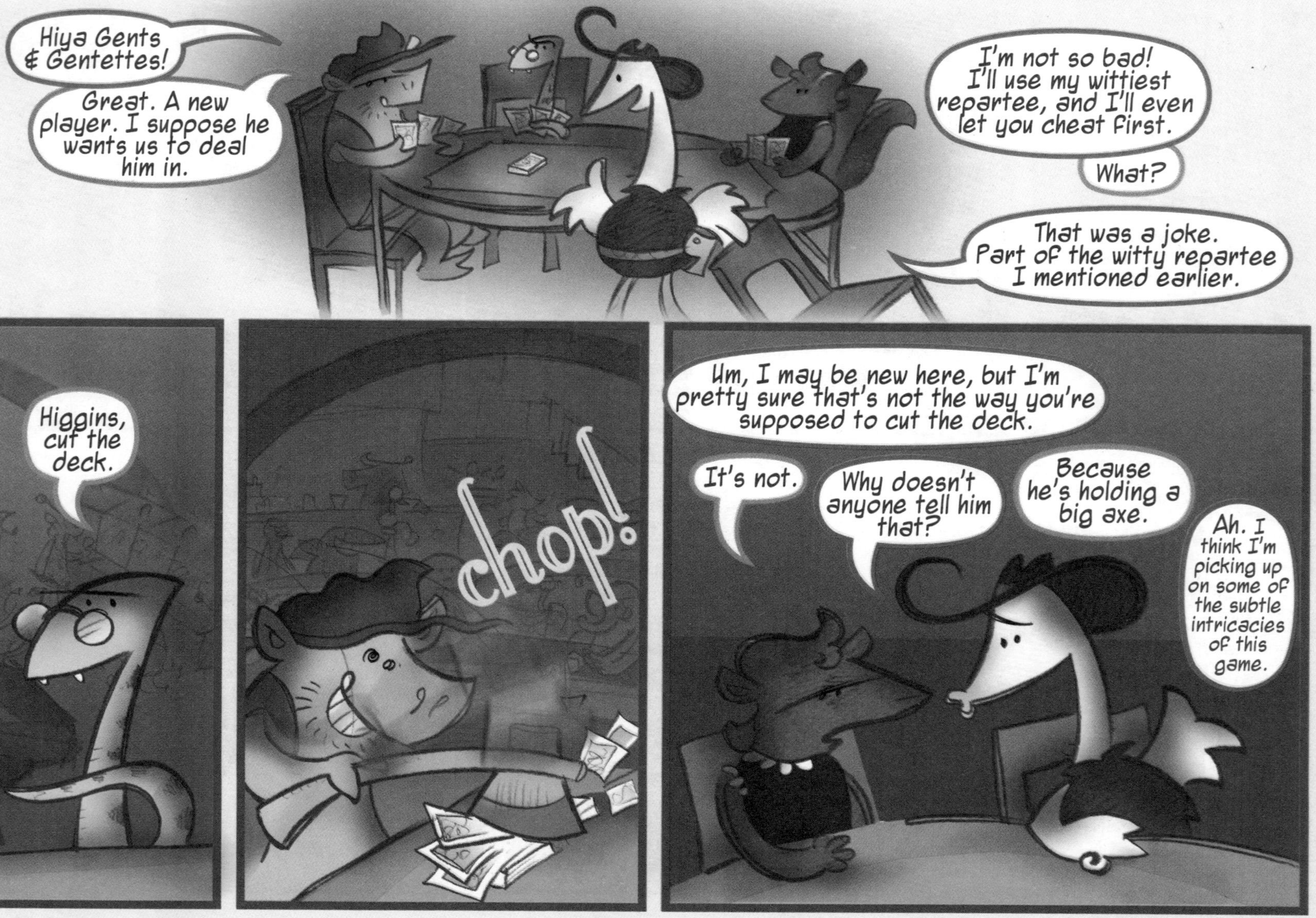
Hiya Gents & Gentettes!
Great. A new player. I suppose he wants us to deal him in.
I'm not so bad! I'll use my wittiest repartee, and I'll even let you cheat first.
What?
That was a joke. Part of the witty repartee I mentioned earlier.
Higgins, cut the deck.
chop!
Um, I may be new here, but I'm pretty sure that's not the way you're supposed to cut the deck.
It's not.
Why doesn't anyone tell him that?
Because he's holding a big axe.
Ah. I think I'm picking up on some of the subtle intricacies of this game.

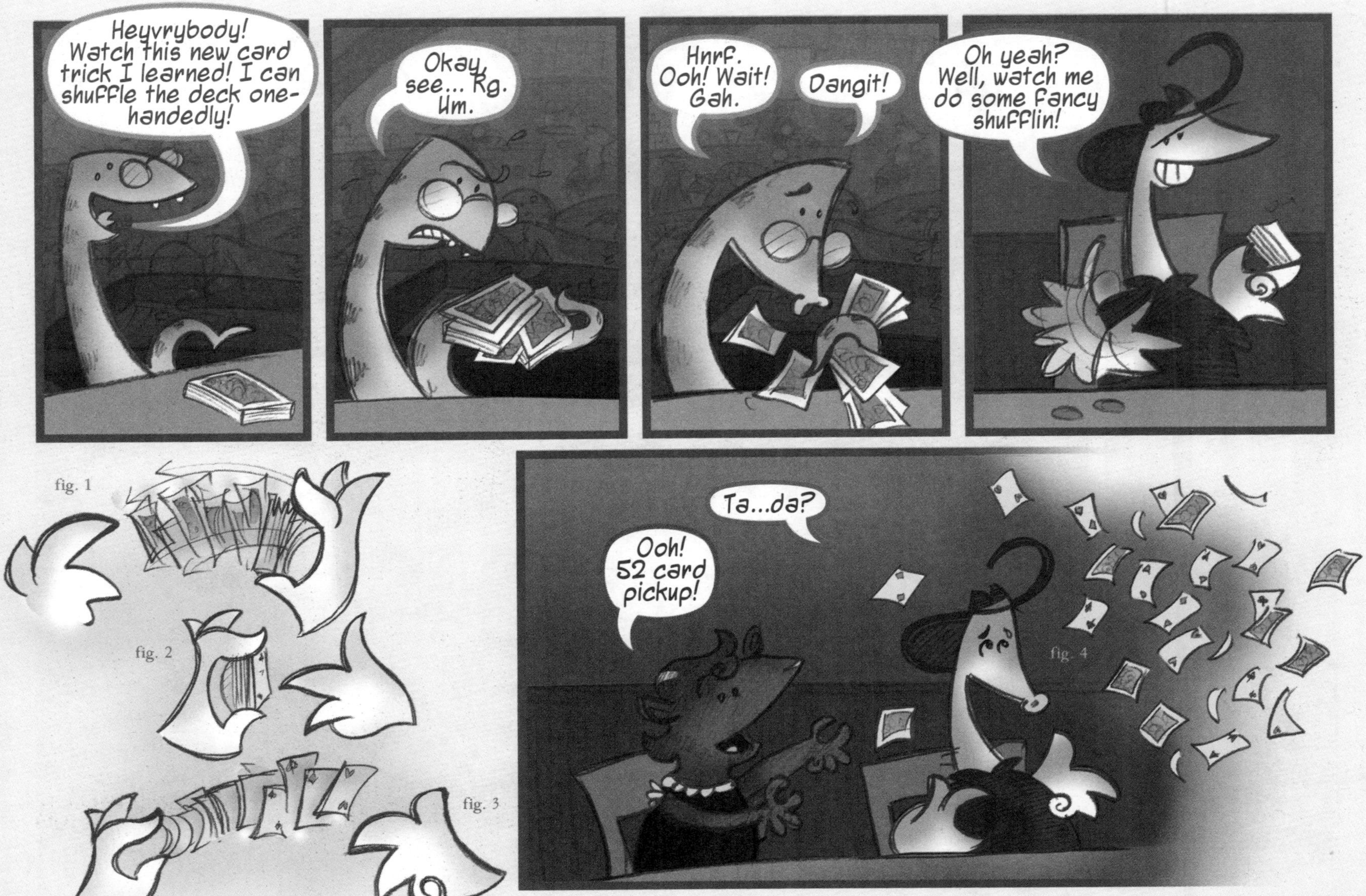
Heyvrybody! Watch this new card trick I learned! I can shuffle the deck one-handedly!
Okay, see... Rg. Um.
Hnrf. Ooh! Wait! Gah.
Dangit!
Oh yeah? Well, watch me do some fancy shufflin!
fig. 1
fig. 2
fig. 3
Ta...da?
Ooh! 52 card pickup!
fig. 4

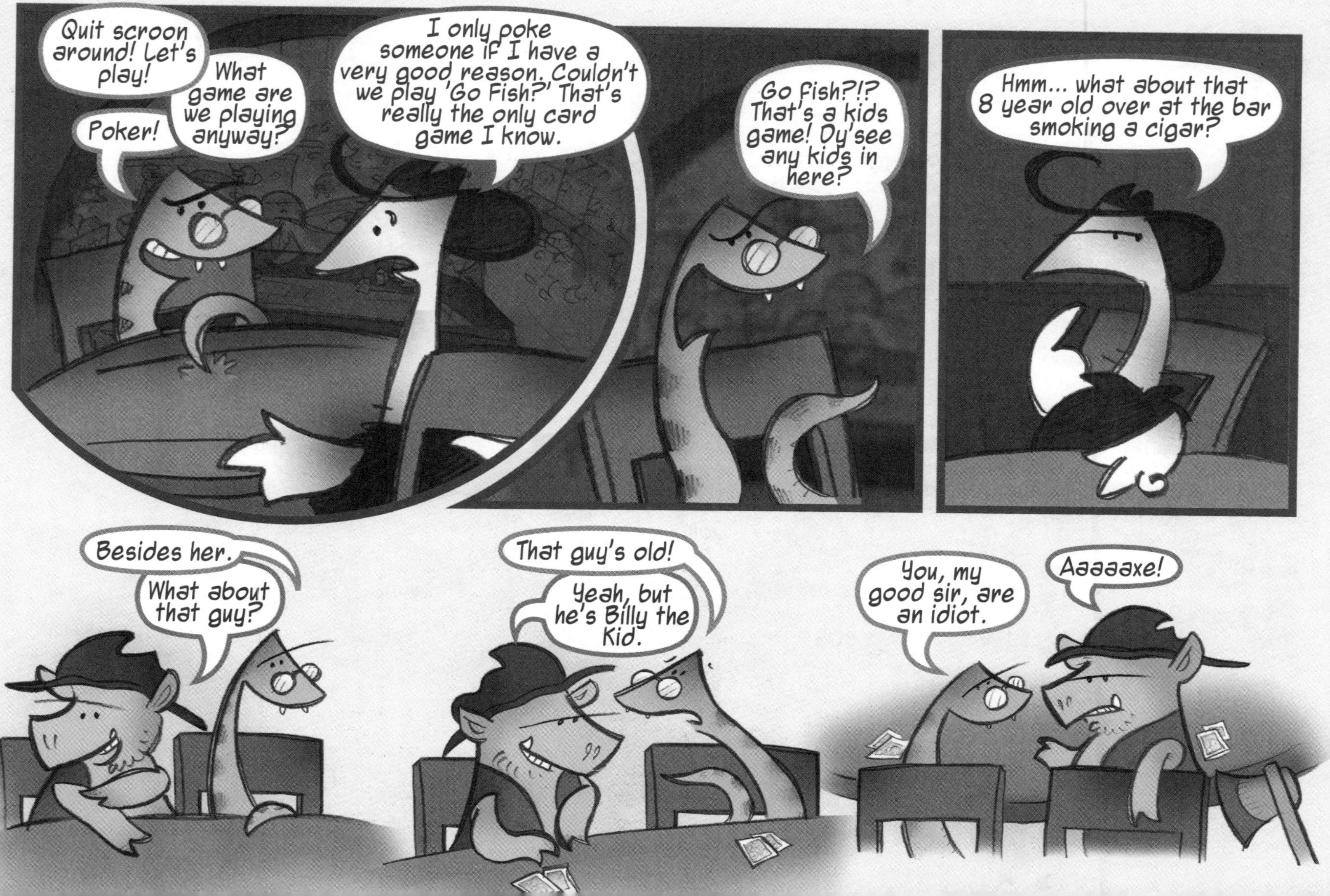
Quit scroon around! Let's play!
What game are we playing anyway?
Poker!
I only poke someone if I have a very good reason. Couldn't we play 'Go Fish?' That's really the only card game I know.
Go fish?!? That's a kids game! Dy'see any kids in here?
Hmm... what about that 8 year old over at the bar smoking a cigar?
Besides her.
What about that guy?
That guy's old!
Yeah, but he's Billy the Kid.
You, my good sir, are an idiot.
Aaaaaxe!

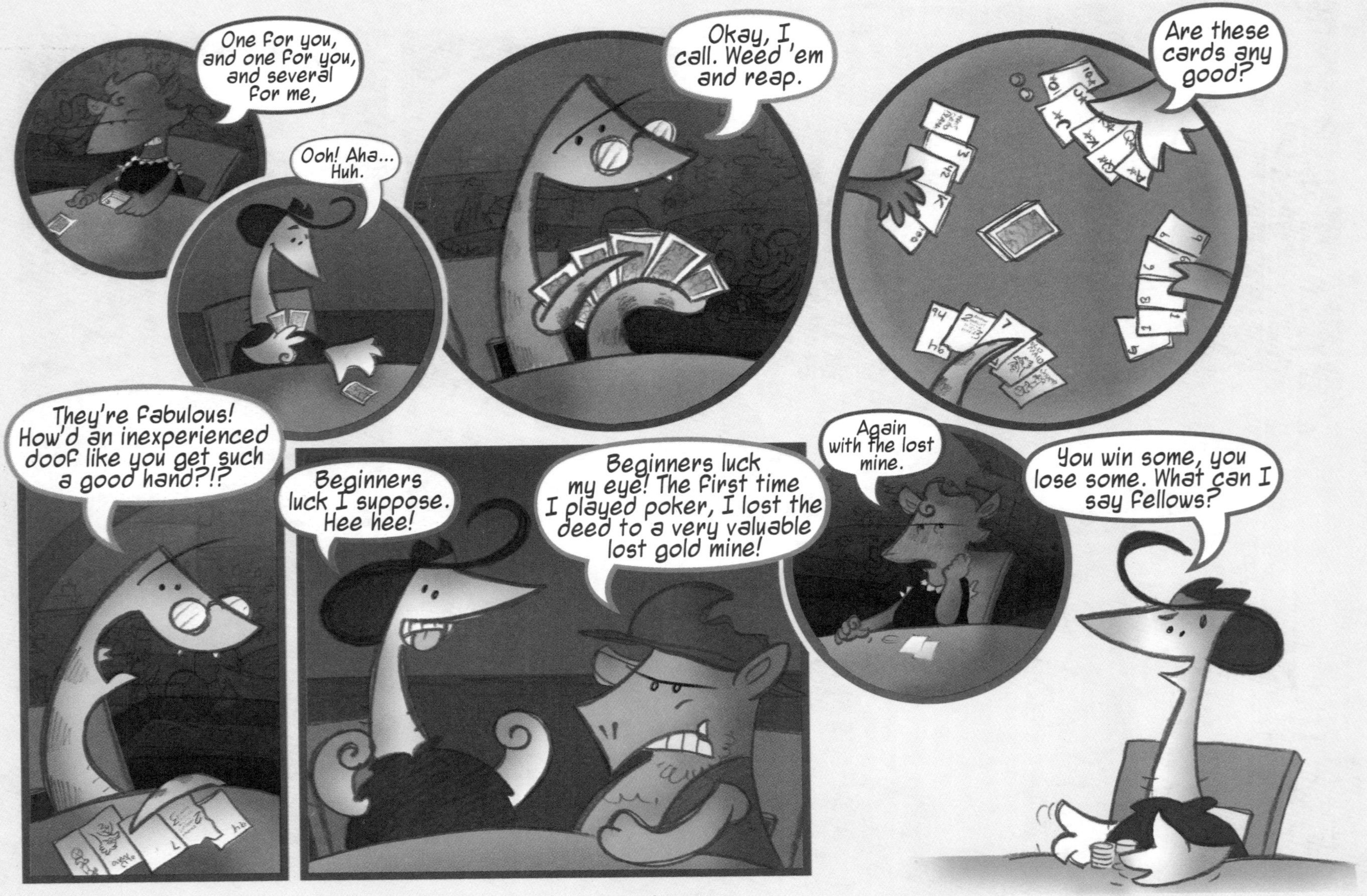

One for you, and one for you, and several for me,
Ooh! Aha... Huh.
Okay, I call. Weed 'em and reap.
Are these cards any good?
They're fabulous! How'd an inexperienced doof like you get such a good hand?!?
Beginners luck I suppose. Hee hee!
Beginners luck my eye! The first time I played poker, I lost the deed to a very valuable lost gold mine!
Again with the lost mine.
You win some, you lose some. What can I say fellows?

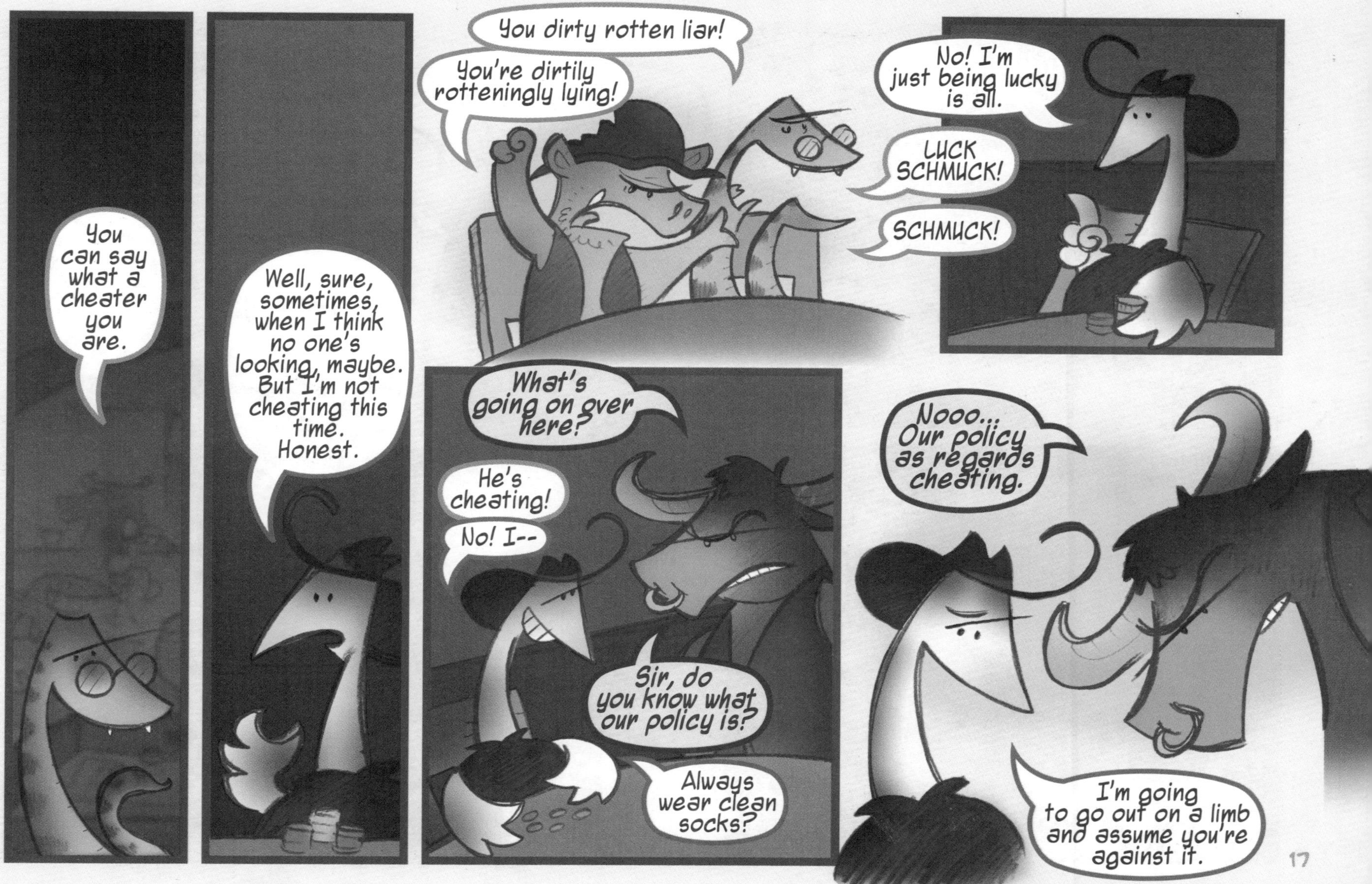

You can say what a cheater you are.
Well, sure, sometimes, when I think no one's looking, maybe. But I'm not cheating this time. Honest.
You dirty rotten liar!
You're dirtily rotteningly lying!
No! I'm just being lucky is all.
LUCK SCHMUCK!
SCHMUCK!
What's going on over here?
He's cheating!
No! I--
Sir, do you know what our policy is?
Always wear clean socks?
Nooo... Our policy as regards cheating.
I'm going to go out on a limb and assume you're against it.

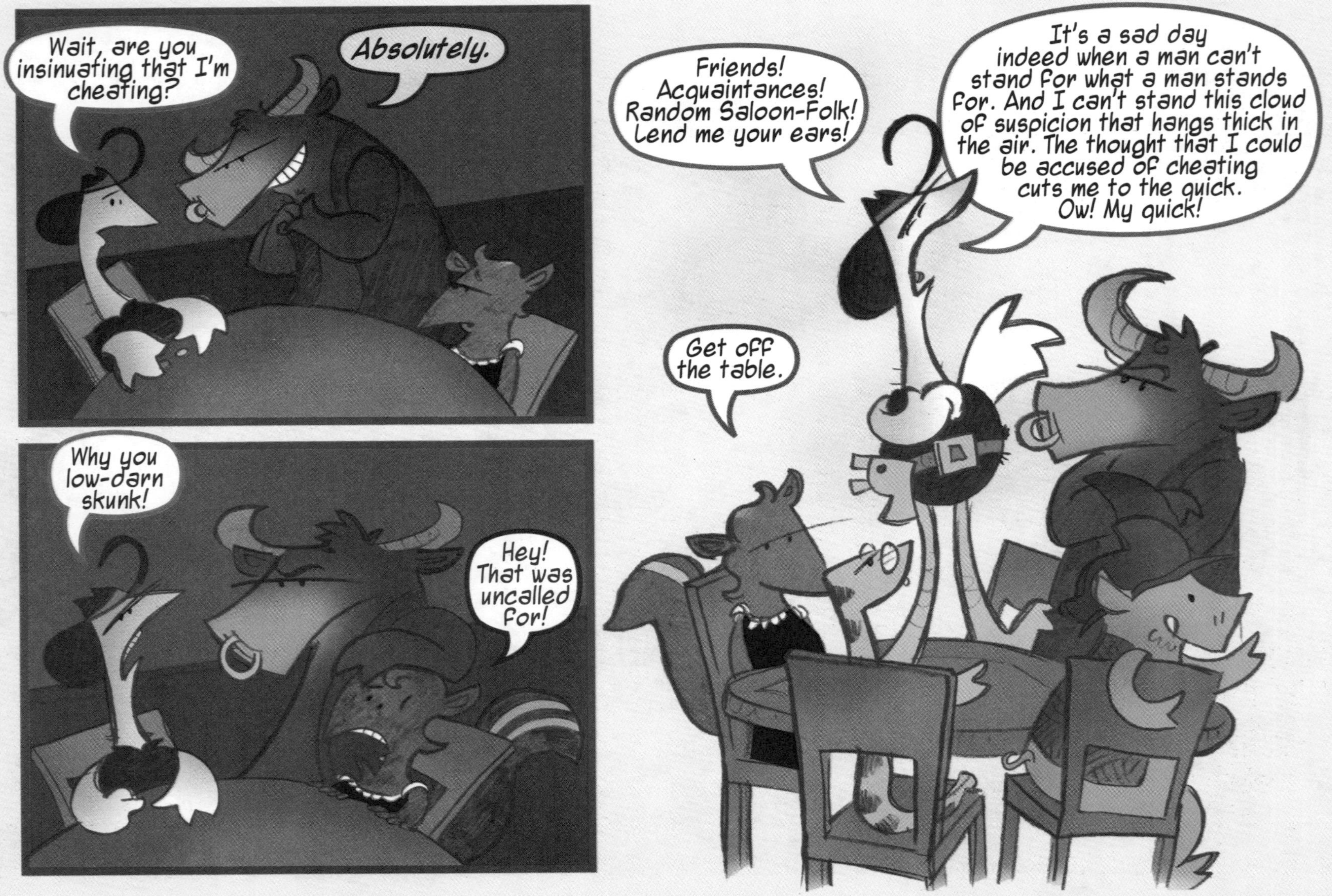
Wait, are you insinuating that I'm cheating?
Absolutely.
Why you low-darn skunk!
Hey! That was uncalled for!
Friends! Acquaintances! Random Saloon-Folk! Lend me your ears!
It's a sad day indeed when a man can't stand for what a man stands for. And I can't stand this cloud of suspicion that hangs thick in the air. The thought that I could be accused of cheating cuts me to the quick. Ow! My quick!
Get off the table.

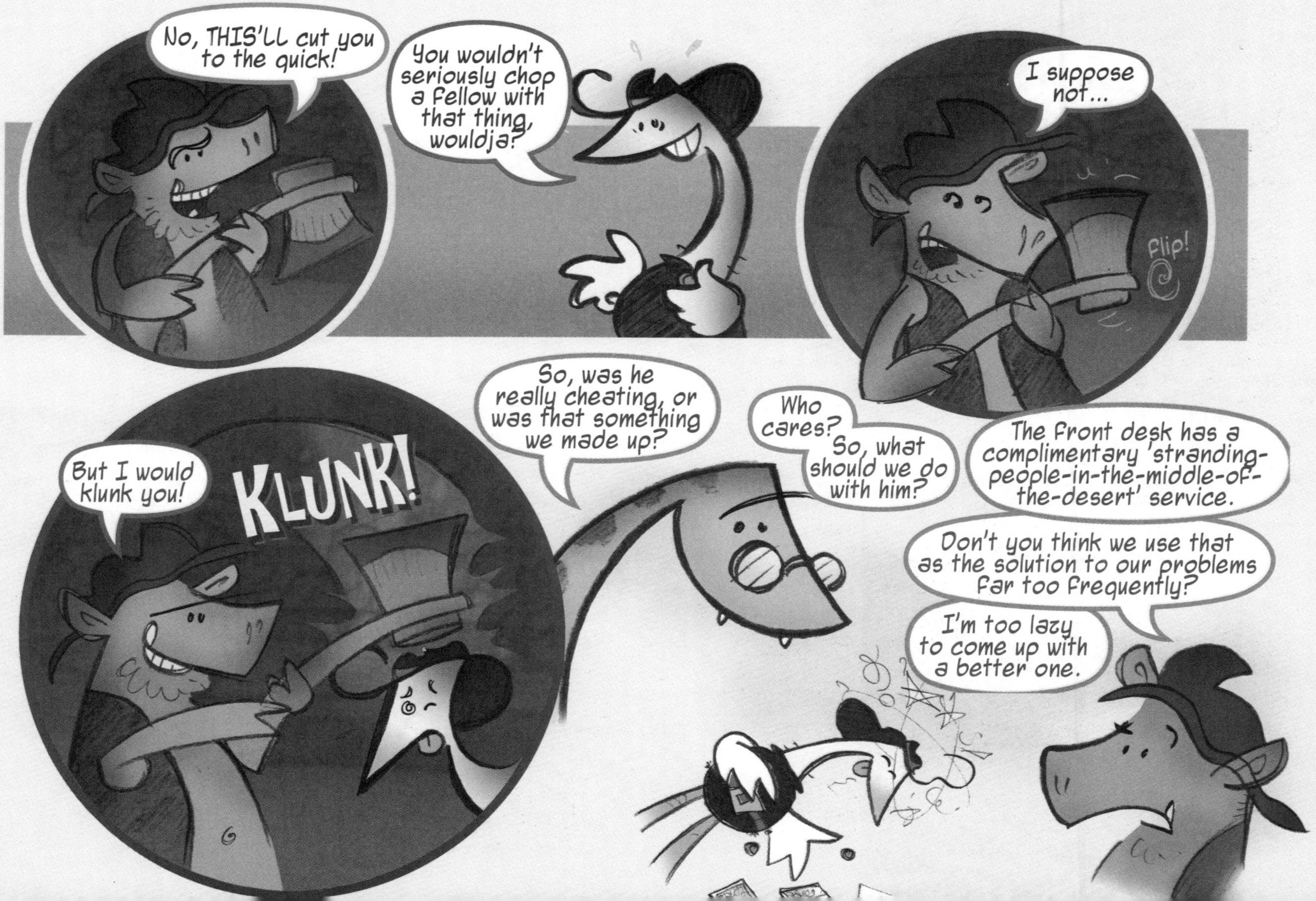
No, THIS'LL cut you to the quick!
You wouldn't seriously chop a fellow with that thing, wouldja?
I suppose not...
Flip!
But I would klunk you!
KLUNK!
So, was he really cheating, or was that something we made up?
Who cares?
So, what should we do with him?
The front desk has a complimentary 'stranding-people-in-the-middle-of-the-desert' service.
Don't you think we use that as the solution to our problems far too frequently?
I'm too lazy to come up with a better one.

chapter 2

stranded in the desert and then not

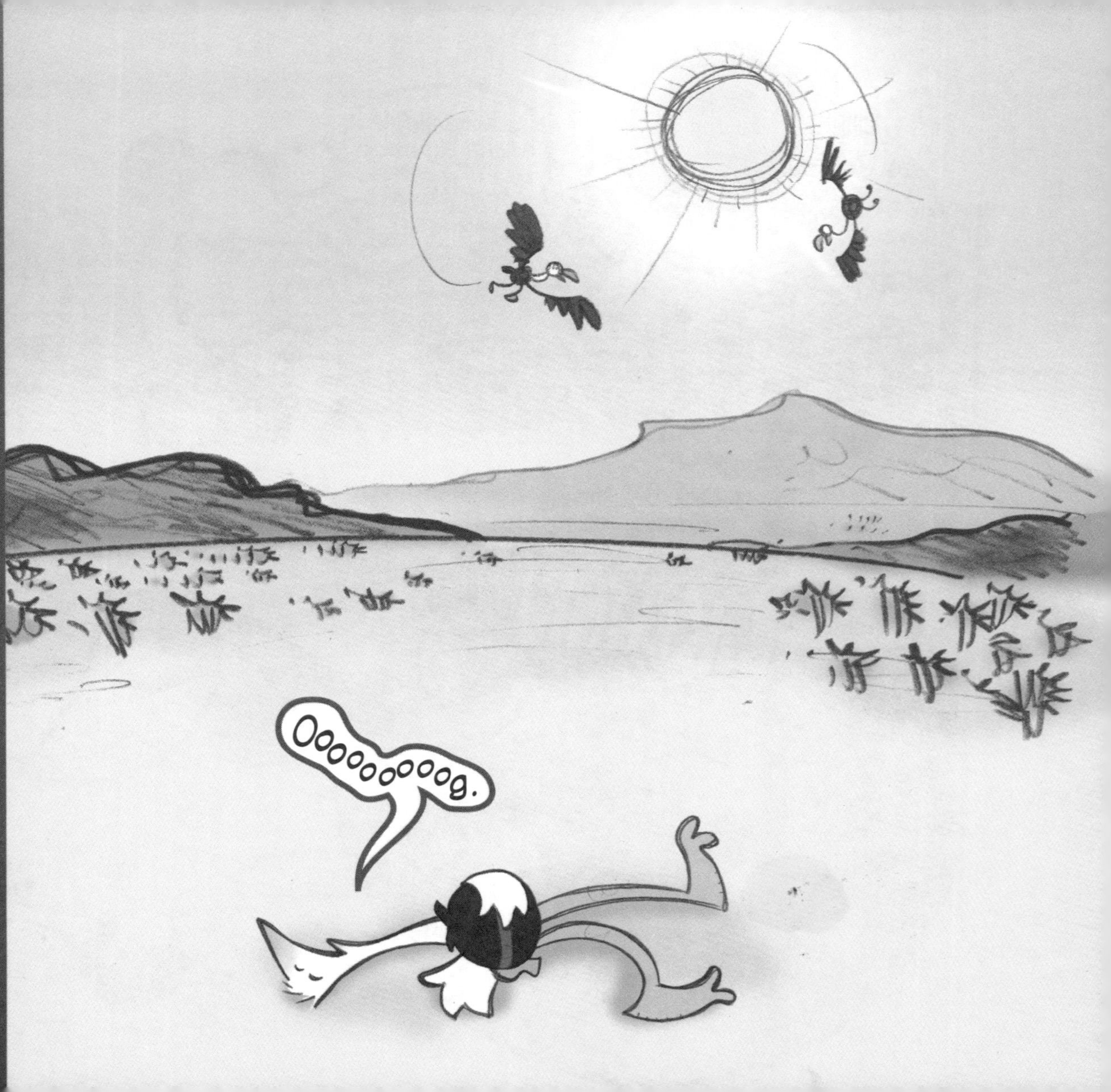
Oooooooooog.

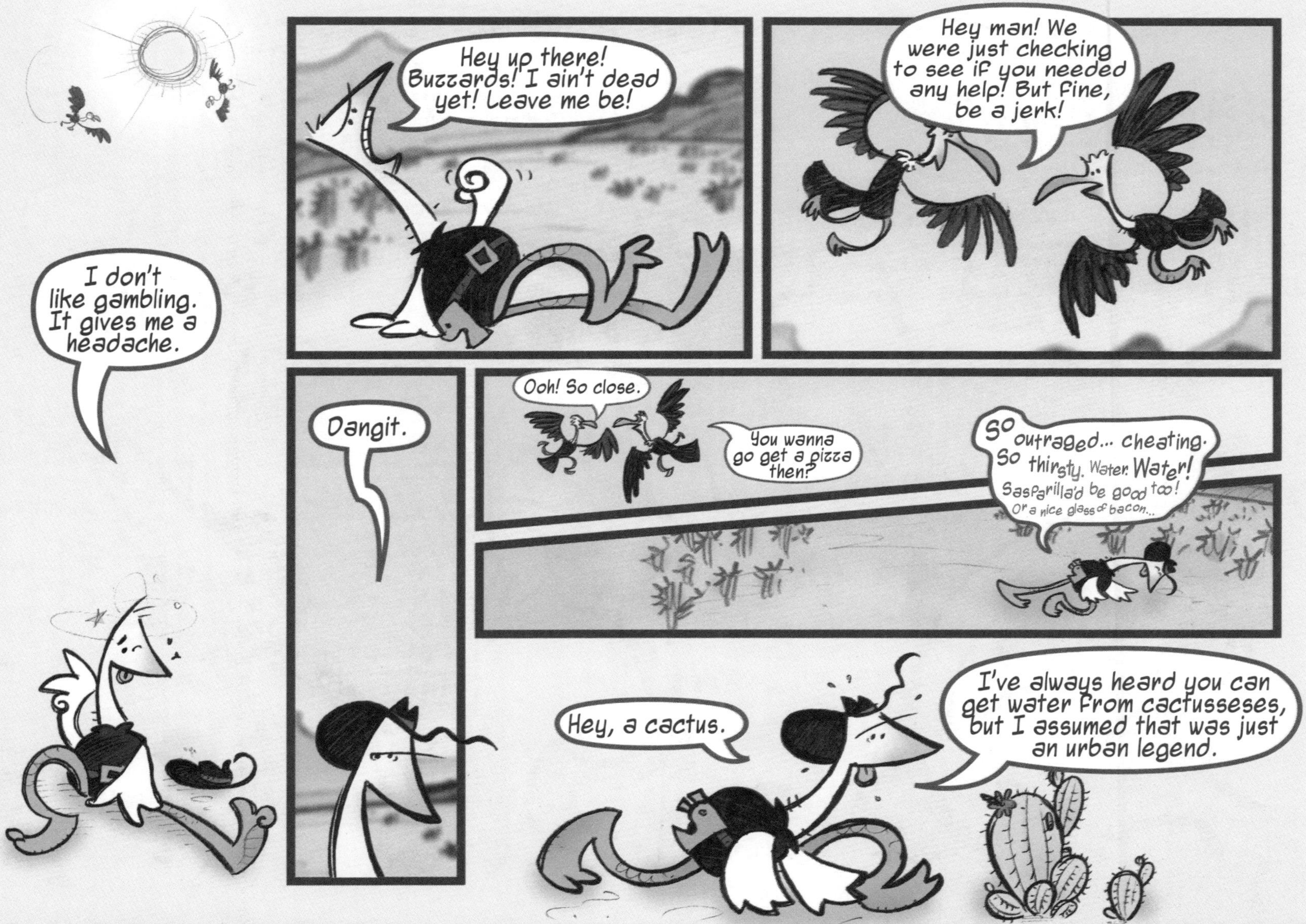
I don't like gambling. It gives me a headache.
Hey up there! Buzzards! I ain't dead yet! Leave me be!
Hey man! We were just checking to see if you needed any help! But fine, be a jerk!
Dangit.
Ooh! So close.
You wanna go get a pizza then?
So outraged... cheating. So thirsty. Water. Water! Sasparilla'd be good too! Or a nice glass of bacon...
Hey, a cactus.
I've always heard you can get water from cactusseses, but I assumed that was just an urban legend.

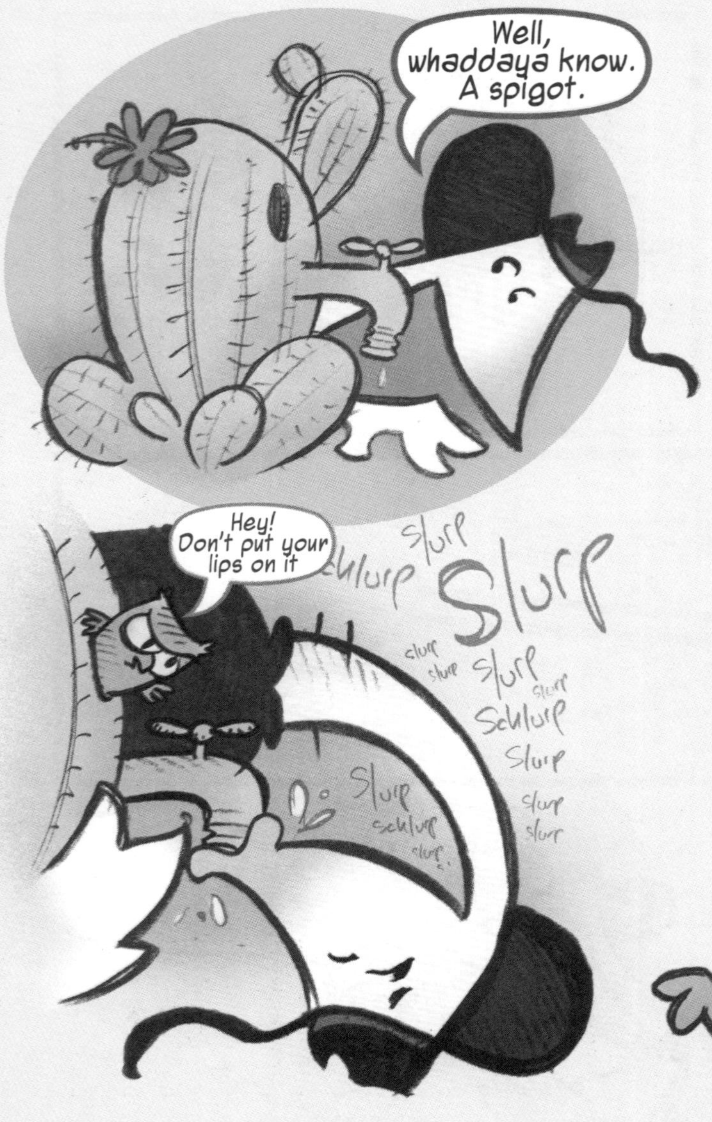

Well, whaddaya know. A spigot.
Hey! Don't put your lips on it
Slurp
Schlurp
Slurp
slurp
slurp
Slurp
slurp
Schlurp
Slurp
Slurp
schlurp
slurp
slurp
slurp

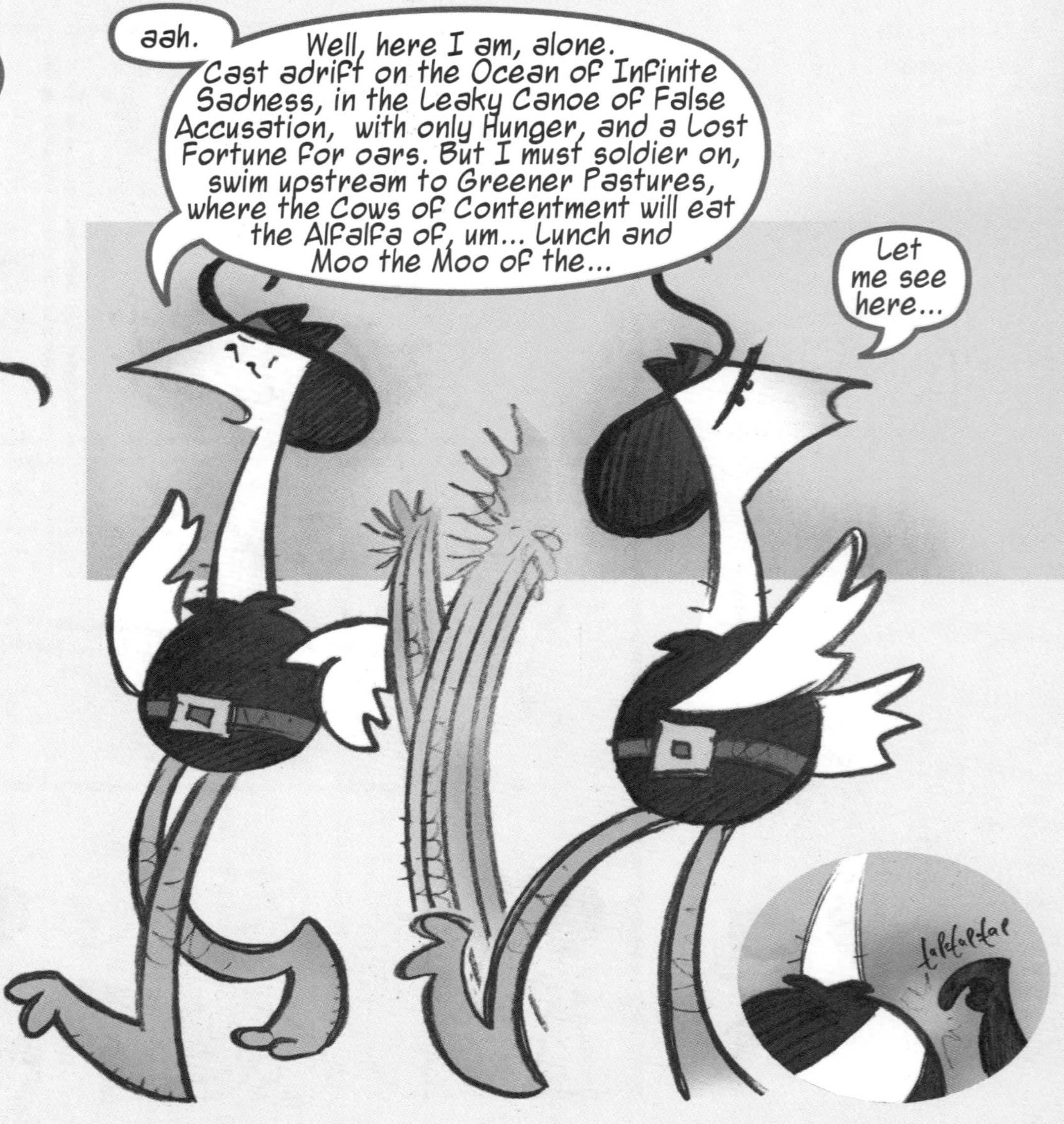

aah.
Well, here I am, alone. Cast adrift on the Ocean of Infinite Sadness, in the Leaky Canoe of False Accusation, with only Hunger, and a Lost Fortune for oars. But I must soldier on, swim upstream to Greener Pastures, where the Cows of Contentment will eat the Alfalfa of, um... Lunch and Moo the Moo of the...
Let me see here...
talfalfal

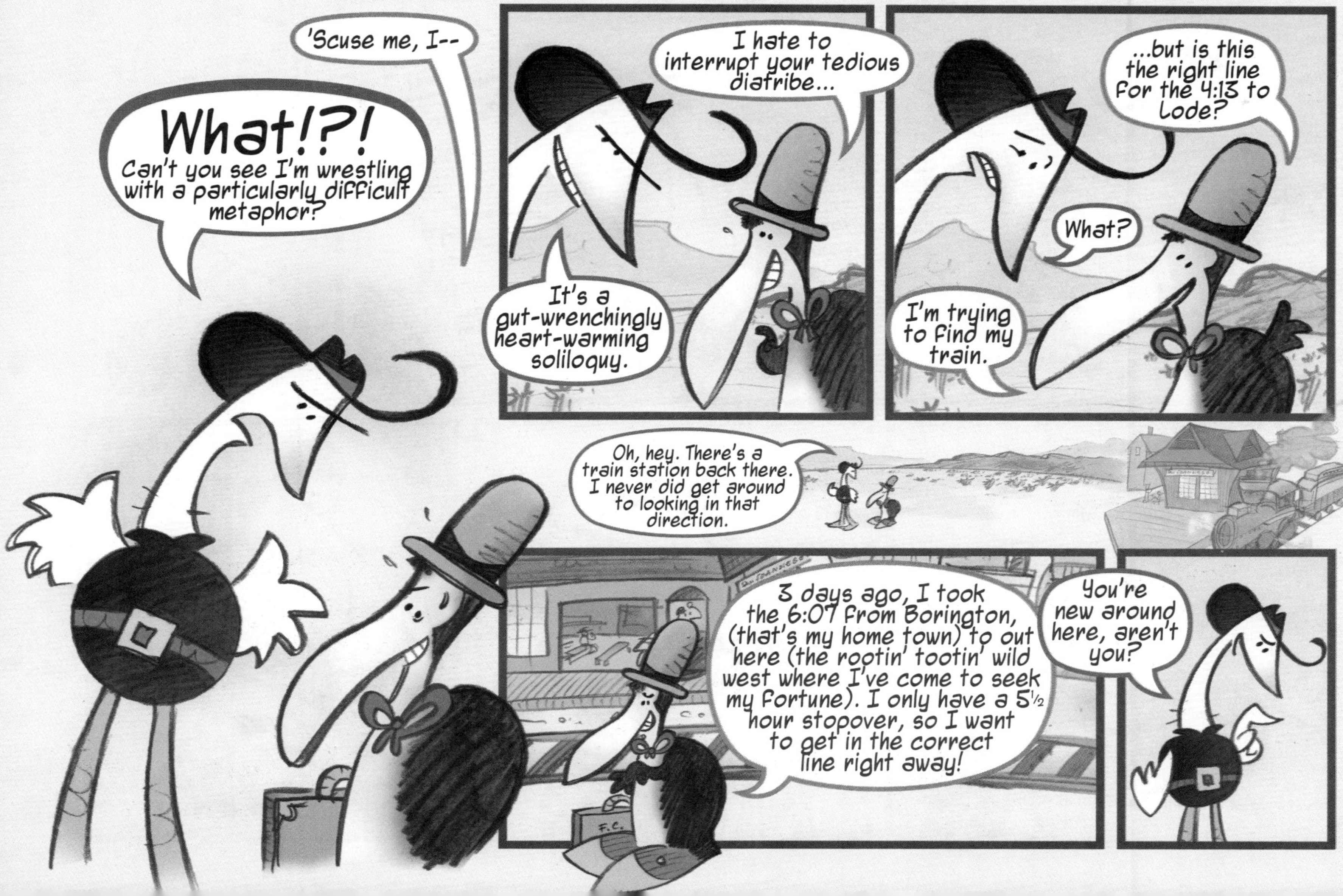
'Scuse me, I--
What!?! Can't you see I'm wrestling with a particularly difficult metaphor?
I hate to interrupt your tedious diatribe...
It's a gut-wrenchingly heart-warming soliloquy.
...but is this the right line for the 4:13 to Lode?
What?
I'm trying to find my train.
Oh, hey. There's a train station back there. I never did get around to looking in that direction.
3 days ago, I took the 6:07 from Borington, (that's my home town) to out here (the rootin' tootin' wild west where I've come to seek my fortune). I only have a 5½ hour stopover, so I want to get in the correct line right away!
You're new around here, aren't you?

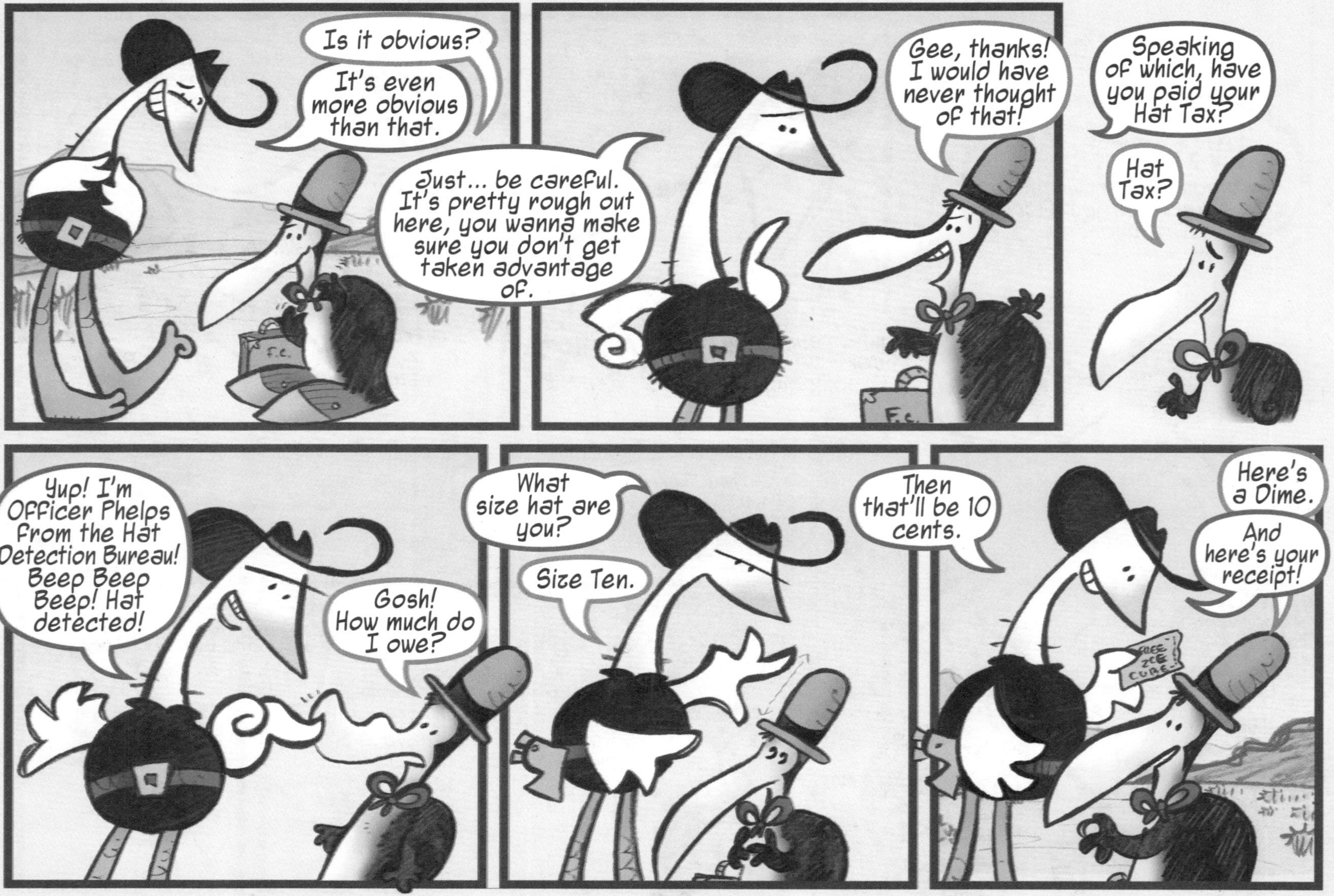
Is it obvious?
It's even more obvious than that.
Just... be careful. It's pretty rough out here, you wanna make sure you don't get taken advantage of.
Gee, thanks! I would have never thought of that!
Speaking of which, have you paid your Hat Tax?
Hat Tax?
Yup! I'm Officer Phelps from the Hat Detection Bureau! Beep Beep Beep! Hat detected!
Gosh! How much do I owe?
What size hat are you?
Size Ten.
Then that'll be 10 cents.
Here's a Dime.
And here's your receipt!
FREE ICE CUBE

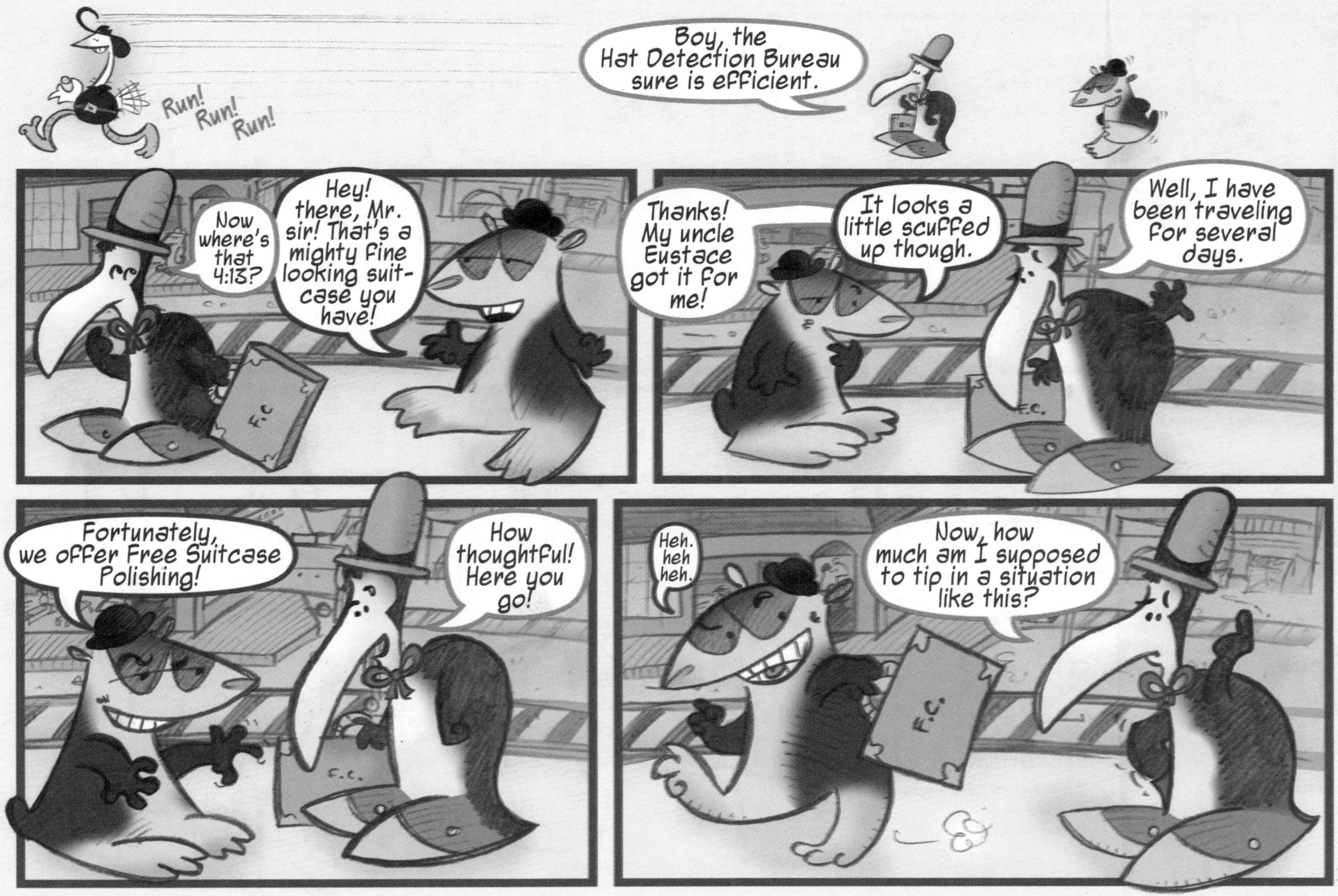
Run! Run! Run!
Boy, the Hat Detection Bureau sure is efficient.
Now where's that 4:13?
Hey! there, Mr. sir! That's a mighty fine looking suit-case you have!
Thanks! My uncle Eustace got it for me!
It looks a little scuffed up though.
Well, I have been traveling for several days.
Fortunately, we offer Free Suitcase Polishing!
How thoughtful! Here you go!
Heh. heh heh.
Now, how much am I supposed to tip in a situation like this?

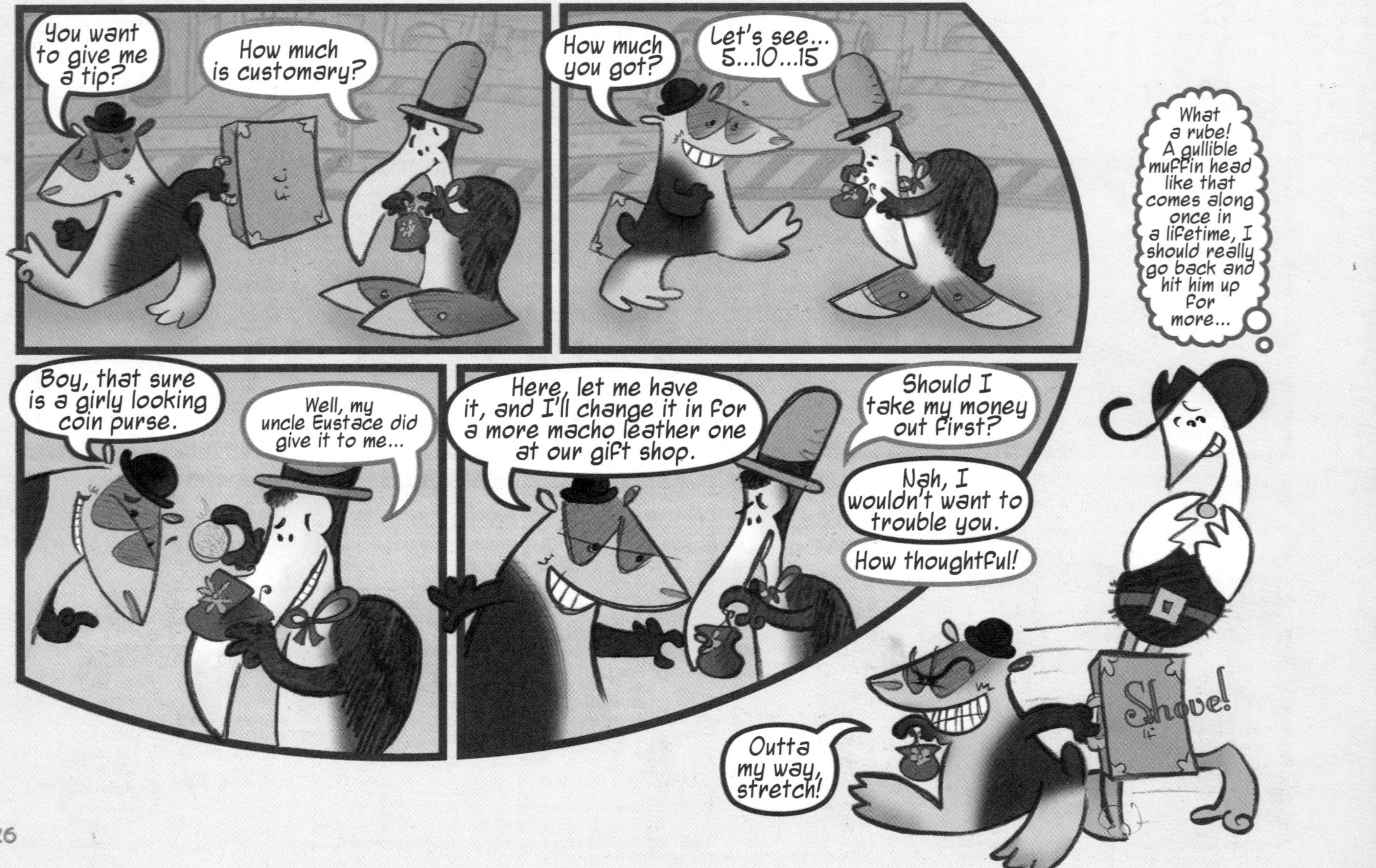
You want to give me a tip?
How much is customary?
How much you got?
Let's see... 5...10...15
Boy, that sure is a girly looking coin purse.
Well, my uncle Eustace did give it to me...
Here, let me have it, and I'll change it in for a more macho leather one at our gift shop.
Should I take my money out first?
Nah, I wouldn't want to trouble you.
How thoughtful!
What a rube! A gullible muffin head like that comes along once in a lifetime, I should really go back and hit him up for more...
Shove!
Outta my way, stretch!

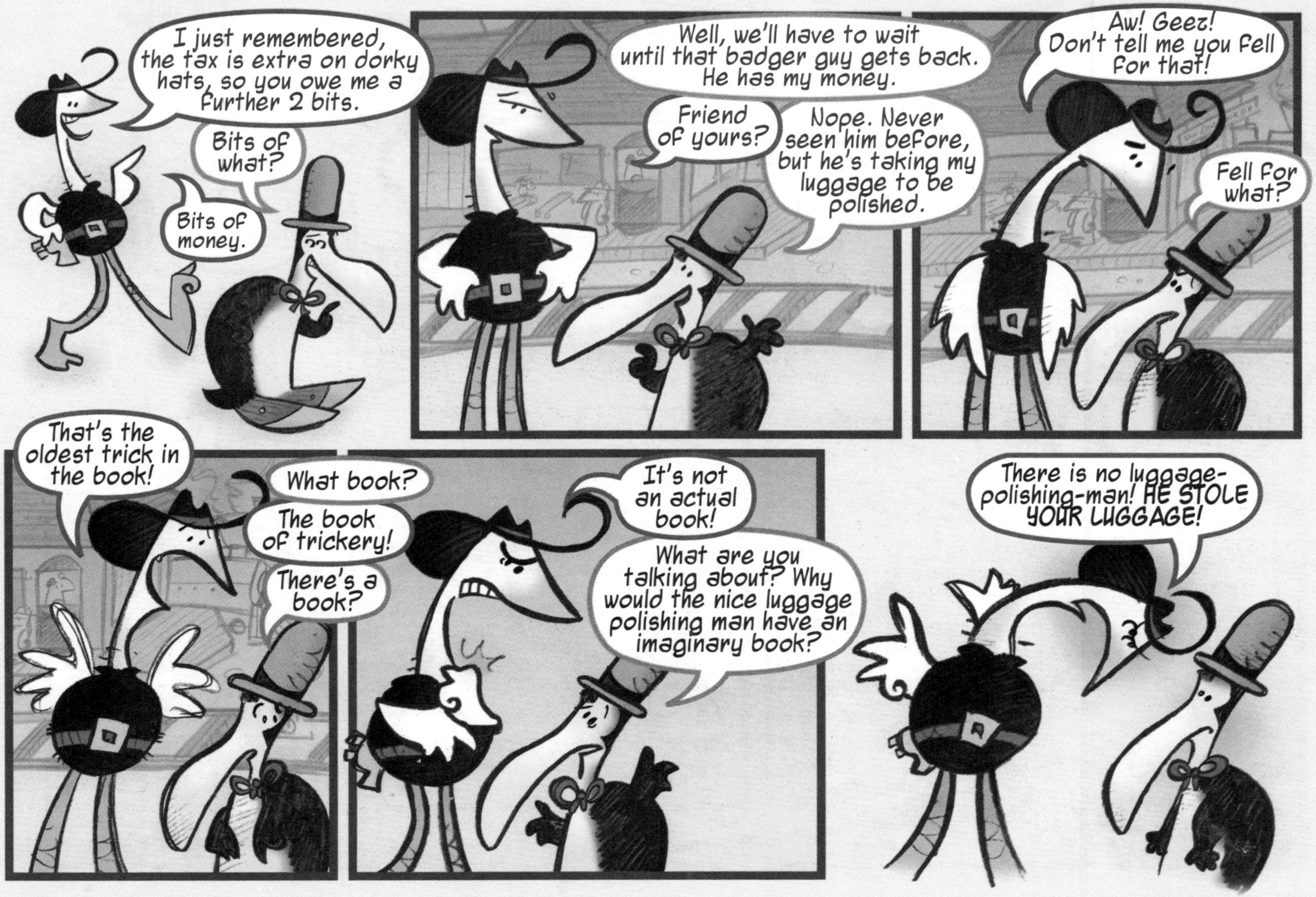

I just remembered, the tax is extra on dorky hats, so you owe me a further 2 bits.
Bits of what?
Bits of money.
Well, we'll have to wait until that badger guy gets back. He has my money.
Friend of yours?
Nope. Never seen him before, but he's taking my luggage to be polished.
Aw! Geez! Don't tell me you fell for that!
Fell for what?
That's the oldest trick in the book!
What book?
The book of trickery!
There's a book?
It's not an actual book!
What are you talking about? Why would the nice luggage polishing man have an imaginary book?
There is no luggage-polishing-man! HE STOLE YOUR LUGGAGE!

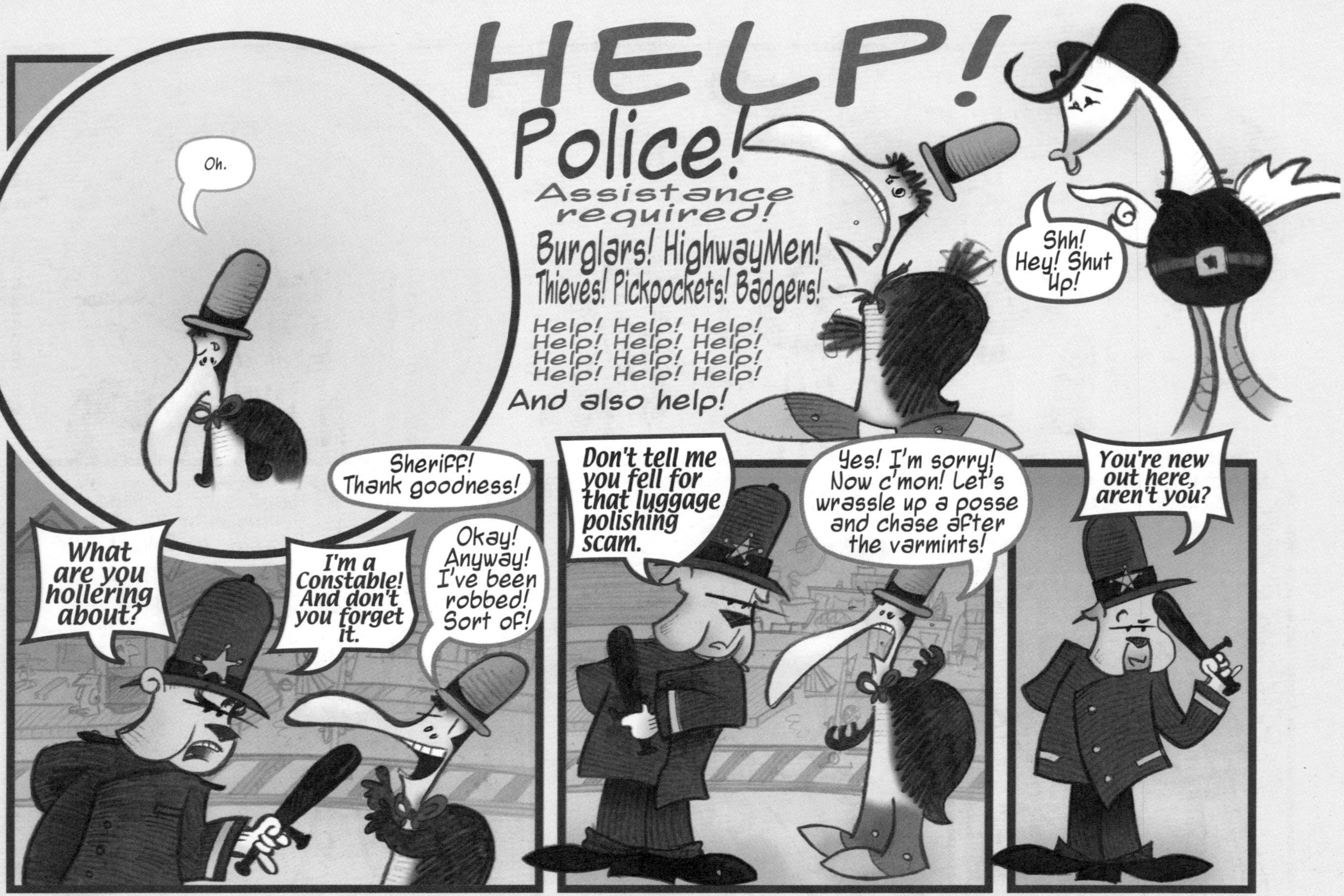

Oh.
HELP!
Police!
Assistance required!
Burglars! HighwayMen!
Thieves! Pickpockets! Badgers!
Help! Help! Help!
Help! Help! Help!
Help! Help! Help!
Help! Help! Help!
And also help!
Shh! Hey! Shut Up!
Sheriff! Thank goodness!
What are you hollering about?
I'm a Constable! And don't you forget it.
Okay! Anyway! I've been robbed! Sort of!
Don't tell me you fell for that luggage polishing scam.
Yes! I'm sorry! Now c'mon! Let's wrassle up a posse and chase after the varmints!
You're new out here, aren't you?

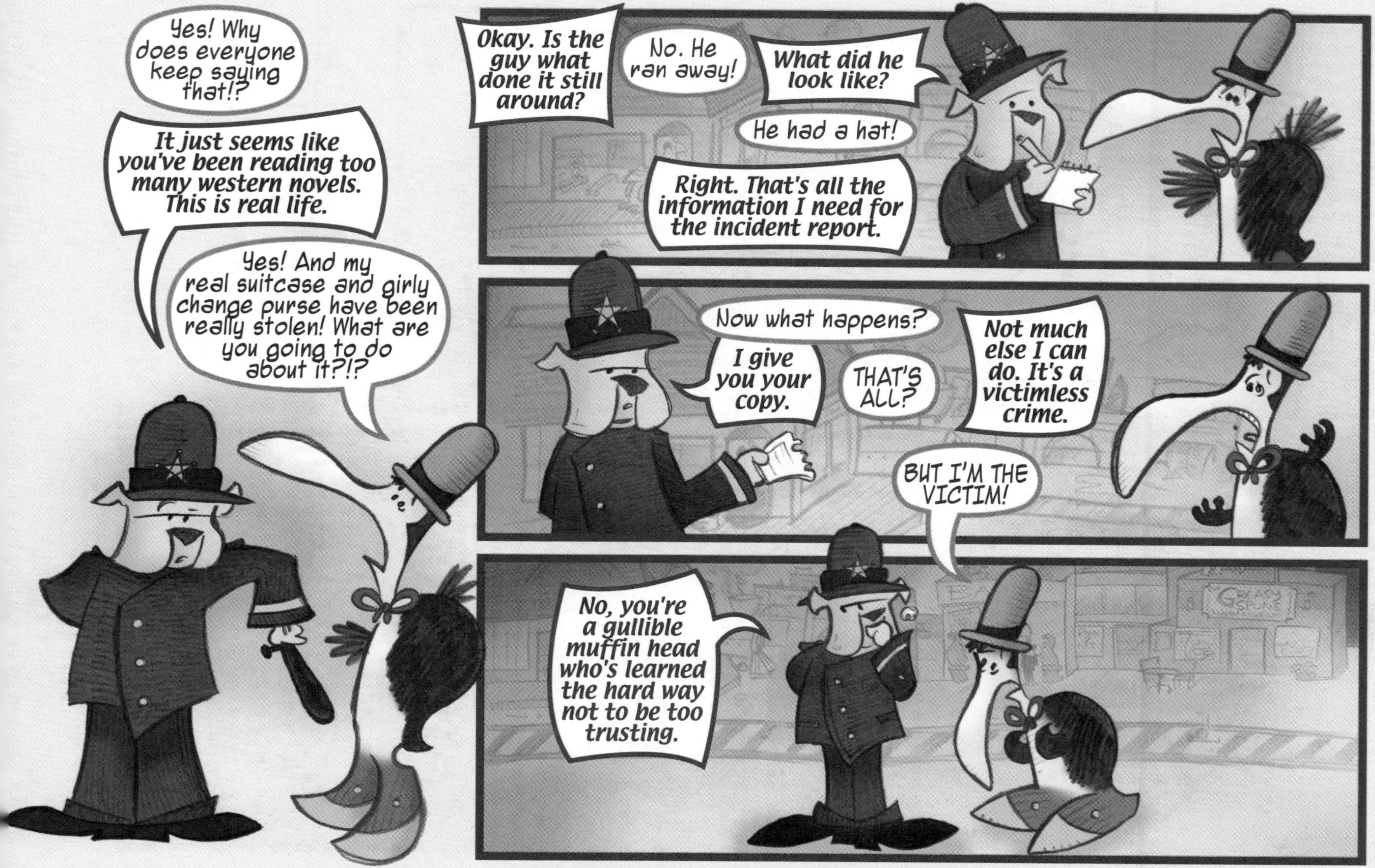
Yes! Why does everyone keep saying that!?
It just seems like you've been reading too many western novels. This is real life.
Yes! And my real suitcase and girly change purse have been really stolen! What are you going to do about it?!?
Okay. Is the guy what done it still around?
No. He ran away!
What did he look like?
He had a hat!
Right. That's all the information I need for the incident report.
Now what happens?
I give you your copy.
THAT'S ALL?
Not much else I can do. It's a victimless crime.
BUT I'M THE VICTIM!
No, you're a gullible muffin head who's learned the hard way not to be too trusting.

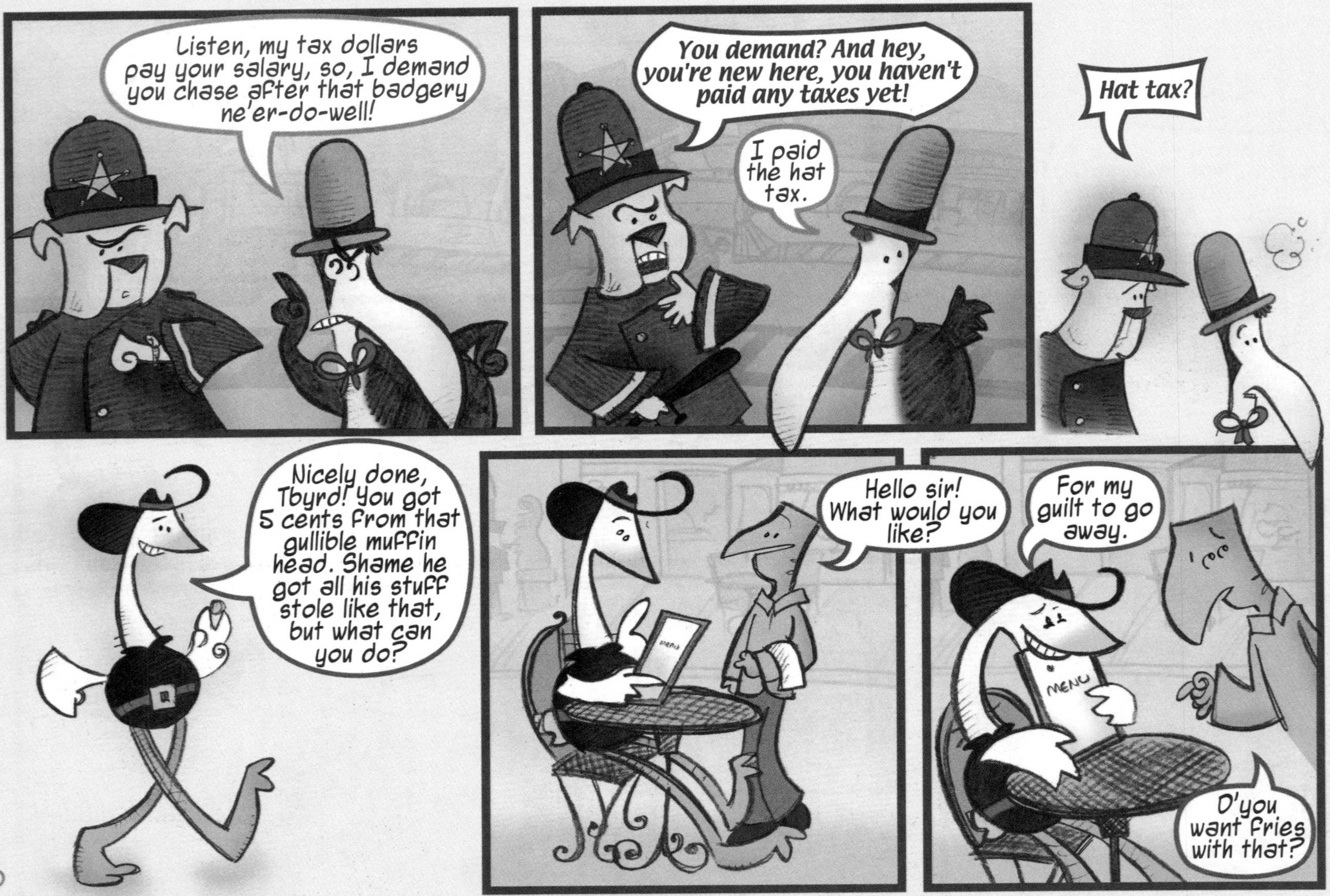

Listen, my tax dollars pay your salary, so, I demand you chase after that badgery ne'er-do-well!
You demand? And hey, you're new here, you haven't paid any taxes yet!
I paid the hat tax.
Hat tax?
Nicely done, Tbyrd! You got 5 cents from that gullible muffin head. Shame he got all his stuff stole like that, but what can you do?
Hello sir! What would you like?
For my guilt to go away.
O'you want fries with that?

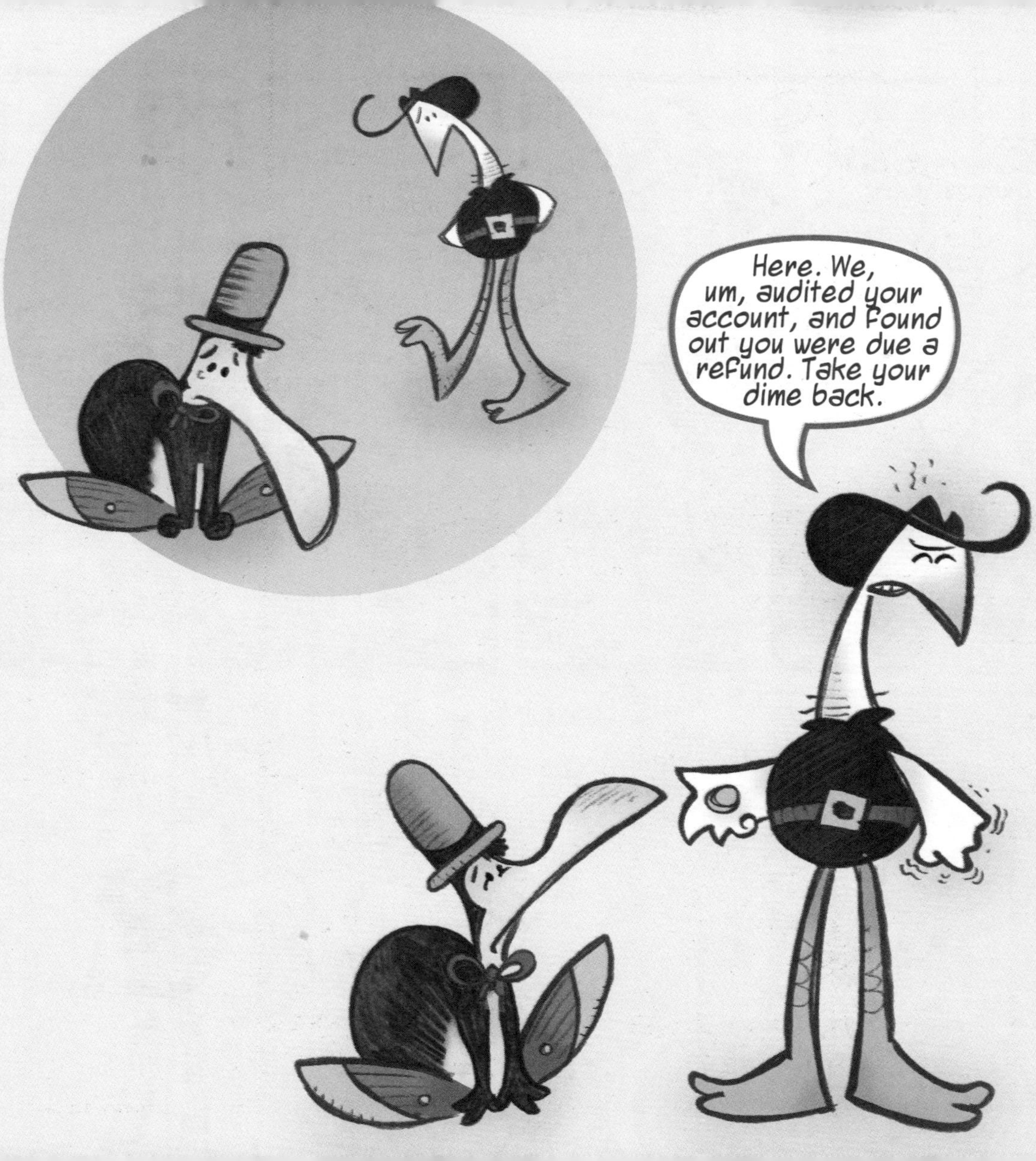
Here. We, um, audited your account, and found out you were due a refund. Take your dime back.

chapter 3

Every line has a silver clouding

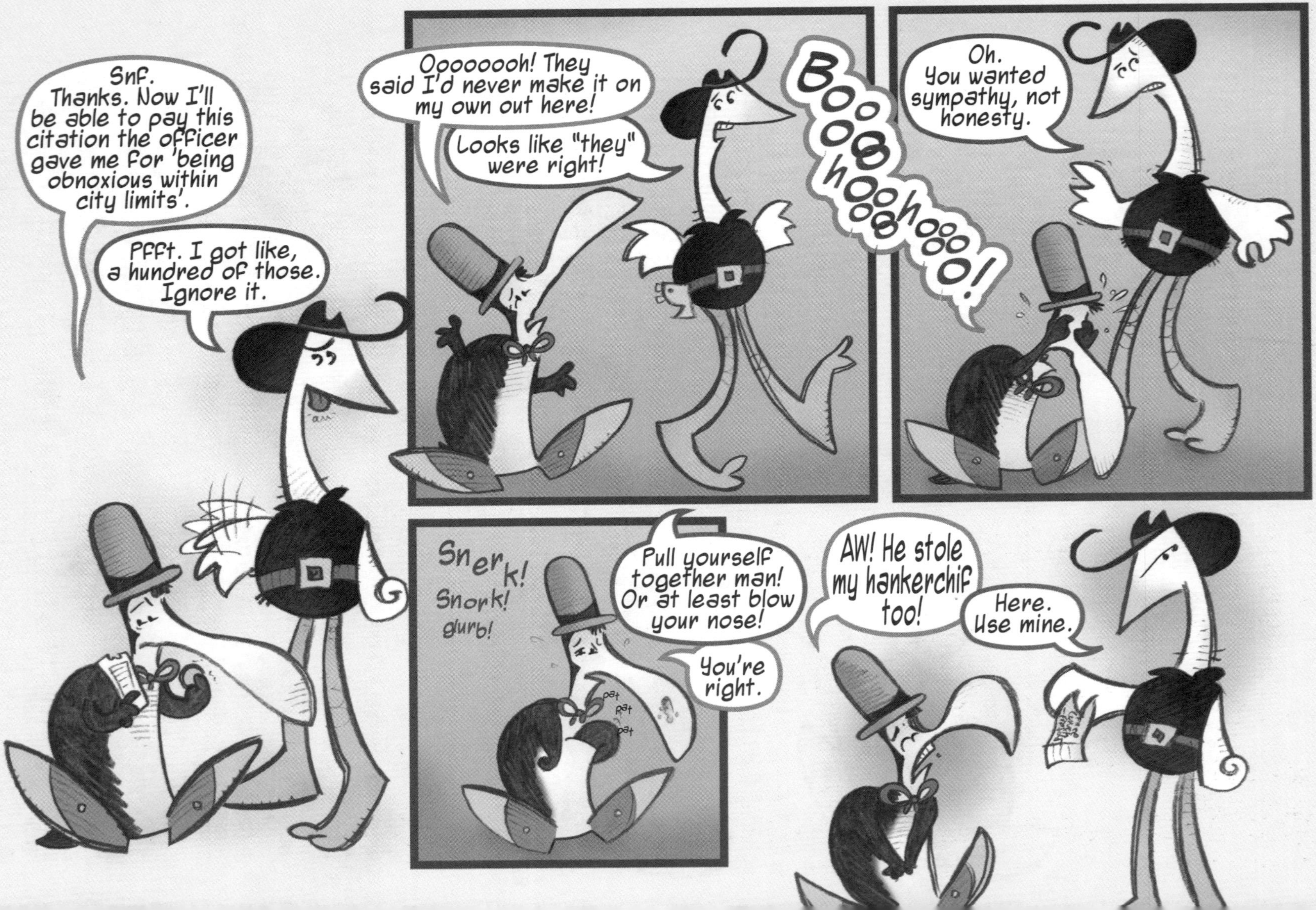
Snf. Thanks. Now I'll be able to pay this citation the officer gave me for 'being obnoxious within city limits'.
Pfft. I got like, a hundred of those. Ignore it.
Oooooooh! They said I'd never make it on my own out here!
Looks like "they" were right!
Booooohoooohoooo!
Oh. You wanted sympathy, not honesty.
Snerk! Snork! glurb!
Pull yourself together man! Or at least blow your nose!
pat pat pat
You're right.
AW! He stole my hankerchif too!
Here. Use mine.

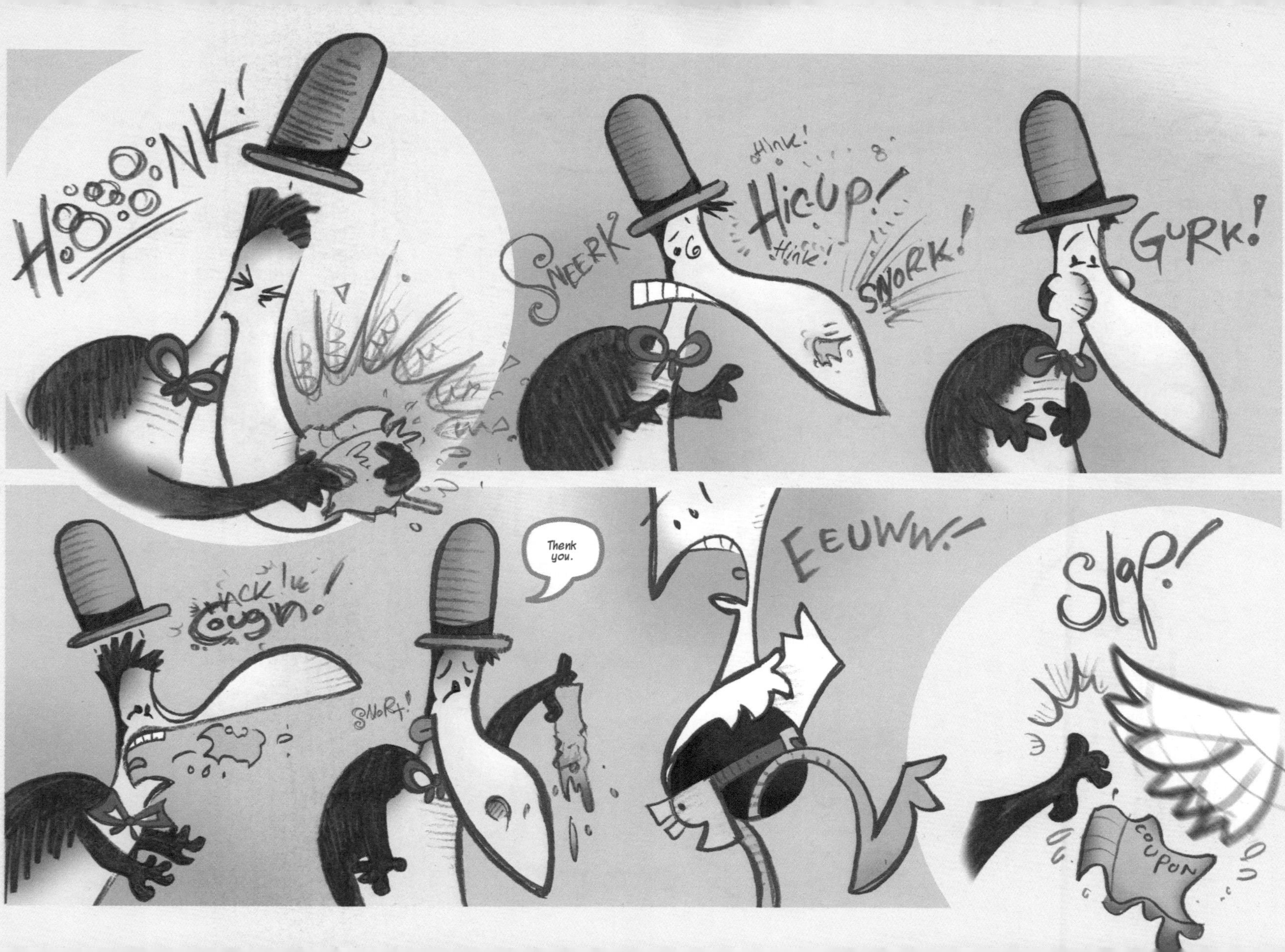
HOOOONK!
SNEERK
Hink!
HIC-UP!
Hink!
SNORK!
GURK!
HACK!
Cough!
SNORT!
Thenk you.
EEUWW!
Slap!
COUPON

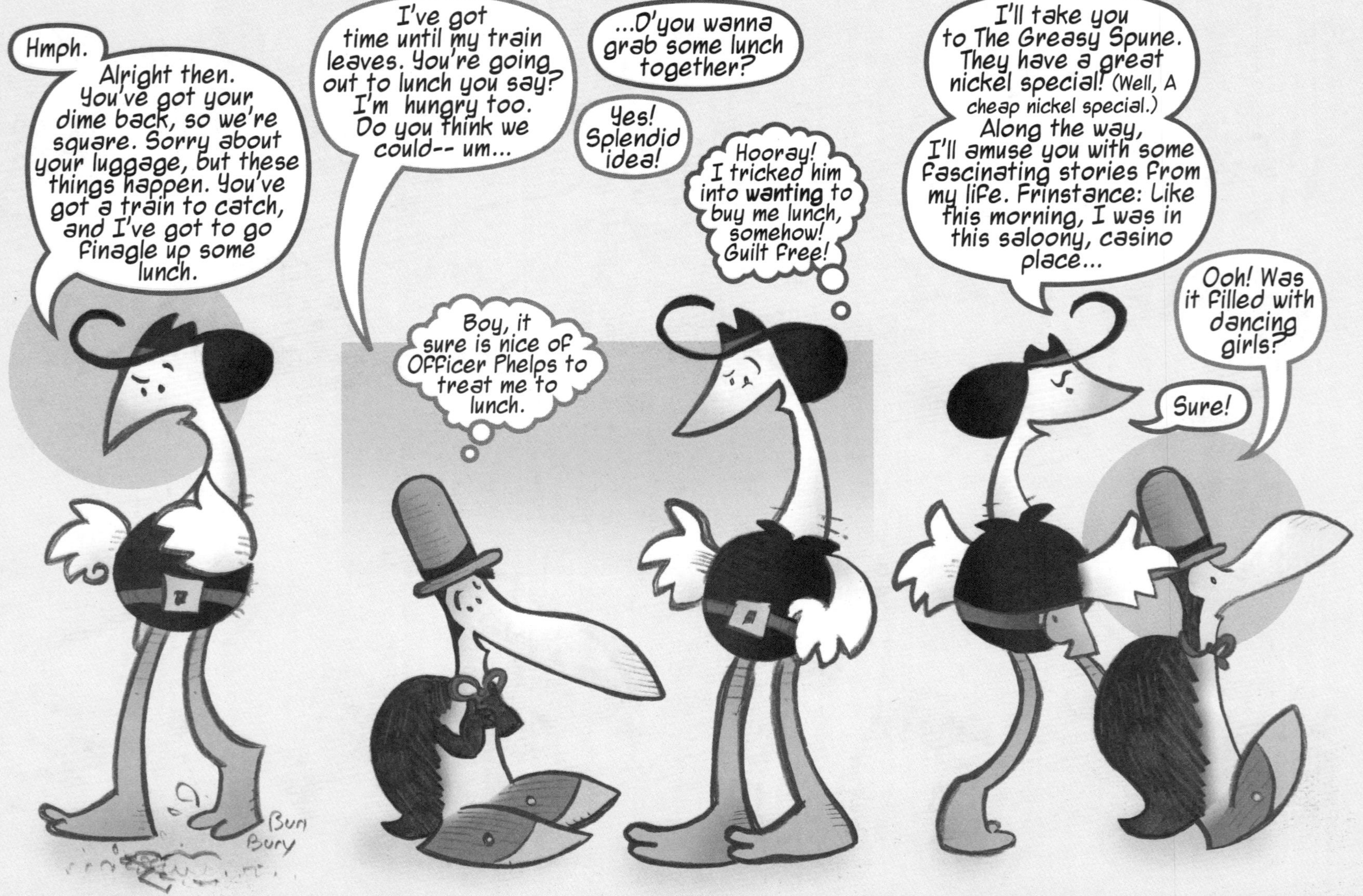
Hmph.
Alright then. You've got your dime back, so we're square. Sorry about your luggage, but these things happen. You've got a train to catch, and I've got to go finagle up some lunch.
I've got time until my train leaves. You're going out to lunch you say? I'm hungry too. Do you think we could-- um...
Boy, it sure is nice of Officer Phelps to treat me to lunch.
...D'you wanna grab some lunch together?
Yes! Splendid idea!
Hooray! I tricked him into **wanting** to buy me lunch, somehow! Guilt free!
I'll take you to The Greasy Spune. They have a great nickel special! (Well, A cheap nickel special.) Along the way, I'll amuse you with some fascinating stories from my life. Frinstance: Like this morning, I was in this saloony, casino place...
Ooh! Was it filled with dancing girls?
Sure!

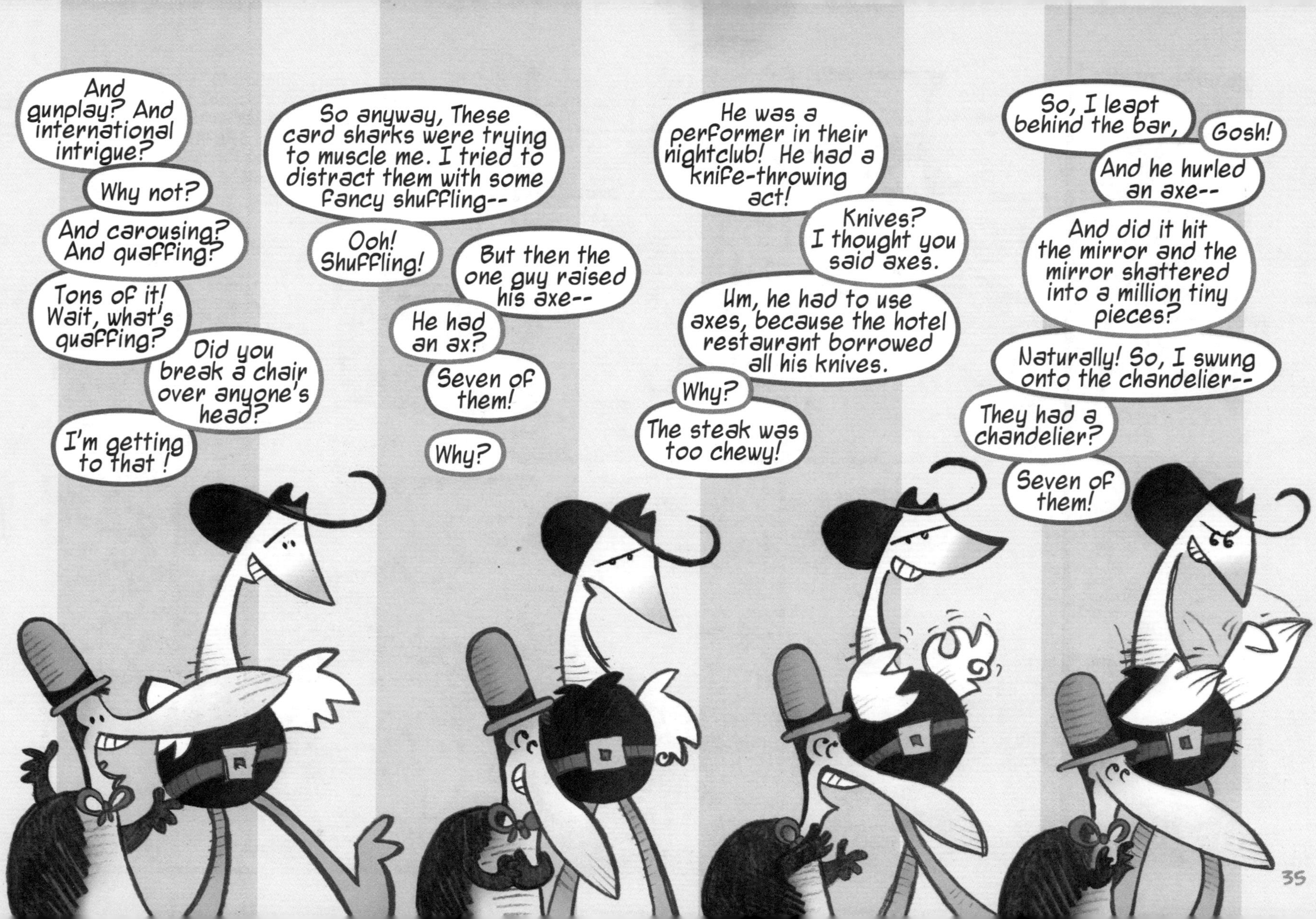
And gunplay? And international intrigue?
Why not?
And carousing? And quaffing?
Tons of it! Wait, what's quaffing?
Did you break a chair over anyone's head?
I'm getting to that!
So anyway, These card sharks were trying to muscle me. I tried to distract them with some fancy shuffling--
Ooh! Shuffling!
But then the one guy raised his axe--
He had an ax?
Seven of them!
Why?
He was a performer in their nightclub! He had a knife-throwing act!
Knives? I thought you said axes.
Um, he had to use axes, because the hotel restaurant borrowed all his knives.
Why?
The steak was too chewy!
So, I leapt behind the bar,
Gosh!
And he hurled an axe--
And did it hit the mirror and the mirror shattered into a million tiny pieces?
Naturally! So, I swung onto the chandelier--
They had a chandelier?
Seven of them!

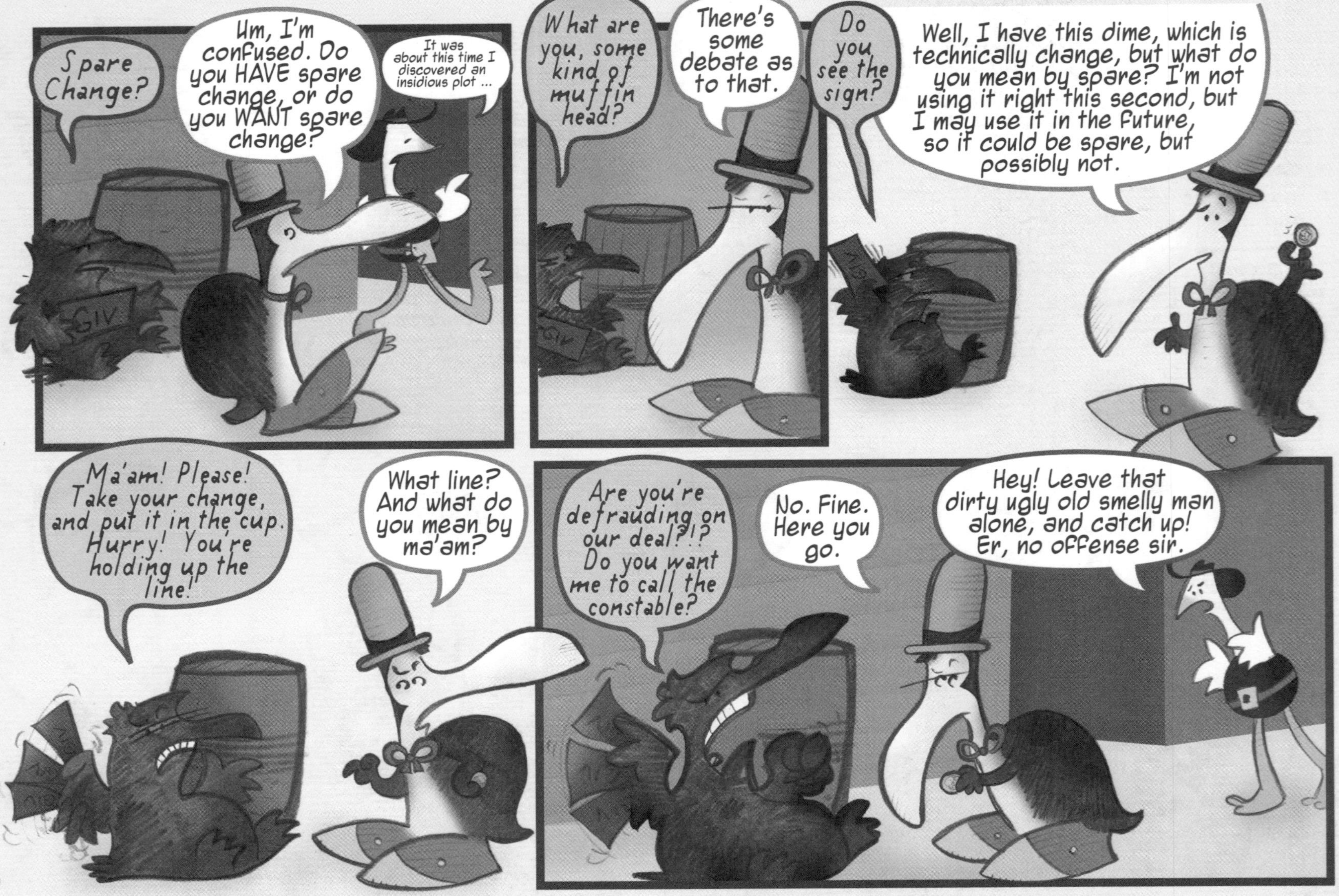
Spare Change?
GIV
Um, I'm confused. Do you HAVE spare change, or do you WANT spare change?
It was about this time I discovered an insidious plot ...
What are you, some kind of muffin head?
There's some debate as to that.
Do you see the sign?
Well, I have this dime, which is technically change, but what do you mean by spare? I'm not using it right this second, but I may use it in the future, so it could be spare, but possibly not.
Ma'am! Please! Take your change, and put it in the cup. Hurry! You're holding up the line!
What line? And what do you mean by ma'am?
Are you're defrauding on our deal?!? Do you want me to call the constable?
No. Fine. Here you go.
Hey! Leave that dirty ugly old smelly man alone, and catch up! Er, no offense sir.

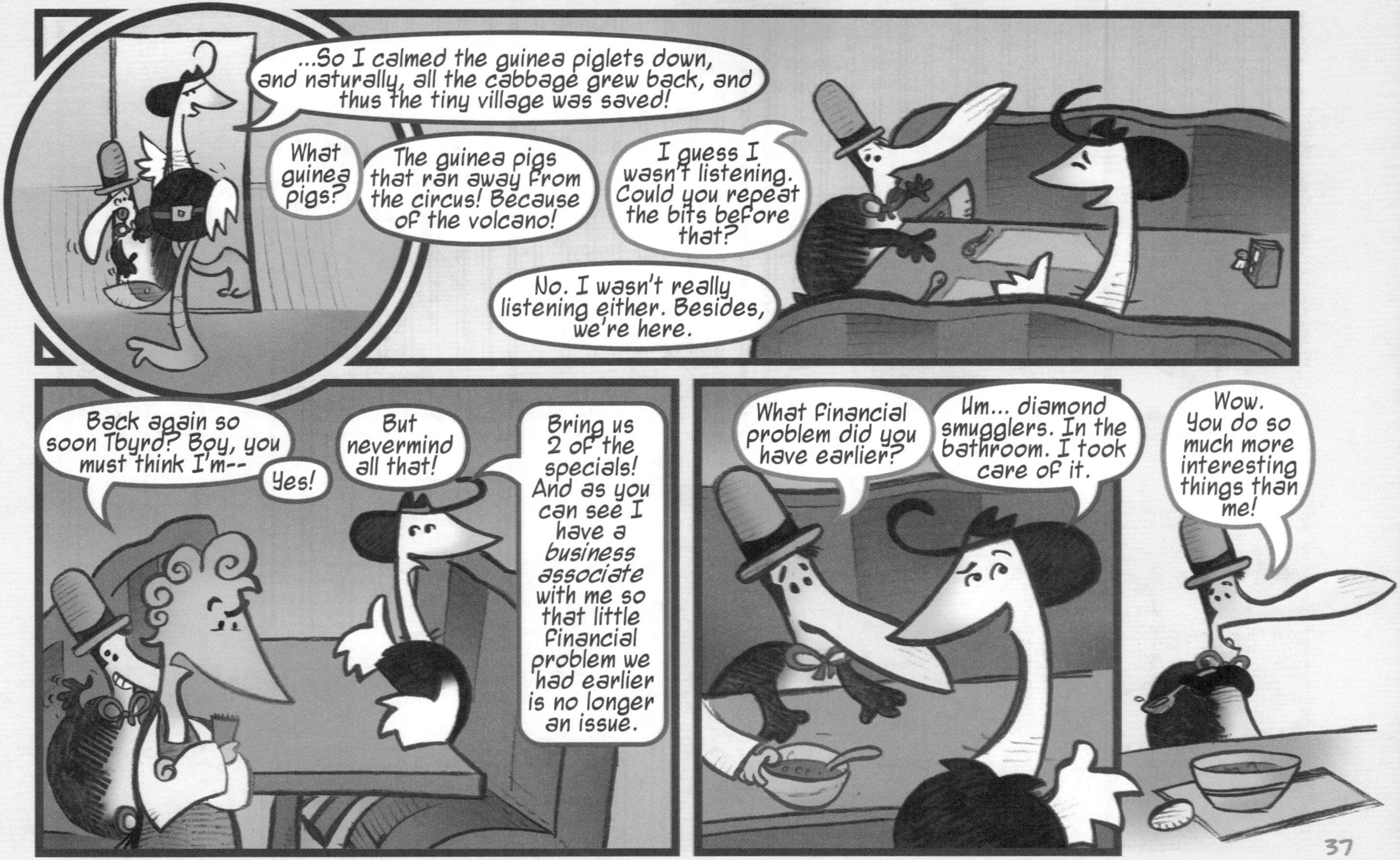
...So I calmed the guinea piglets down, and naturally, all the cabbage grew back, and thus the tiny village was saved!
What guinea pigs?
The guinea pigs that ran away from the circus! Because of the volcano!
I guess I wasn't listening. Could you repeat the bits before that?
No. I wasn't really listening either. Besides, we're here.
Back again so soon Tbyrd? Boy, you must think I'm--
Yes!
But nevermind all that!
Bring us 2 of the specials! And as you can see I have a *business associate* with me so that little financial problem we had earlier is no longer an issue.
What financial problem did you have earlier?
Um... diamond smugglers. In the bathroom. I took care of it.
Wow. You do so much more interesting things than me!

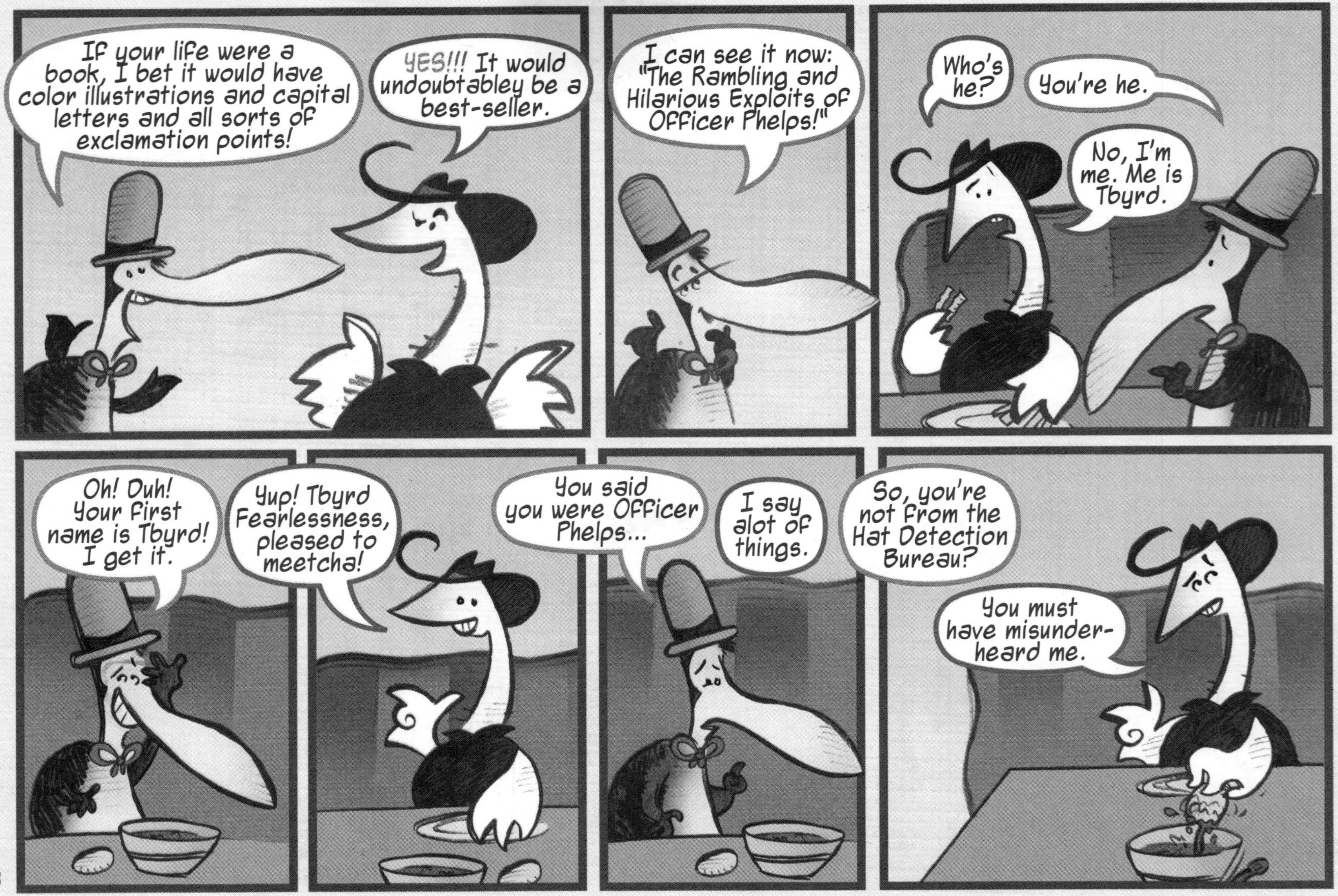
If your life were a book, I bet it would have color illustrations and capital letters and all sorts of exclamation points!
YES!!! It would undoubtabley be a best-seller.
I can see it now: "The Rambling and Hilarious Exploits of Officer Phelps!"
Who's he?
You're he.
No, I'm me. Me is Tbyrd.
Oh! Duh! Your first name is Tbyrd! I get it.
Yup! Tbyrd Fearlessness, pleased to meetcha!
You said you were Officer Phelps...
I say alot of things.
So, you're not from the Hat Detection Bureau?
You must have misunderheard me.

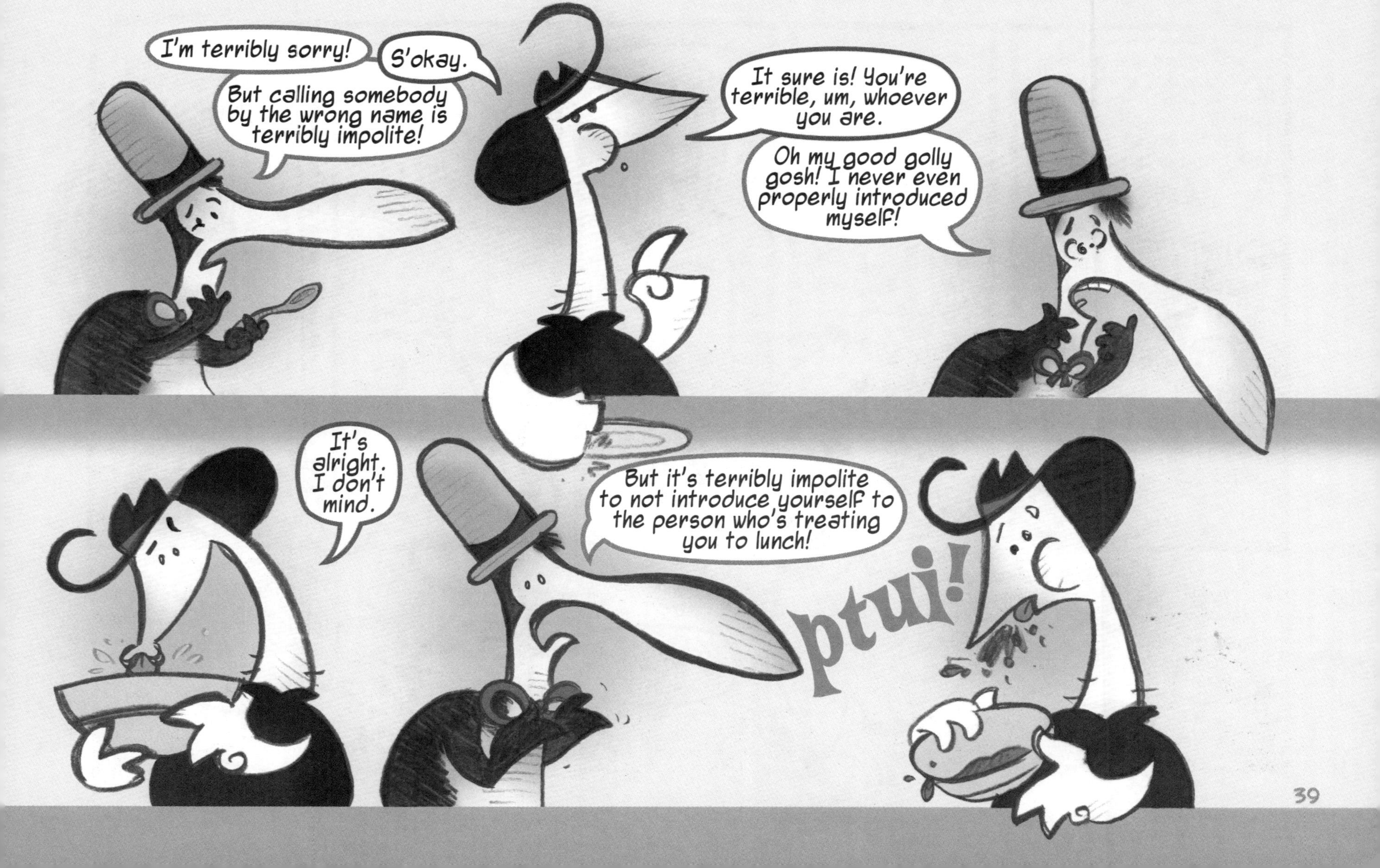
I'm terribly sorry!
S'okay.
But calling somebody by the wrong name is terribly impolite!
It sure is! You're terrible, um, whoever you are.
Oh my good golly gosh! I never even properly introduced myself!
It's alright. I don't mind.
But it's terribly impolite to not introduce yourself to the person who's treating you to lunch!
ptui!

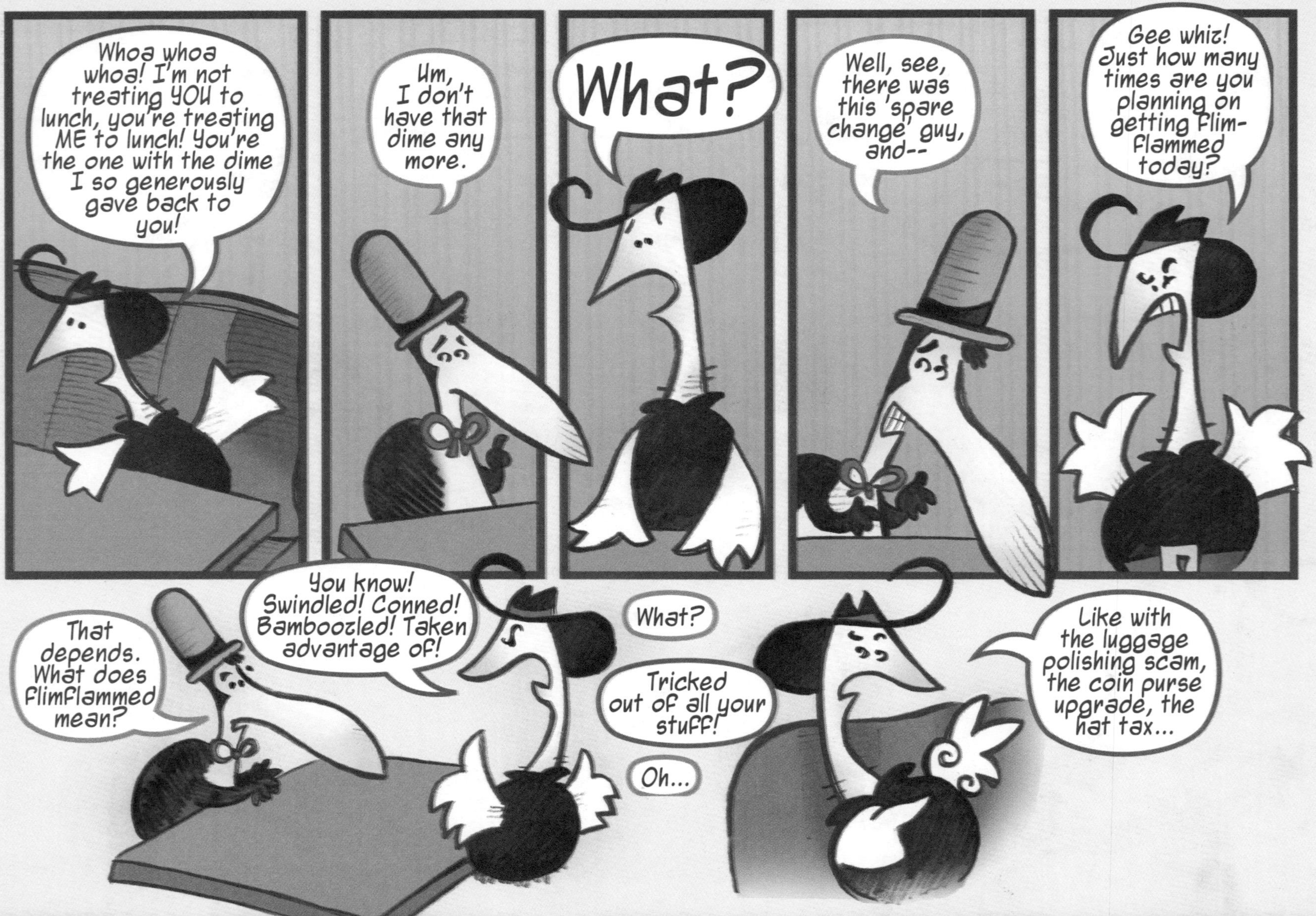
Whoa whoa whoa! I'm not treating YOU to lunch, you're treating ME to lunch! You're the one with the dime I so generously gave back to you!
Um, I don't have that dime any more.
What?
Well, see, there was this 'spare change' guy, and--
Gee whiz! Just how many times are you planning on getting flim-flammed today?
That depends. What does flimflammed mean?
You know! Swindled! Conned! Bamboozled! Taken advantage of!
What?
Tricked out of all your stuff!
Oh...
Like with the luggage polishing scam, the coin purse upgrade, the hat tax...

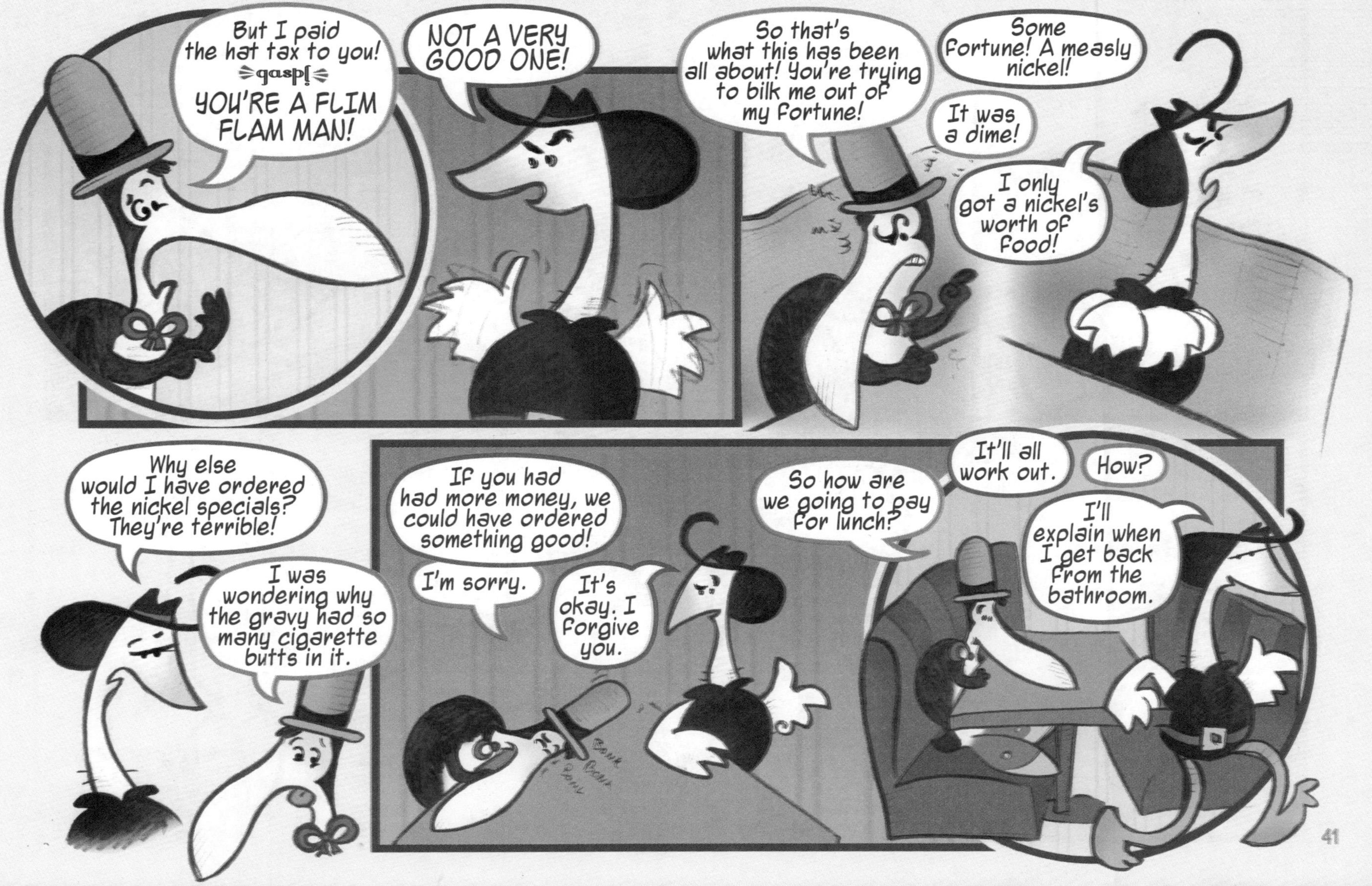

But I paid the hat tax to you! gasp! YOU'RE A FLIM FLAM MAN!
NOT A VERY GOOD ONE!
So that's what this has been all about! You're trying to bilk me out of my fortune!
Some fortune! A measly nickel!
It was a dime!
I only got a nickel's worth of food!
Why else would I have ordered the nickel specials? They're terrible!
I was wondering why the gravy had so many cigarette butts in it.
If you had had more money, we could have ordered something good!
I'm sorry.
It's okay. I forgive you.
So how are we going to pay for lunch?
It'll all work out.
How?
I'll explain when I get back from the bathroom.

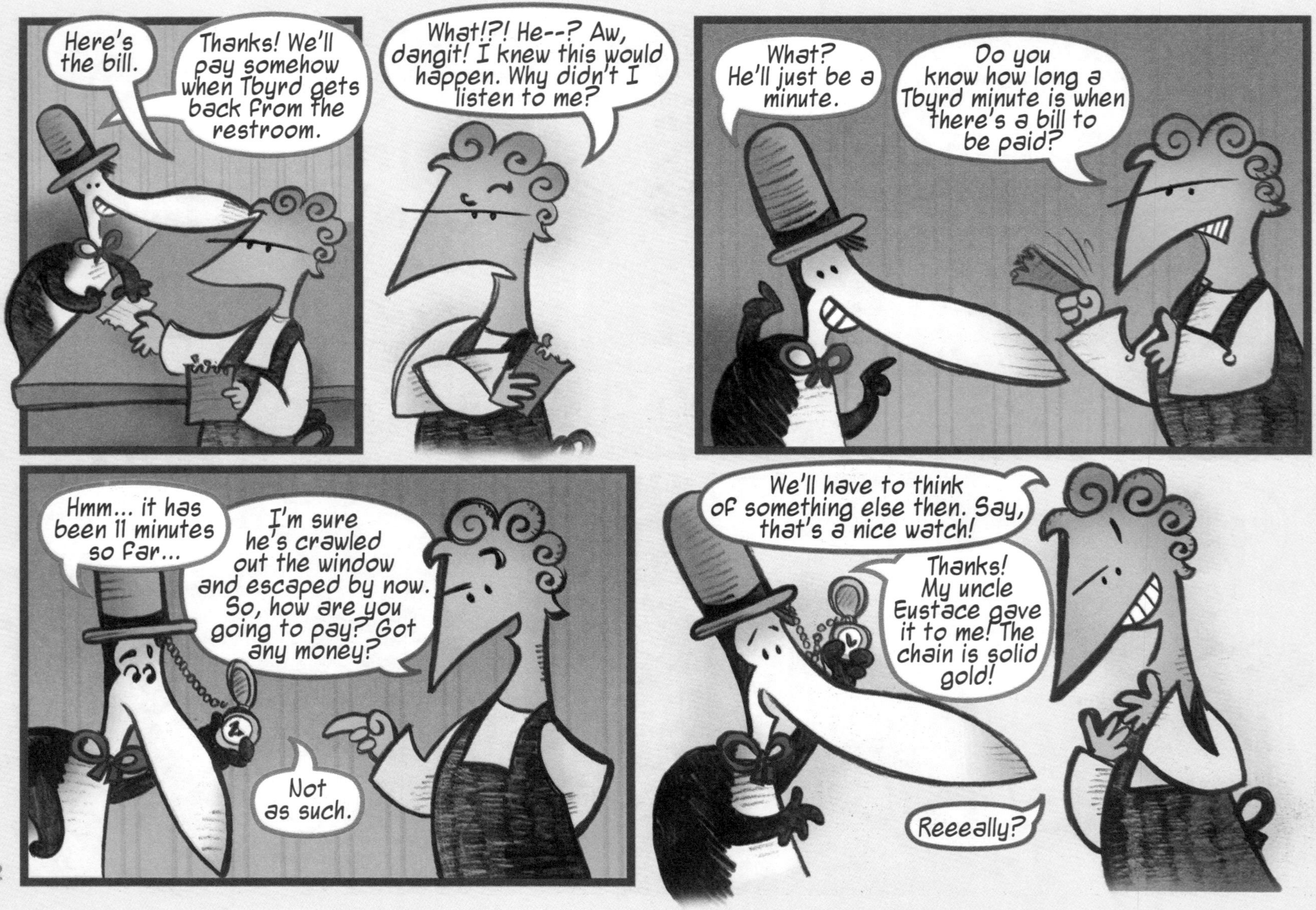
Here's the bill.
Thanks! We'll pay somehow when Tbyrd gets back from the restroom.
What!?! He--? Aw, dangit! I knew this would happen. Why didn't I listen to me?
What? He'll just be a minute.
Do you know how long a Tbyrd minute is when there's a bill to be paid?
Hmm... it has been 11 minutes so far...
I'm sure he's crawled out the window and escaped by now. So, how are you going to pay? Got any money?
Not as such.
We'll have to think of something else then. Say, that's a nice watch!
Thanks! My uncle Eustace gave it to me! The chain is solid gold!
Reeeally?

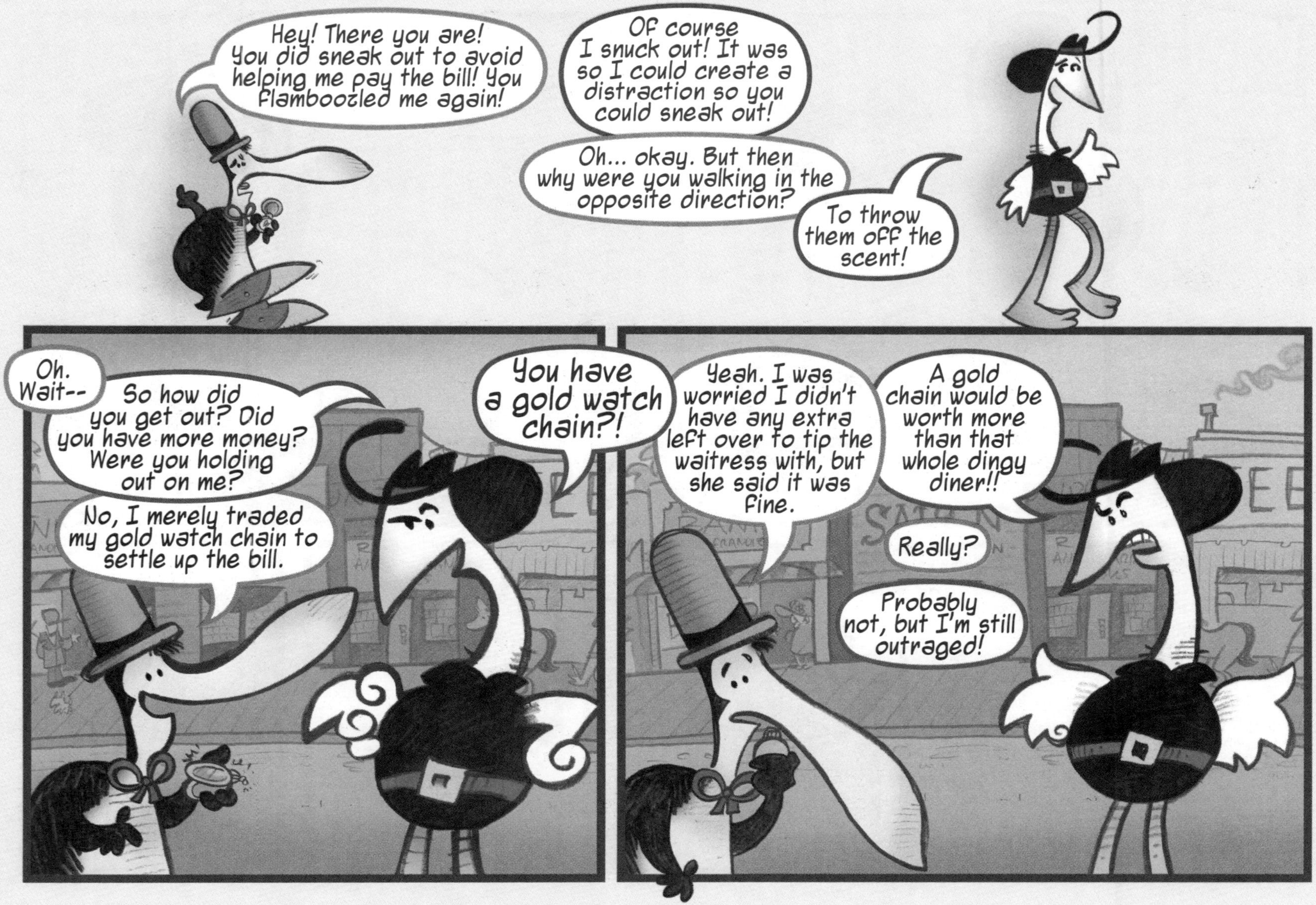
Hey! There you are! You did sneak out to avoid helping me pay the bill! You flamboozled me again!
Of course I snuck out! It was so I could create a distraction so you could sneak out!
Oh... okay. But then why were you walking in the opposite direction?
To throw them off the scent!
Oh. Wait--
So how did you get out? Did you have more money? Were you holding out on me?
No, I merely traded my gold watch chain to settle up the bill.
You have a gold watch chain?!
Yeah. I was worried I didn't have any extra left over to tip the waitress with, but she said it was fine.
A gold chain would be worth more than that whole dingy diner!!
Really?
Probably not, but I'm still outraged!

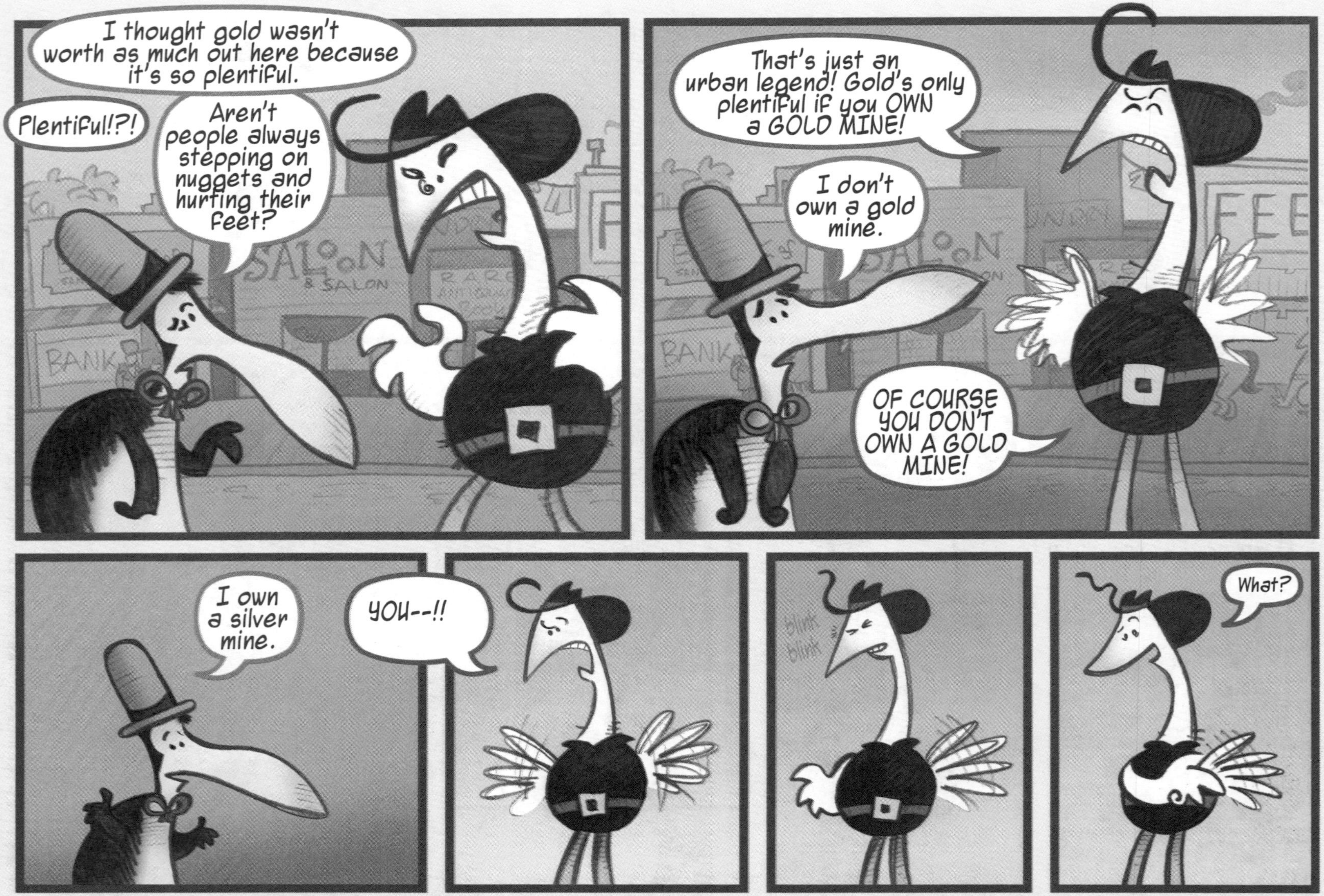
I thought gold wasn't worth as much out here because it's so plentiful.
Plentiful!?!
Aren't people always stepping on nuggets and hurting their feet?
SALOON
& SALON
BANK
That's just an urban legend! Gold's only plentiful if you OWN a GOLD MINE!
I don't own a gold mine.
OF COURSE YOU DON'T OWN A GOLD MINE!
I own a silver mine.
YOU--!!
blink blink
What?

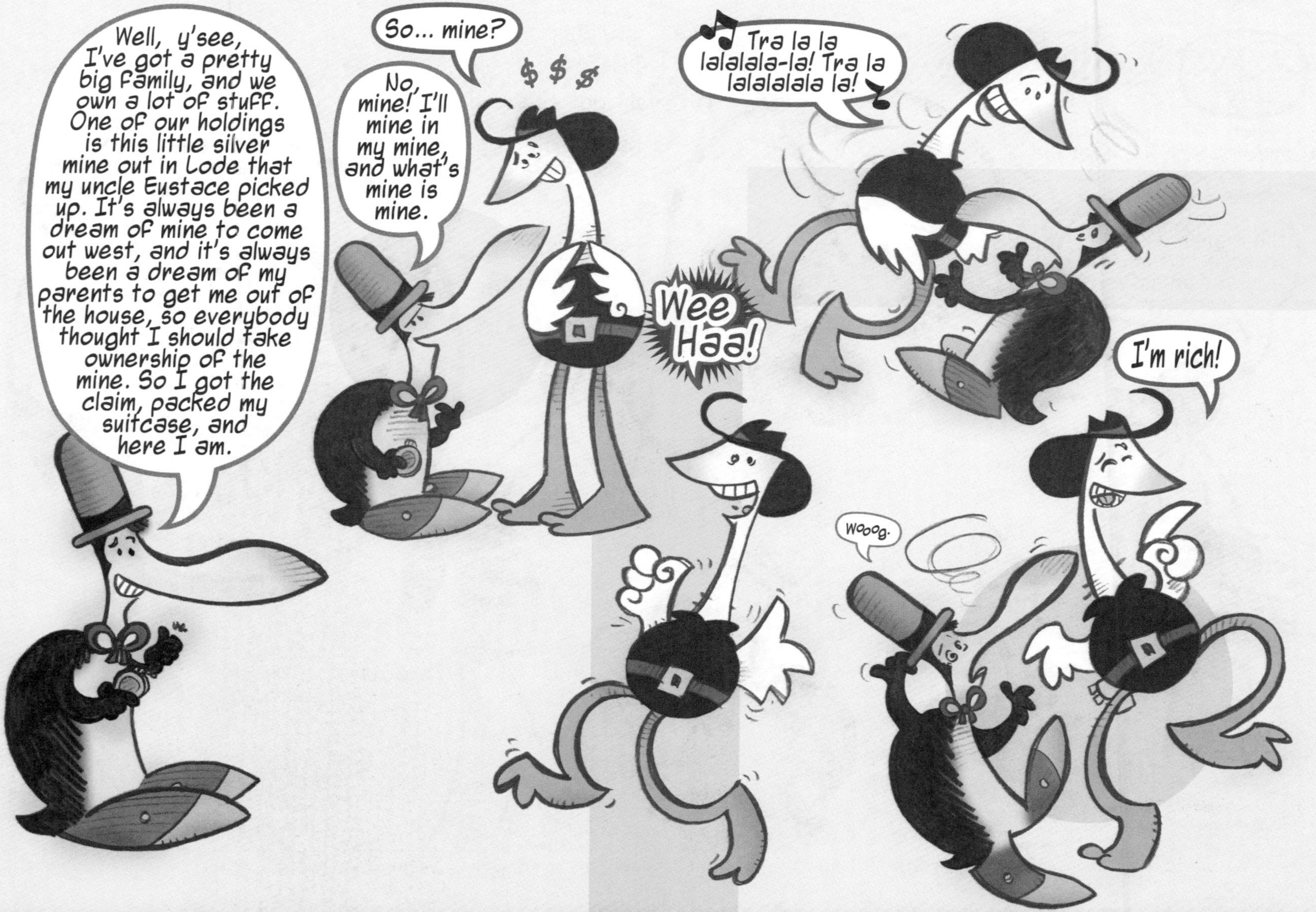
Well, y'see, I've got a pretty big family, and we own a lot of stuff. One of our holdings is this little silver mine out in Lode that my uncle Eustace picked up. It's always been a dream of mine to come out west, and it's always been a dream of my parents to get me out of the house, so everybody thought I should take ownership of the mine. So I got the claim, packed my suitcase, and here I am.
So... mine?
No, mine! I'll mine in my mine, and what's mine is mine.
$ $ $
Wee Haa!
Tra la la lalalala-la! Tra la lalalalala la!
I'm rich!
Wooog.

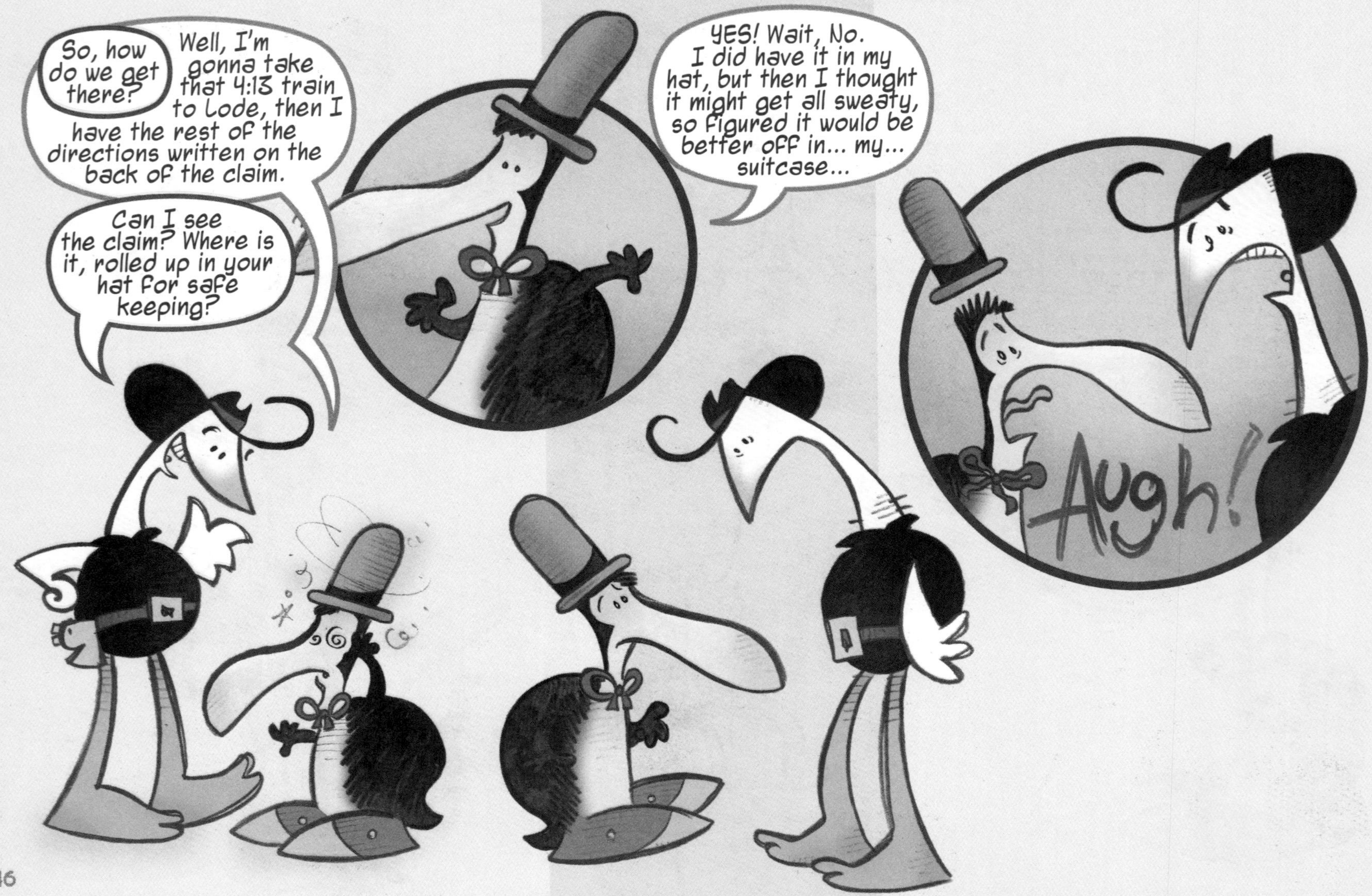
So, how do we get there?
Well, I'm gonna take that 4:13 train to Lode, then I have the rest of the directions written on the back of the claim.
Can I see the claim? Where is it, rolled up in your hat for safe keeping?
YES! Wait, No. I did have it in my hat, but then I thought it might get all sweaty, so figured it would be better off in... my... suitcase...
Augh!

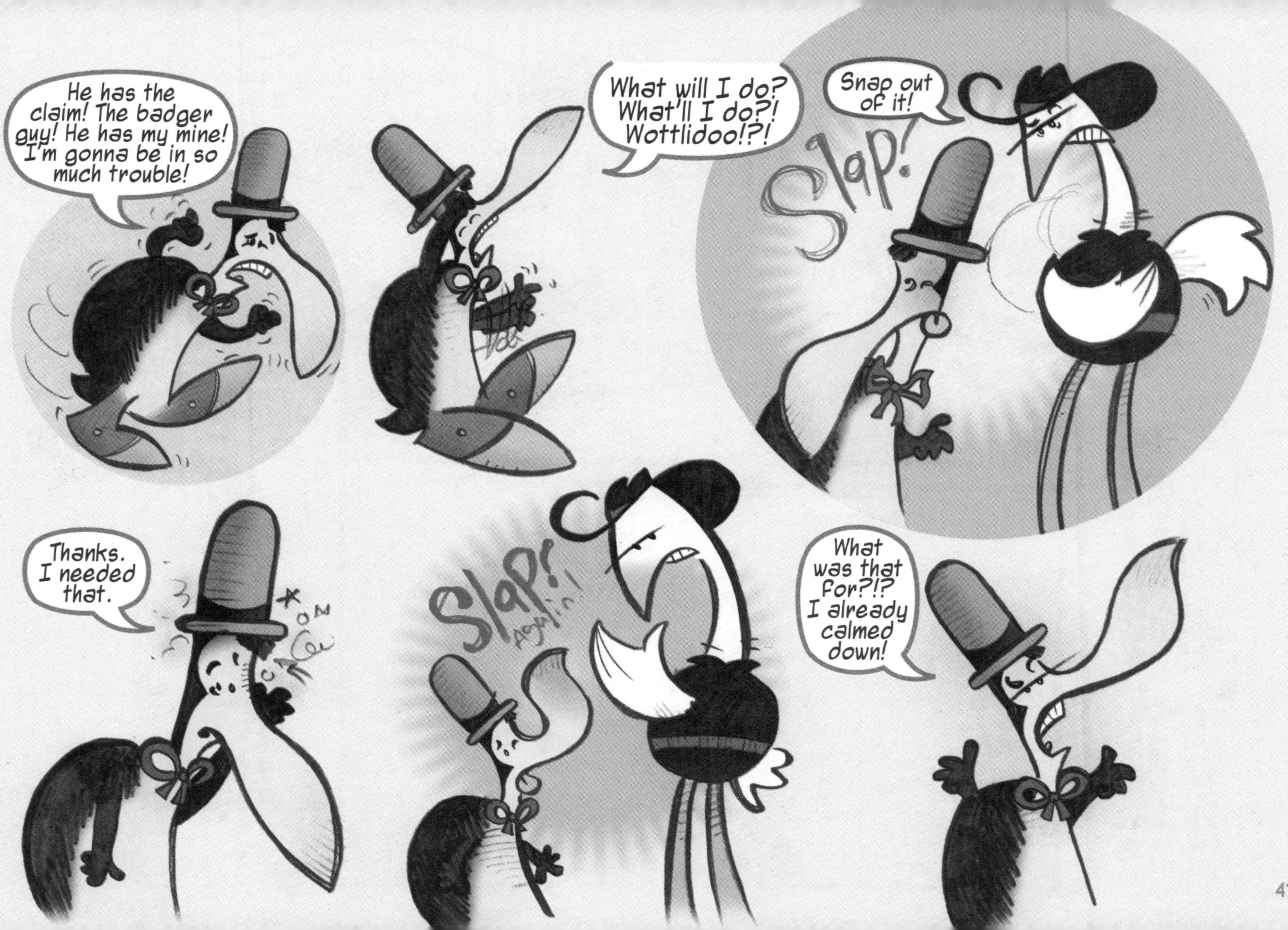
He has the claim! The badger guy! He has my mine! I'm gonna be in so much trouble!
What will I do? What'll I do?! Wottlidoo!?!
Snap out of it!
Slap!
Thanks. I needed that.
Slap! again!
What was that for?!? I already calmed down!

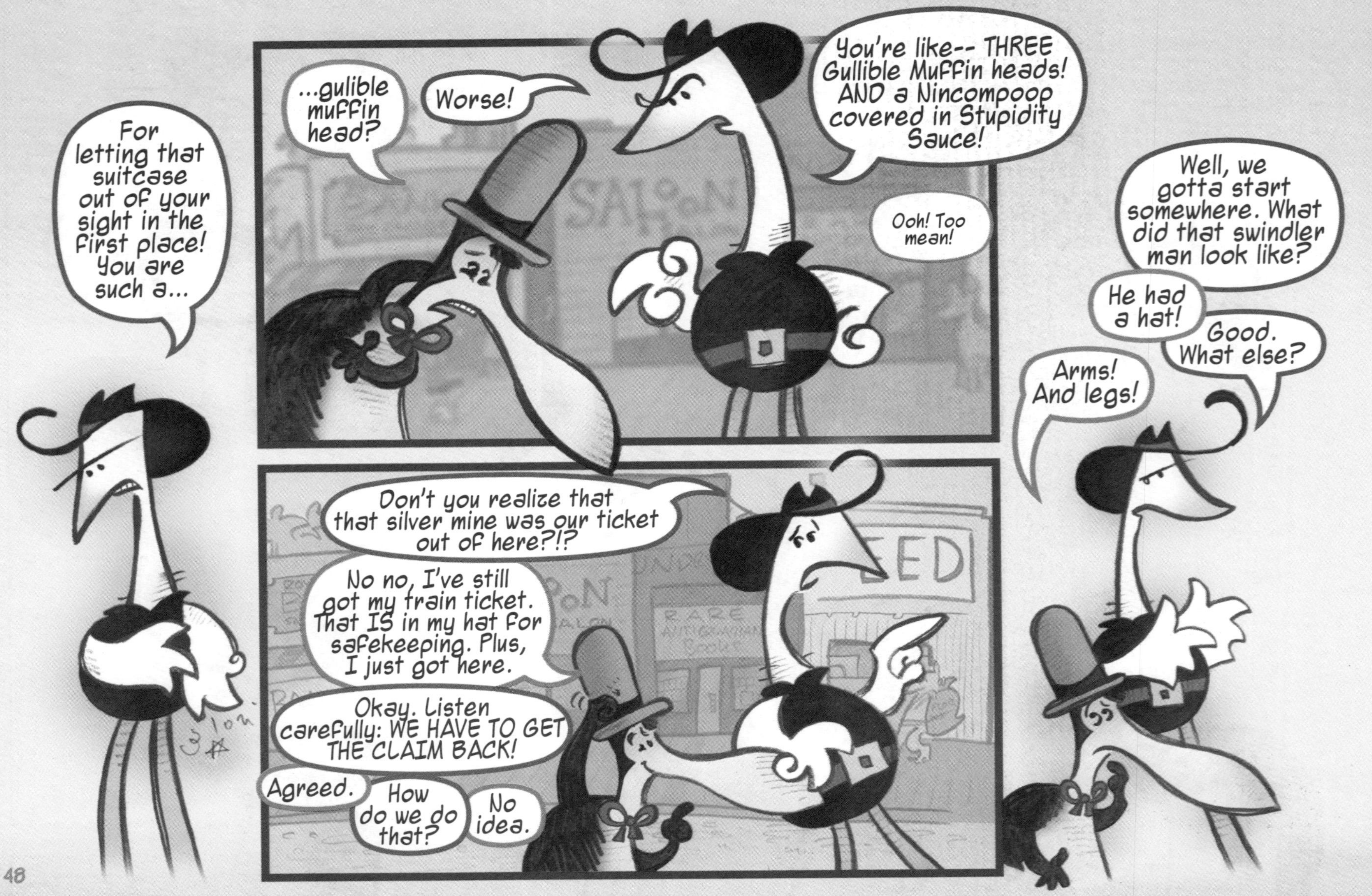

For letting that suitcase out of your sight in the first place! You are such a...
...gulible muffin head?
Worse!
You're like-- THREE Gullible Muffin heads! AND a Nincompoop covered in Stupidity Sauce!
Ooh! Too mean!
Don't you realize that that silver mine was our ticket out of here?!?
No no, I've still got my train ticket. That IS in my hat for safekeeping. Plus, I just got here.
Okay. Listen carefully: WE HAVE TO GET THE CLAIM BACK!
Agreed.
How do we do that?
No idea.
Well, we gotta start somewhere. What did that swindler man look like?
He had a hat!
Good. What else?
Arms! And legs!

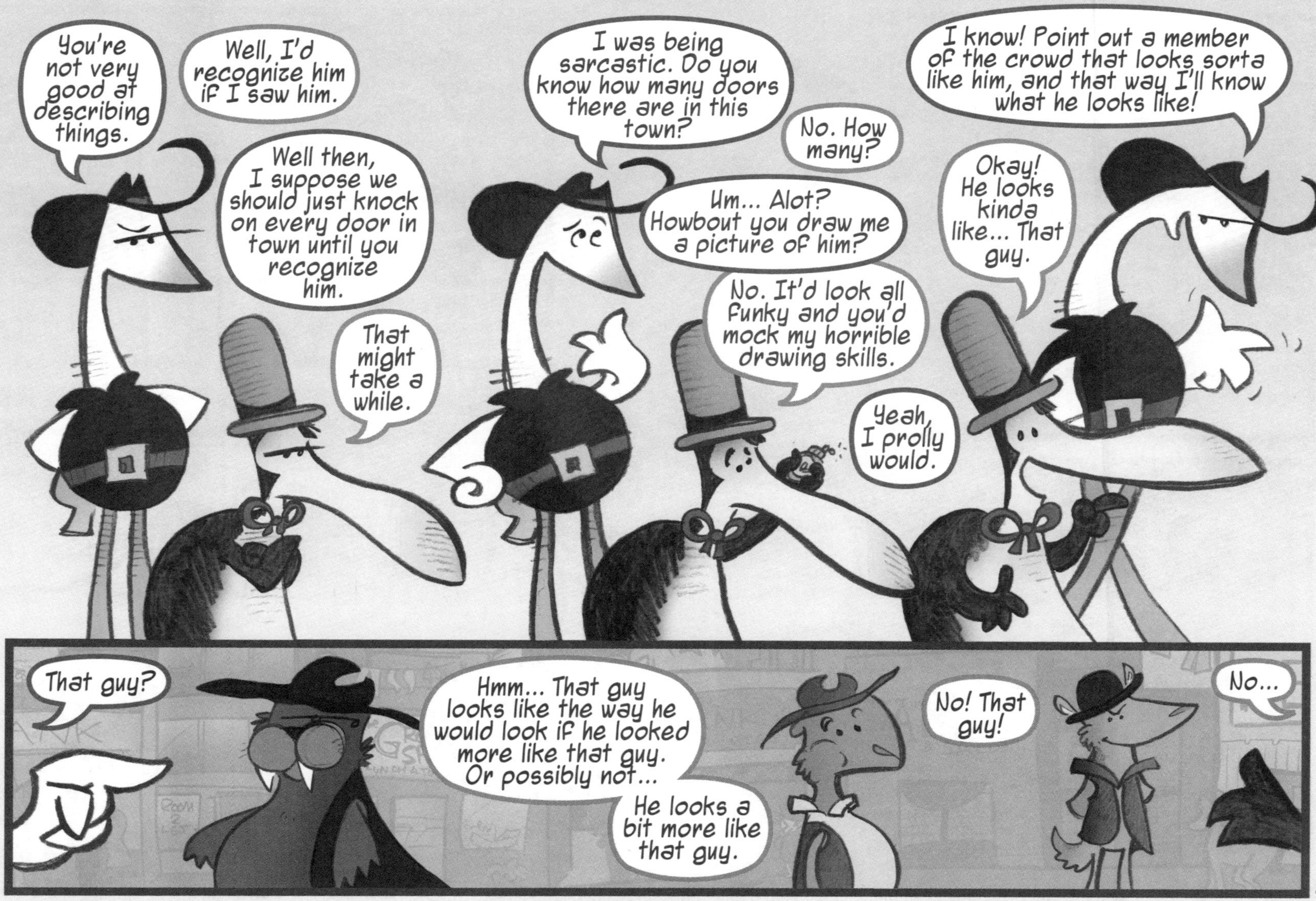
You're not very good at describing things.
Well, I'd recognize him if I saw him.
Well then, I suppose we should just knock on every door in town until you recognize him.
That might take a while.
I was being sarcastic. Do you know how many doors there are in this town?
No. How many?
Um... Alot? Howbout you draw me a picture of him?
No. It'd look all funky and you'd mock my horrible drawing skills.
Yeah, I prolly would.
I know! Point out a member of the crowd that looks sorta like him, and that way I'll know what he looks like!
Okay! He looks kinda like... That guy.
That guy?
Hmm... That guy looks like the way he would look if he looked more like that guy. Or possibly not...
He looks a bit more like that guy.
No! That guy!
No...

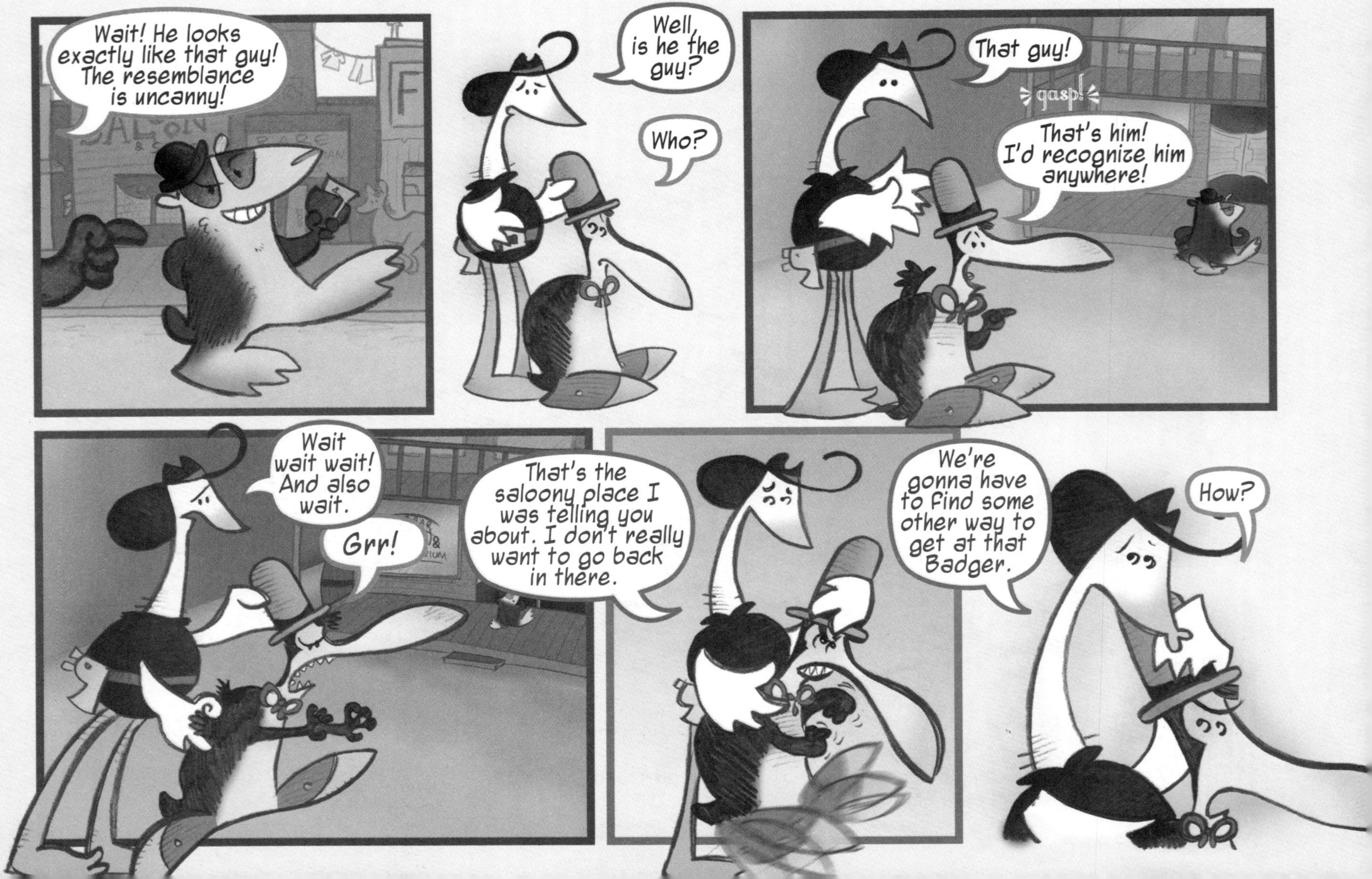
Wait! He looks exactly like that guy! The resemblance is uncanny!
Well, is he the guy?
Who?
That guy!
gasp!
That's him! I'd recognize him anywhere!
Wait wait wait! And also wait.
Grr!
That's the saloony place I was telling you about. I don't really want to go back in there.
We're gonna have to find some other way to get at that Badger.
How?

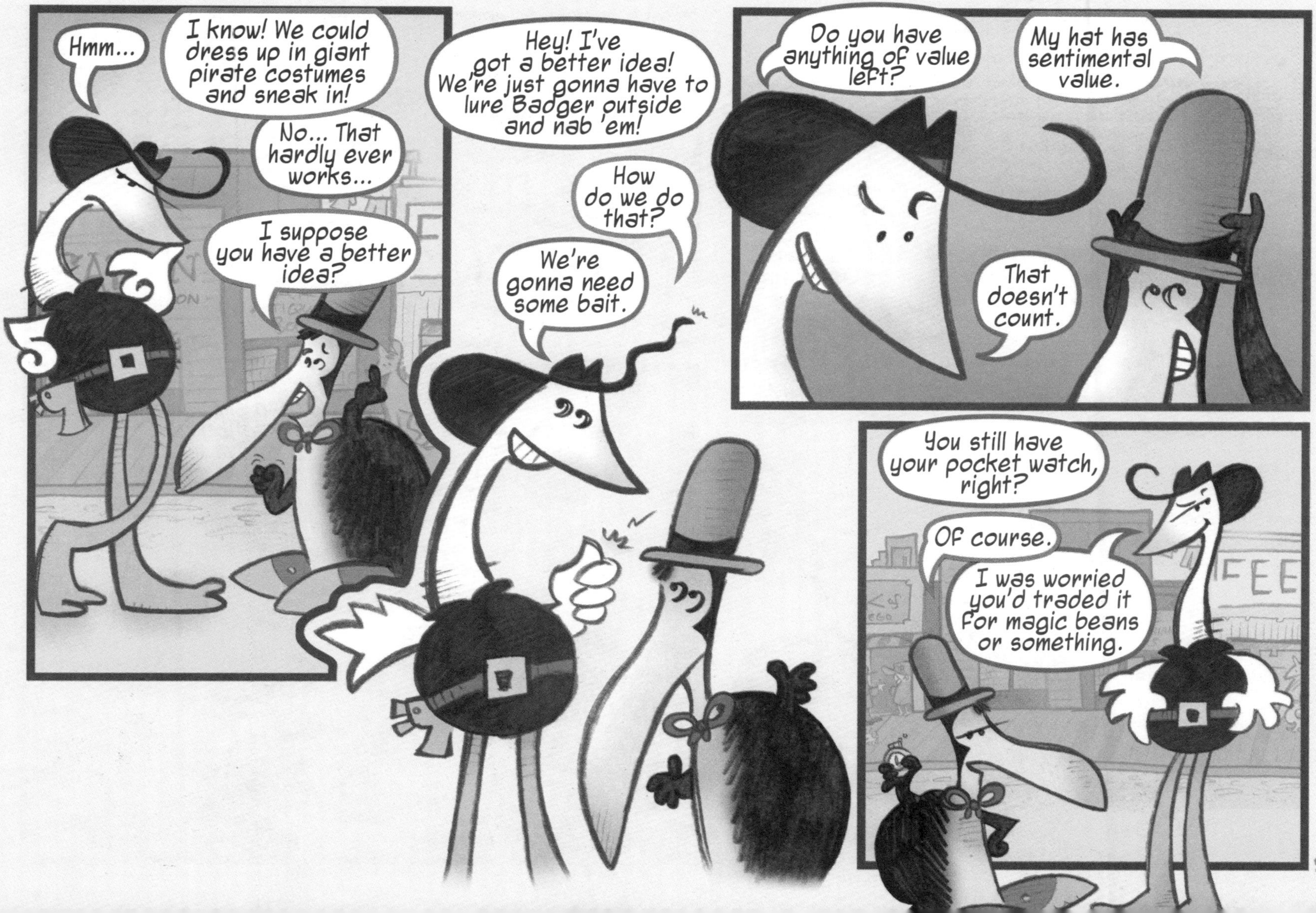

Hmm...
I know! We could dress up in giant pirate costumes and sneak in!
No... That hardly ever works...
I suppose you have a better idea?
5
Hey! I've got a better idea! We're just gonna have to lure Badger outside and nab 'em!
How do we do that?
We're gonna need some bait.
Do you have anything of value left?
My hat has sentimental value.
That doesn't count.
You still have your pocket watch, right?
Of course.
I was worried you'd traded it for magic beans or something.

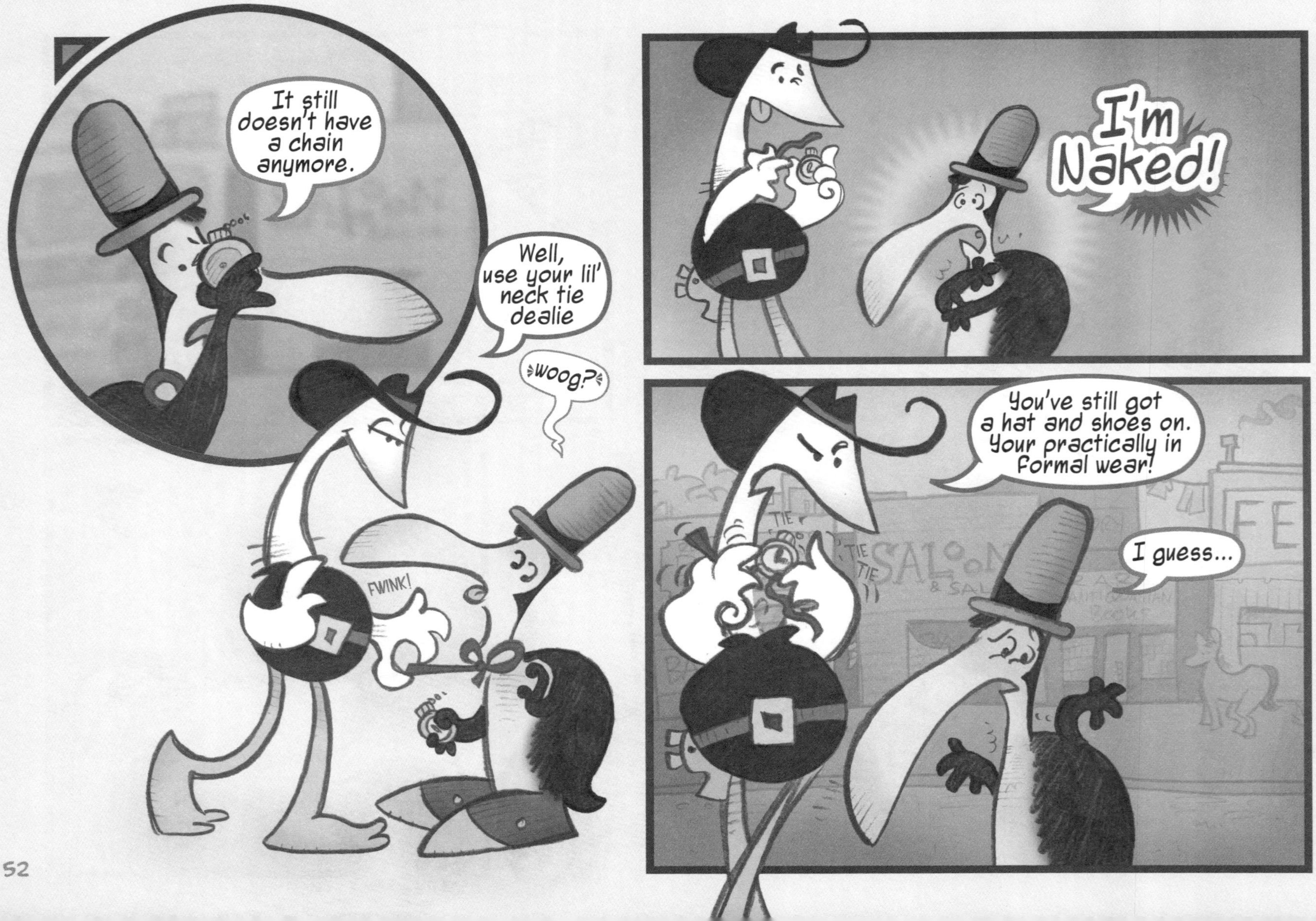
It still doesn't have a chain anymore.
Well, use your lil' neck tie dealie
woog?
FWINK!
I'm Naked!
You've still got a hat and shoes on. Your practically in formal wear!
I guess...

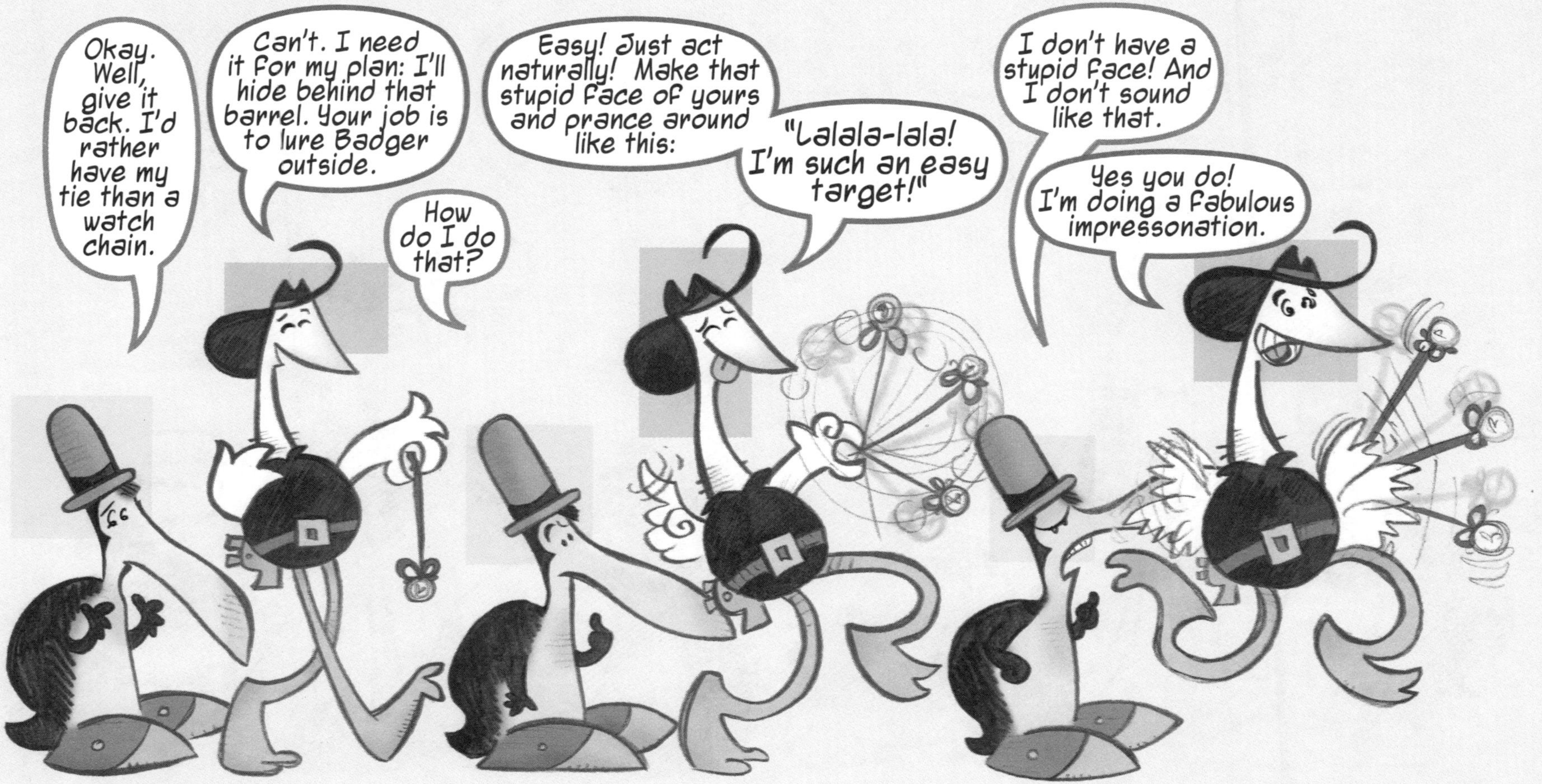
Okay. Well, give it back. I'd rather have my tie than a watch chain.
Can't. I need it for my plan: I'll hide behind that barrel. Your job is to lure Badger outside.
How do I do that?
Easy! Just act naturally! Make that stupid face of yours and prance around like this:
"Lalala-lala! I'm such an easy target!"
I don't have a stupid face! And I don't sound like that.
Yes you do! I'm doing a fabulous impressonation.

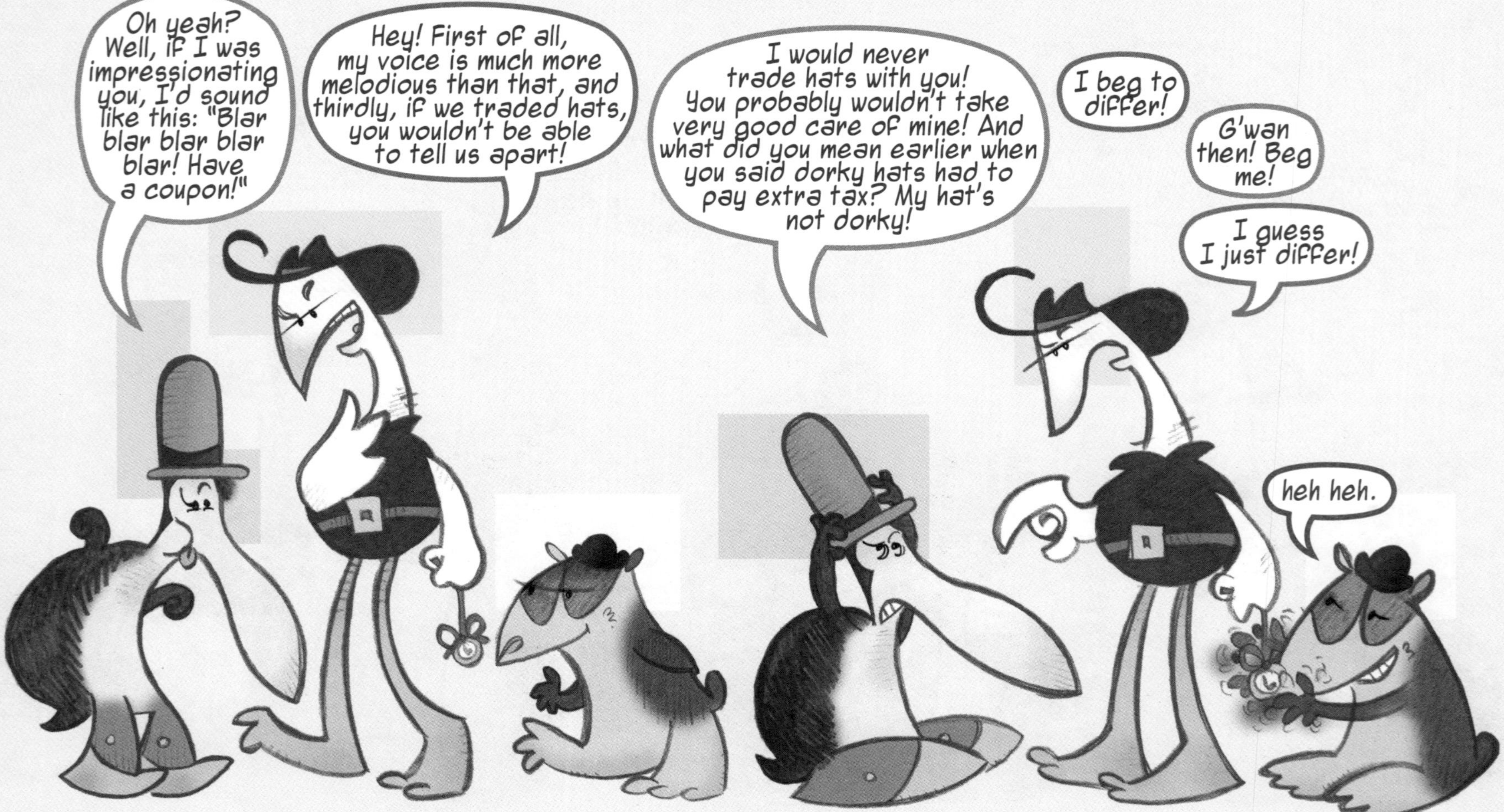
Oh yeah? Well, if I was impressionating you, I'd sound like this: "Blar blar blar blar blar! Have a coupon!"
Hey! First of all, my voice is much more melodious than that, and thirdly, if we traded hats, you wouldn't be able to tell us apart!
I would never trade hats with you! You probably wouldn't take very good care of mine! And what did you mean earlier when you said dorky hats had to pay extra tax? My hat's not dorky!
I beg to differ!
G'wan then! Beg me!
I guess I just differ!
heh heh.

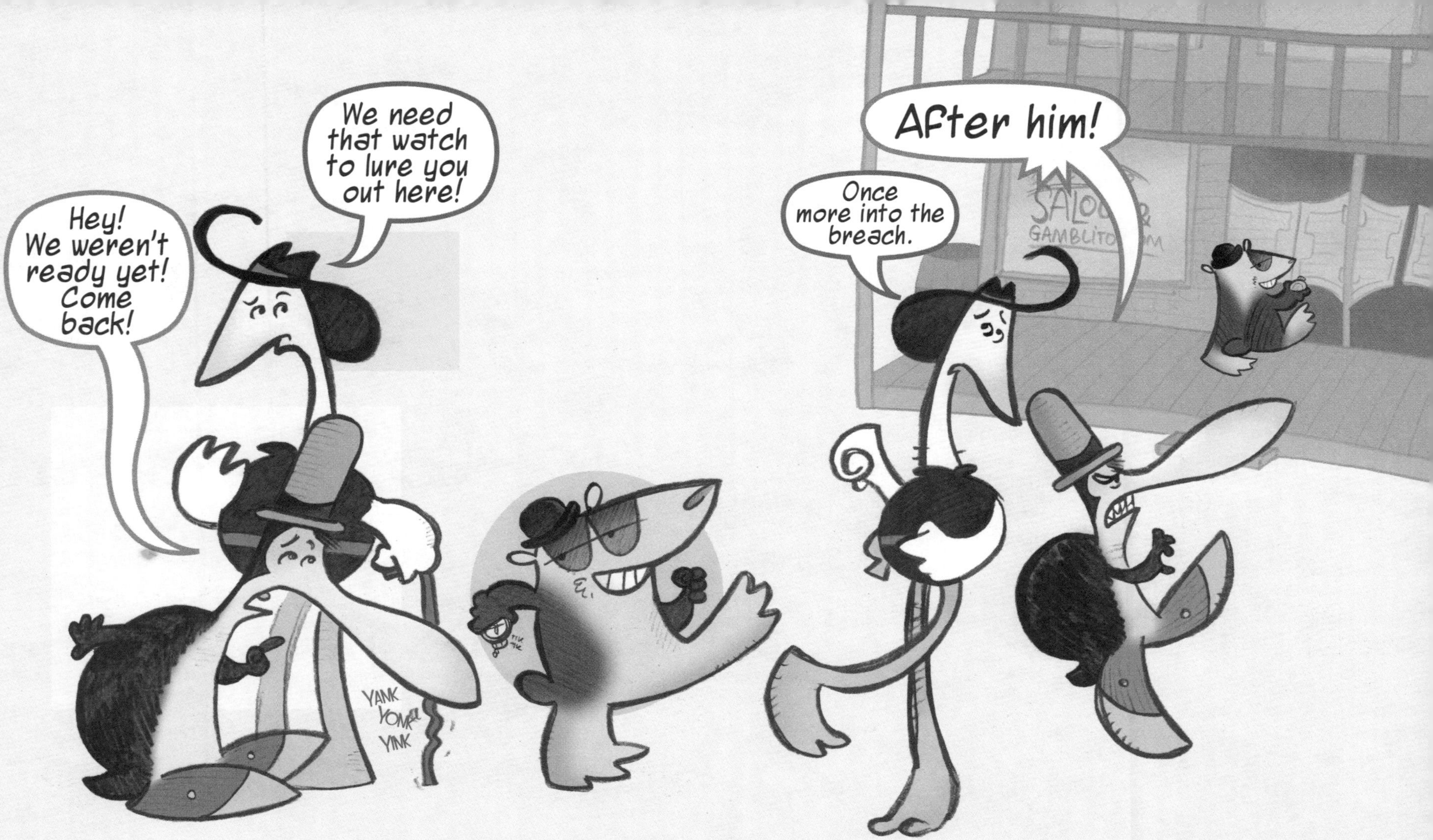
Hey! We weren't ready yet! Come back!
We need that watch to lure you out here!
YANK
YONK
YINK
Once more into the breach.
After him!
SALOO
GAMBLITO

chapter 4

FLAMBOOZLED!

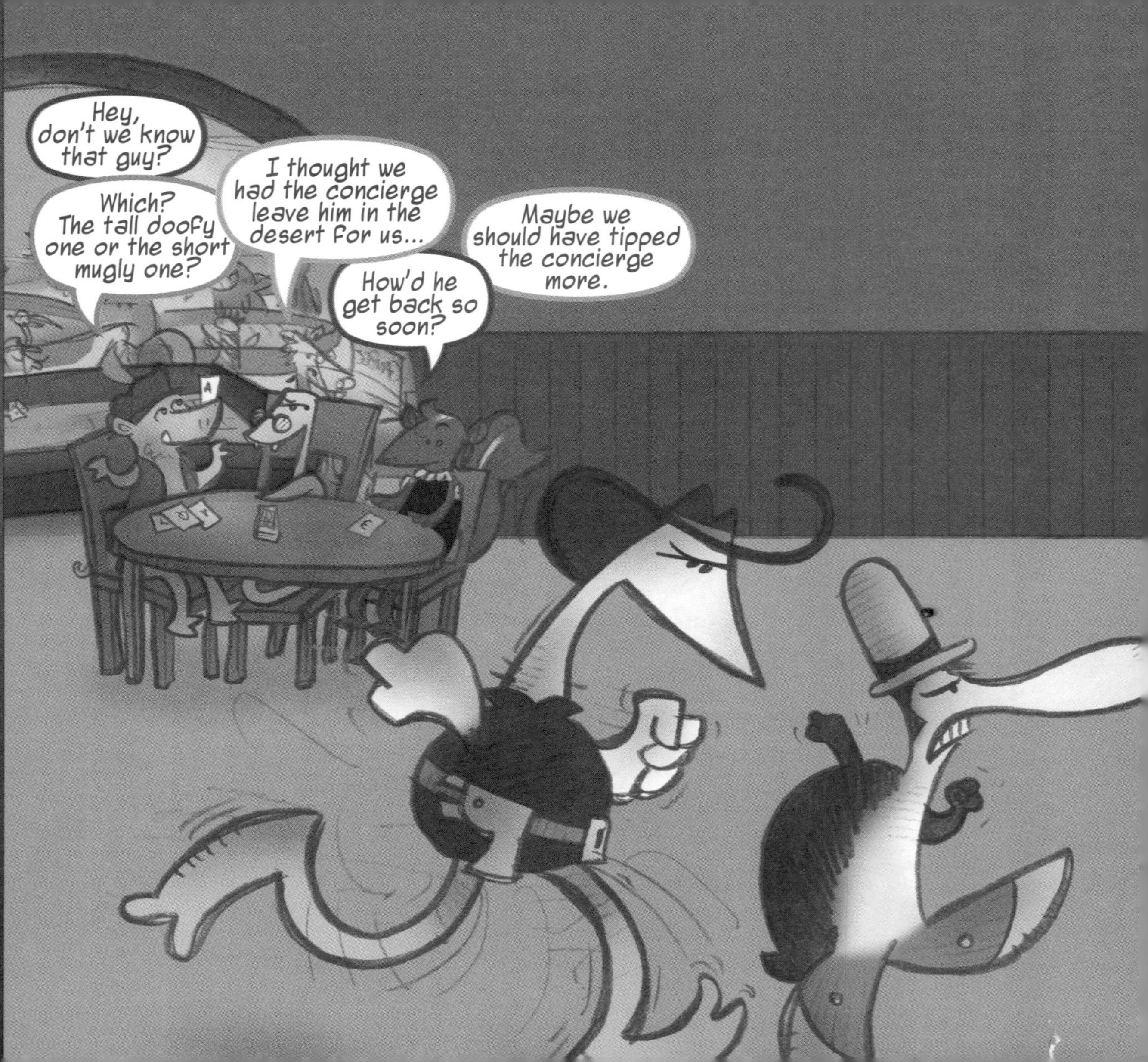

Hey, don't we know that guy?
Which? The tall doofy one or the short mugly one?
I thought we had the concierge leave him in the desert for us...
How'd he get back so soon?
Maybe we should have tipped the concierge more.

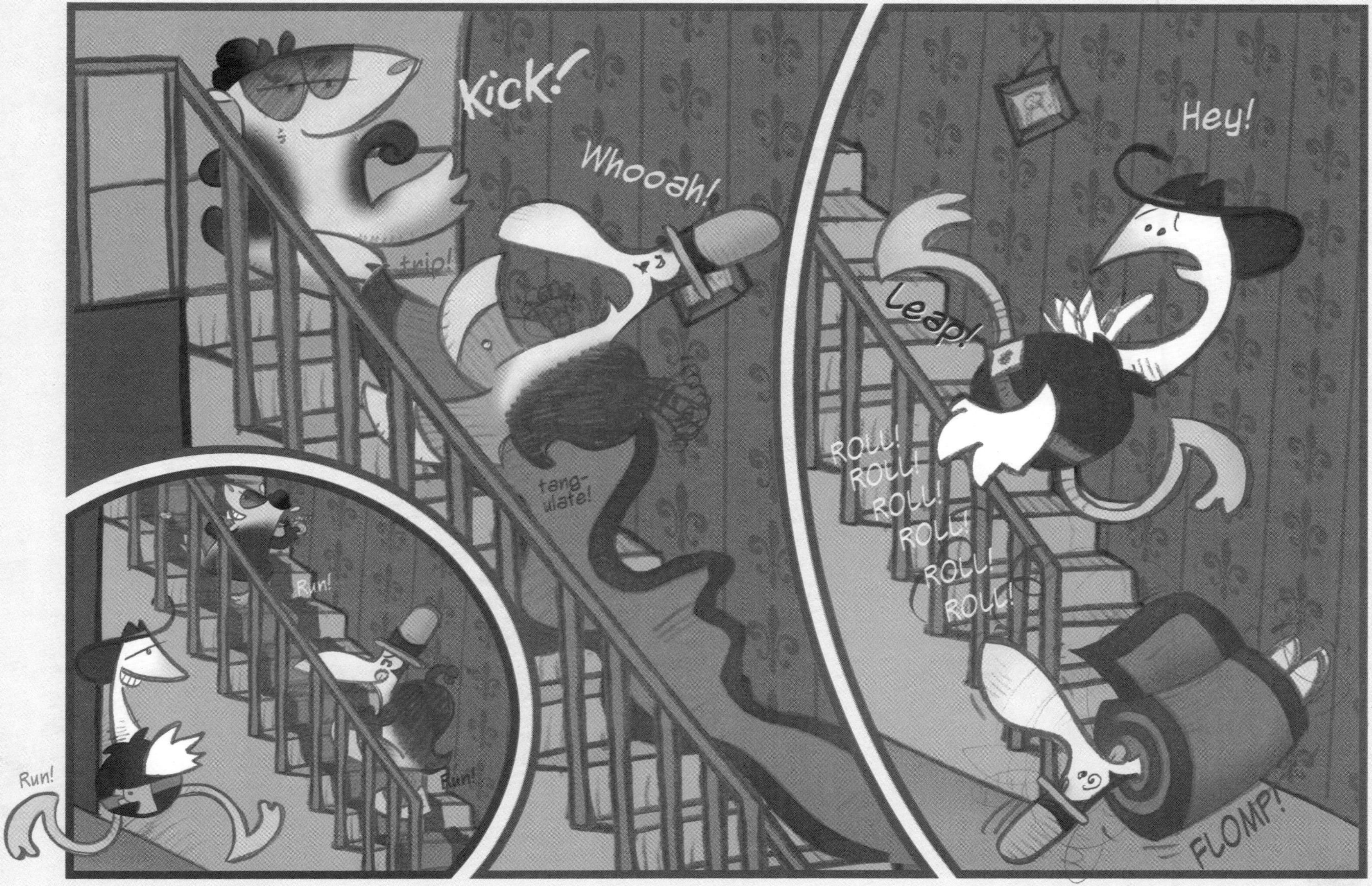
Kick!
Whooah!
trip!
tang-
ulate!
Run!
Run!
Run!
Hey!
Leap!
ROLL!
ROLL!
ROLL!
ROLL!
ROLL!
ROLL!
FLOMP!

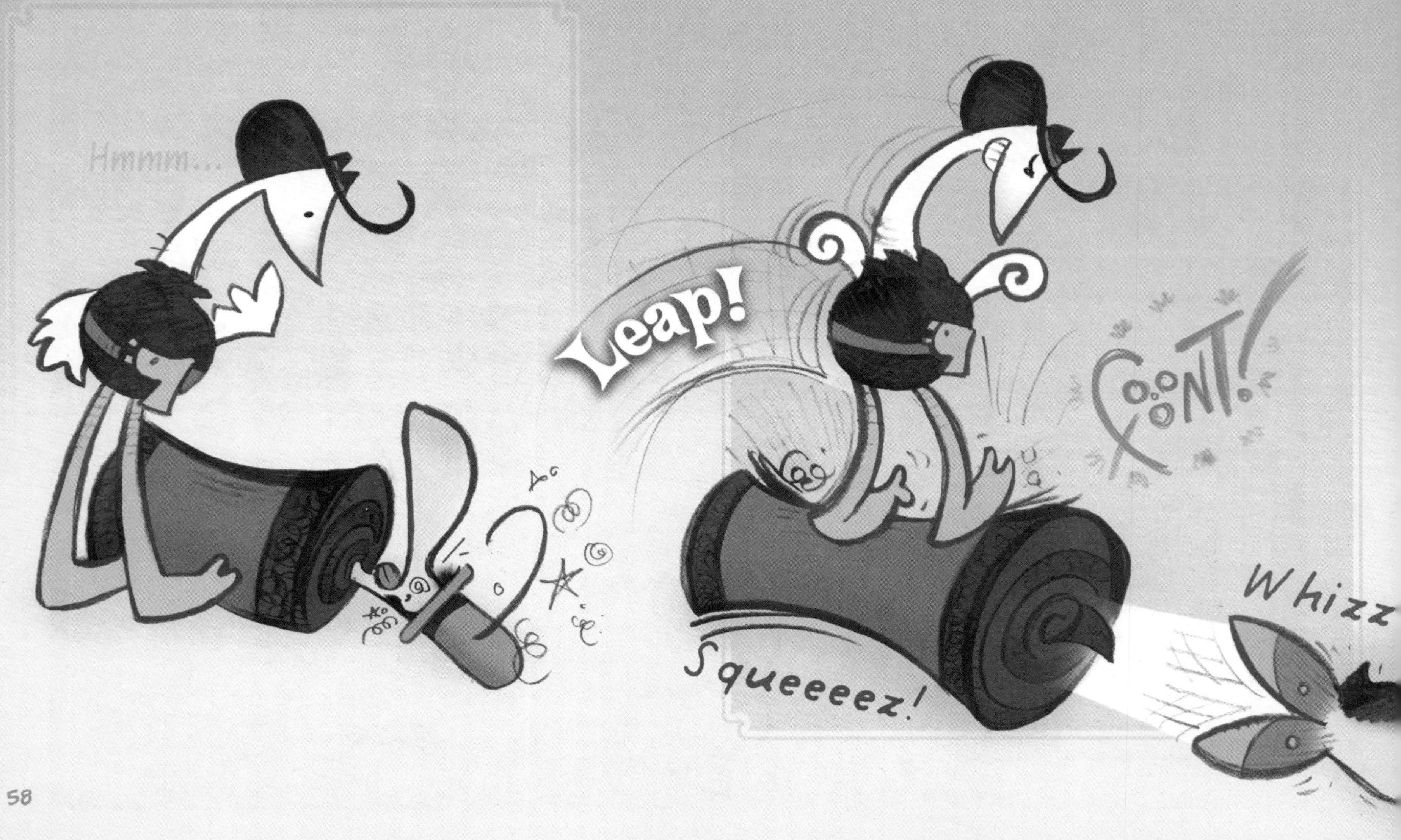
Hmmm...
Leap!
COOONT!
Squeeeeez!
Whizz

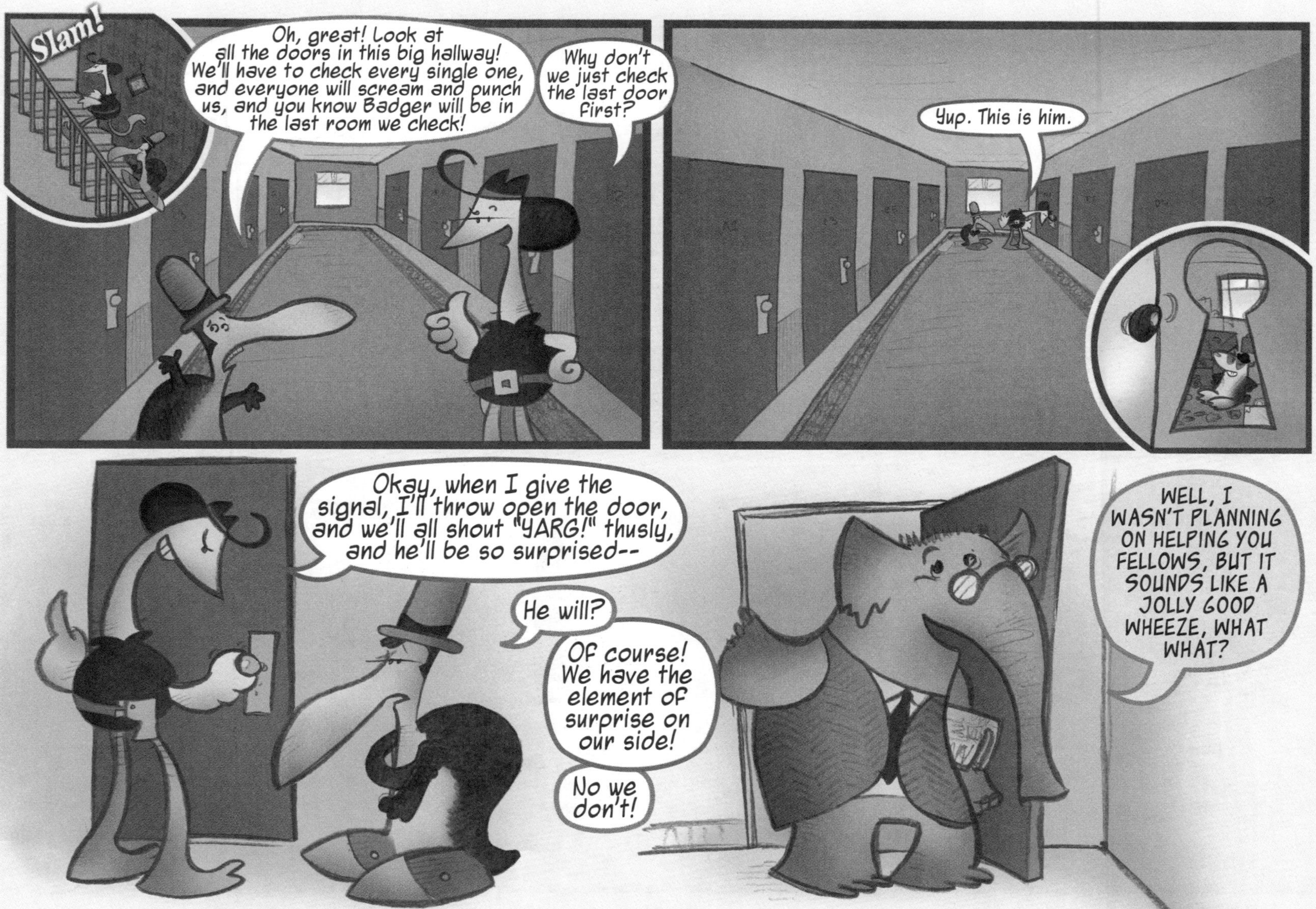
Slam!
Oh, great! Look at all the doors in this big hallway! We'll have to check every single one, and everyone will scream and punch us, and you know Badger will be in the last room we check!
Why don't we just check the last door first?
Yup. This is him.
Okay, when I give the signal, I'll throw open the door, and we'll all shout "YARG!" thusly, and he'll be so surprised--
He will?
Of course! We have the element of surprise on our side!
No we don't!
WELL, I WASN'T PLANNING ON HELPING YOU FELLOWS, BUT IT SOUNDS LIKE A JOLLY GOOD WHEEZE, WHAT WHAT?

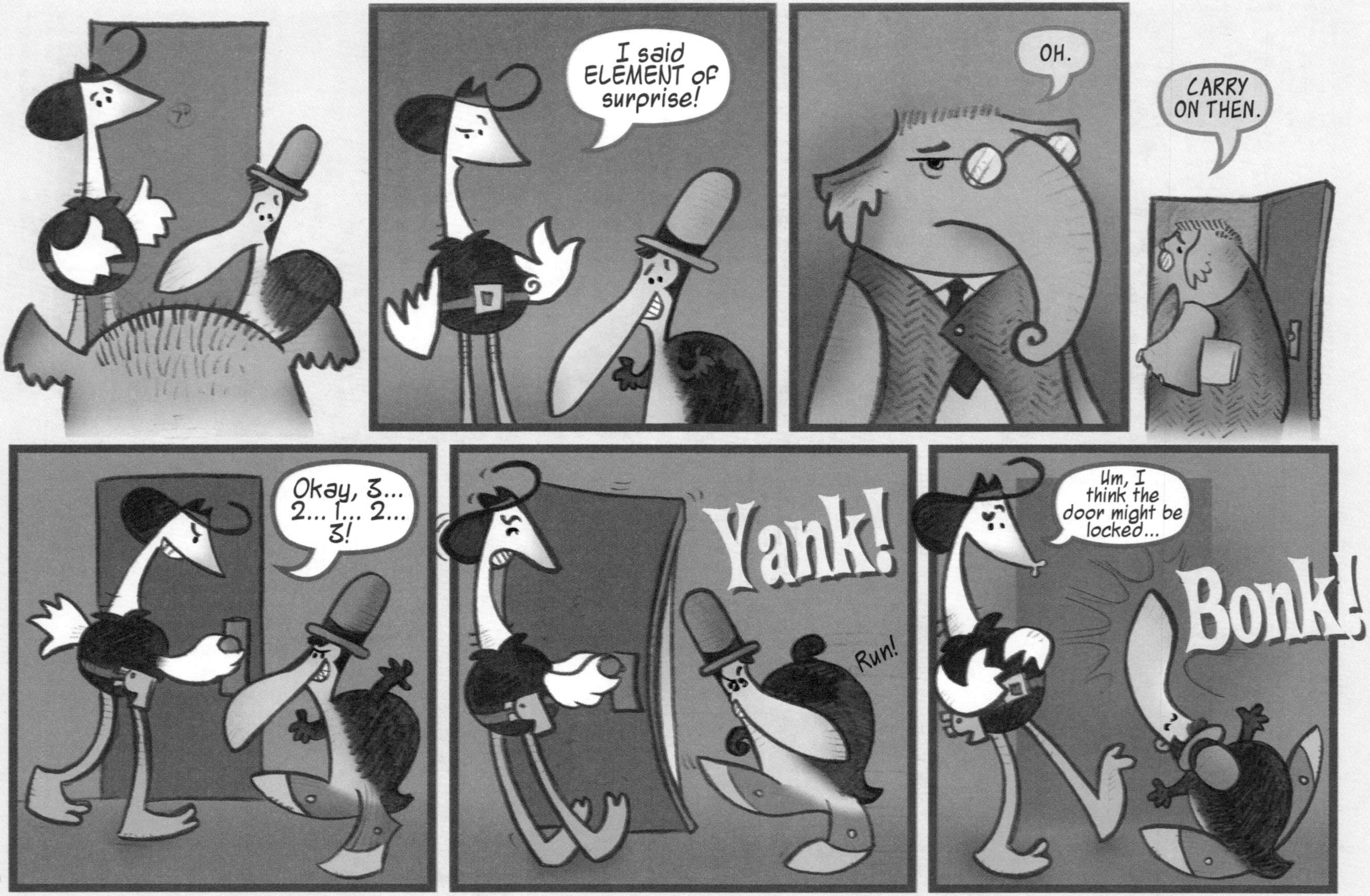
I said ELEMENT of surprise!
OH.
CARRY ON THEN.
Okay, 3... 2... 1... 2... 3!
Yank!
Run!
Um, I think the door might be locked...
Bonk!

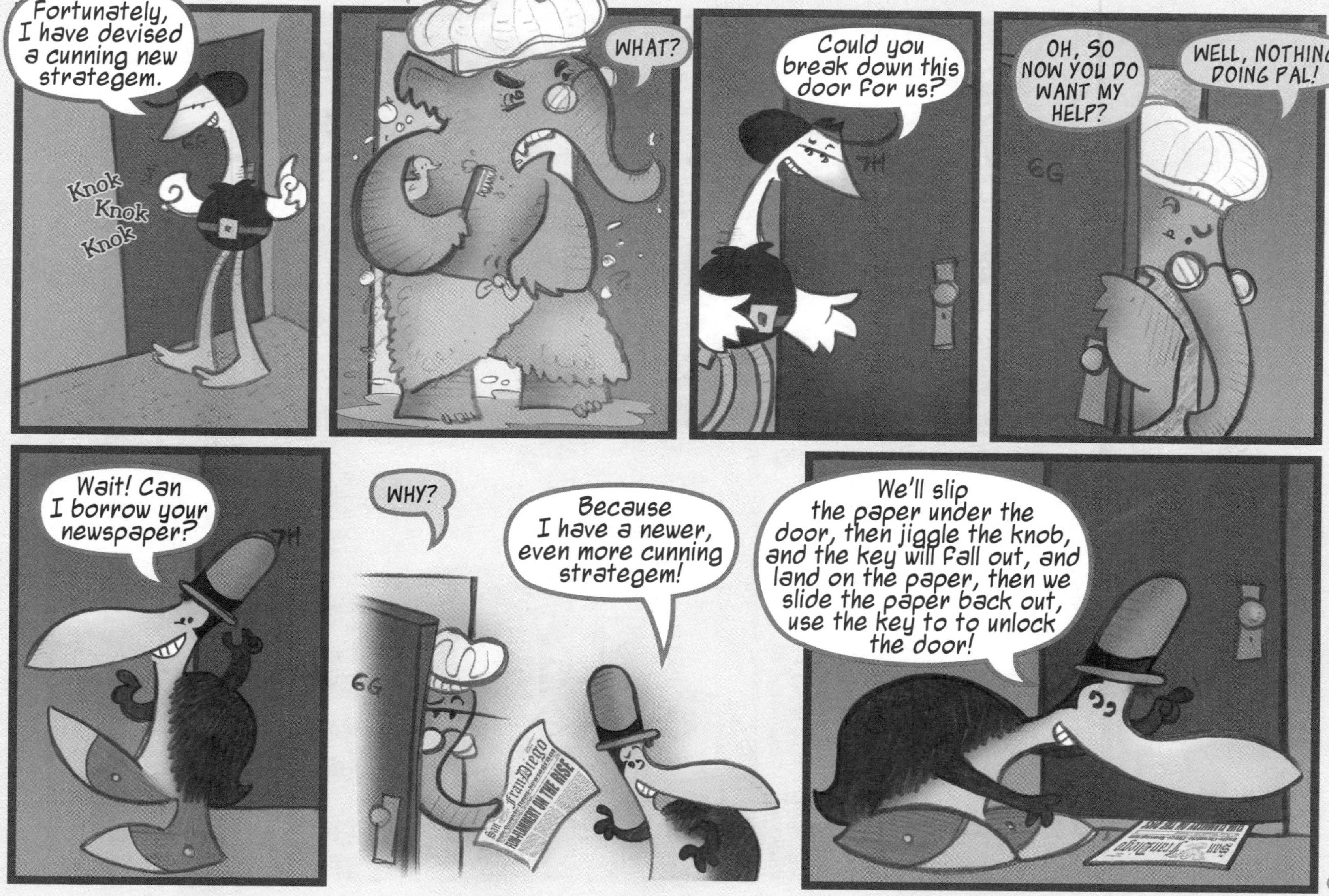
Fortunately, I have devised a cunning new strategem.
6G
Knok Knok Knok
WHAT?
Could you break down this door for us?
7H
OH, SO NOW YOU DO WANT MY HELP?
6G
WELL, NOTHING DOING PAL!
Wait! Can I borrow your newspaper?
7H
WHY?
6G
Because I have a newer, even more cunning strategem!
We'll slip the paper under the door, then jiggle the knob, and the key will fall out, and land on the paper, then we slide the paper back out, use the key to to unlock the door!

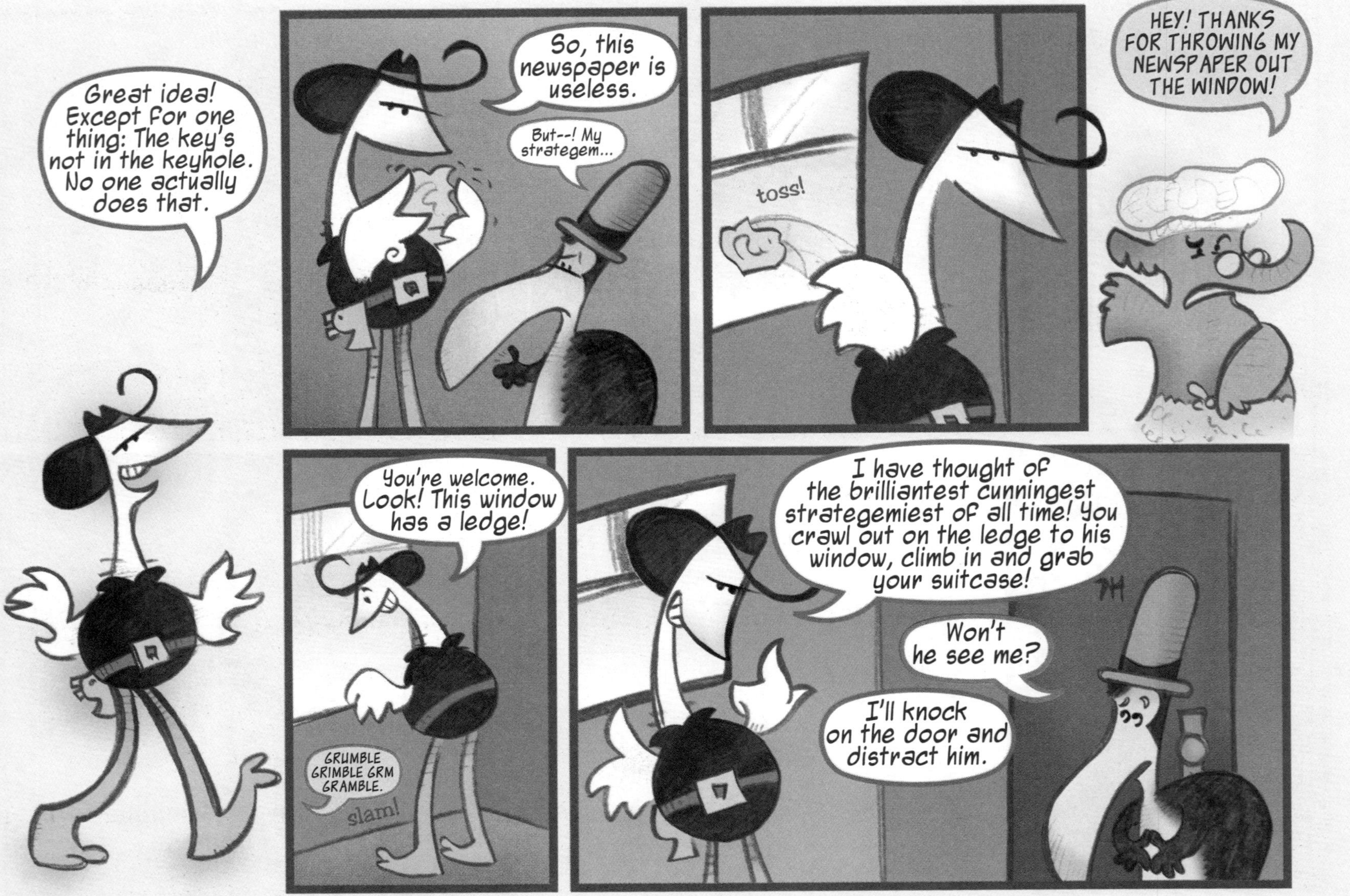

Great idea! Except for one thing: The key's not in the keyhole. No one actually does that.
So, this newspaper is useless.
But--! My strategem...
toss!
HEY! THANKS FOR THROWING MY NEWSPAPER OUT THE WINDOW!
You're welcome. Look! This window has a ledge!
GRUMBLE GRIMBLE GRM GRAMBLE.
slam!
I have thought of the brilliantest cunningest strategemiest of all time! You crawl out on the ledge to his window, climb in and grab your suitcase!
Won't he see me?
I'll knock on the door and distract him.

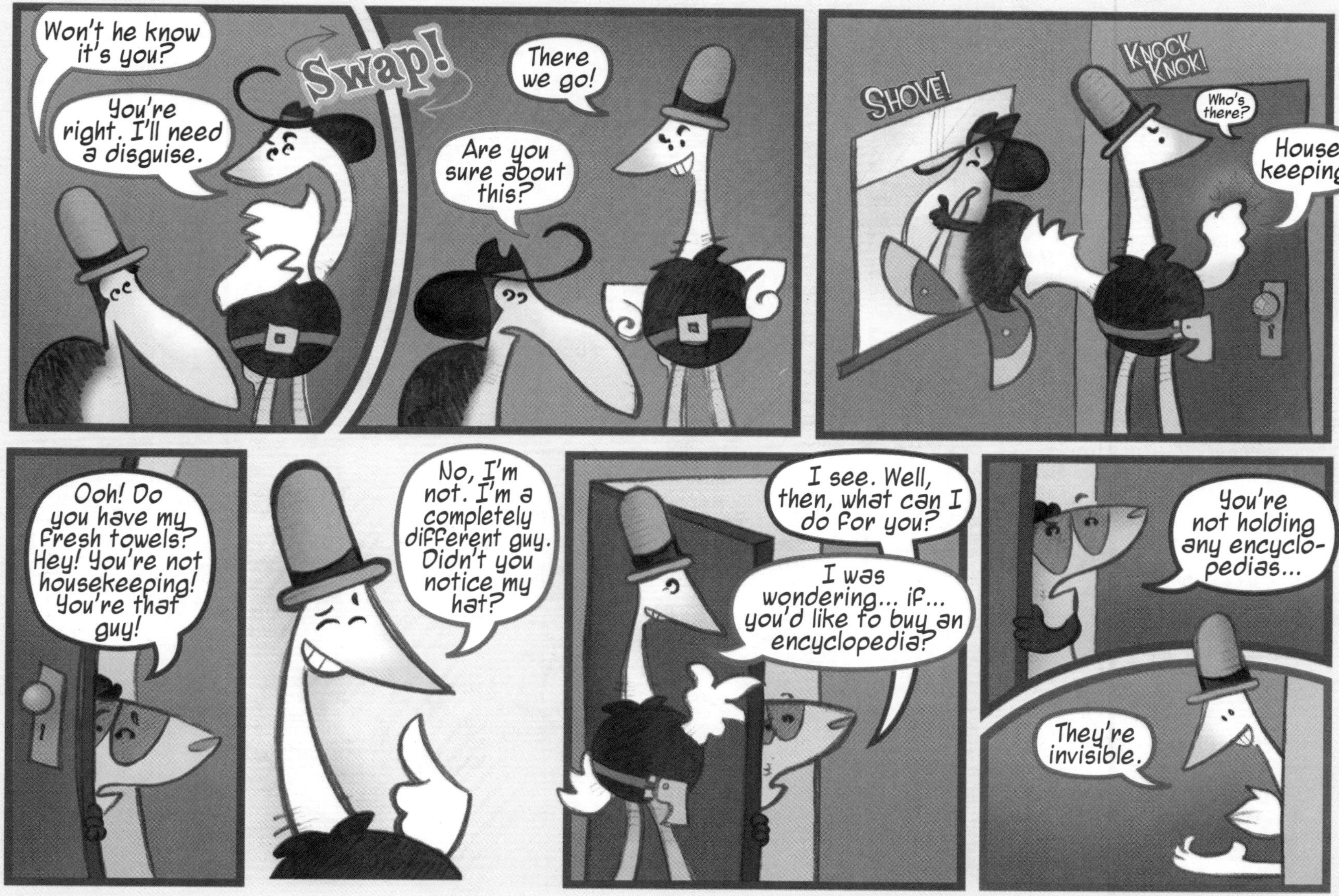
Won't he know it's you?
You're right. I'll need a disguise.
Swap!
There we go!
Are you sure about this?
SHOVE!
KNOCK KNOK!
Who's there?
House keeping!
Ooh! Do you have my fresh towels? Hey! You're not housekeeping! You're that guy!
No, I'm not. I'm a completely different guy. Didn't you notice my hat?
I see. Well, then, what can I do for you?
I was wondering... if... you'd like to buy an encyclopedia?
You're not holding any encyclopedias...
They're invisible.

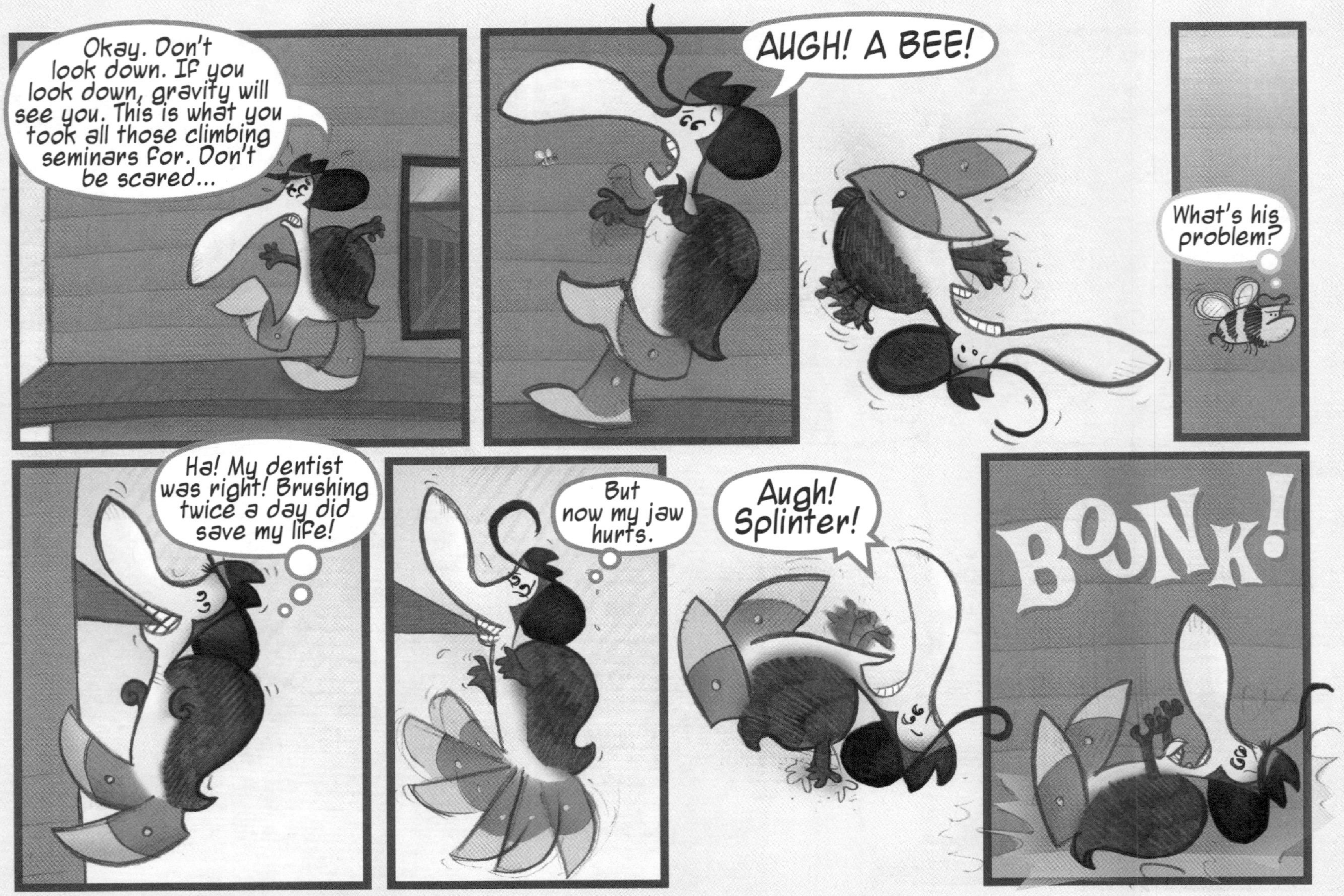
Okay. Don't look down. If you look down, gravity will see you. This is what you took all those climbing seminars for. Don't be scared...
AUGH! A BEE!
What's his problem?
Ha! My dentist was right! Brushing twice a day did save my life!
But now my jaw hurts.
Augh! Splinter!
BOONK!

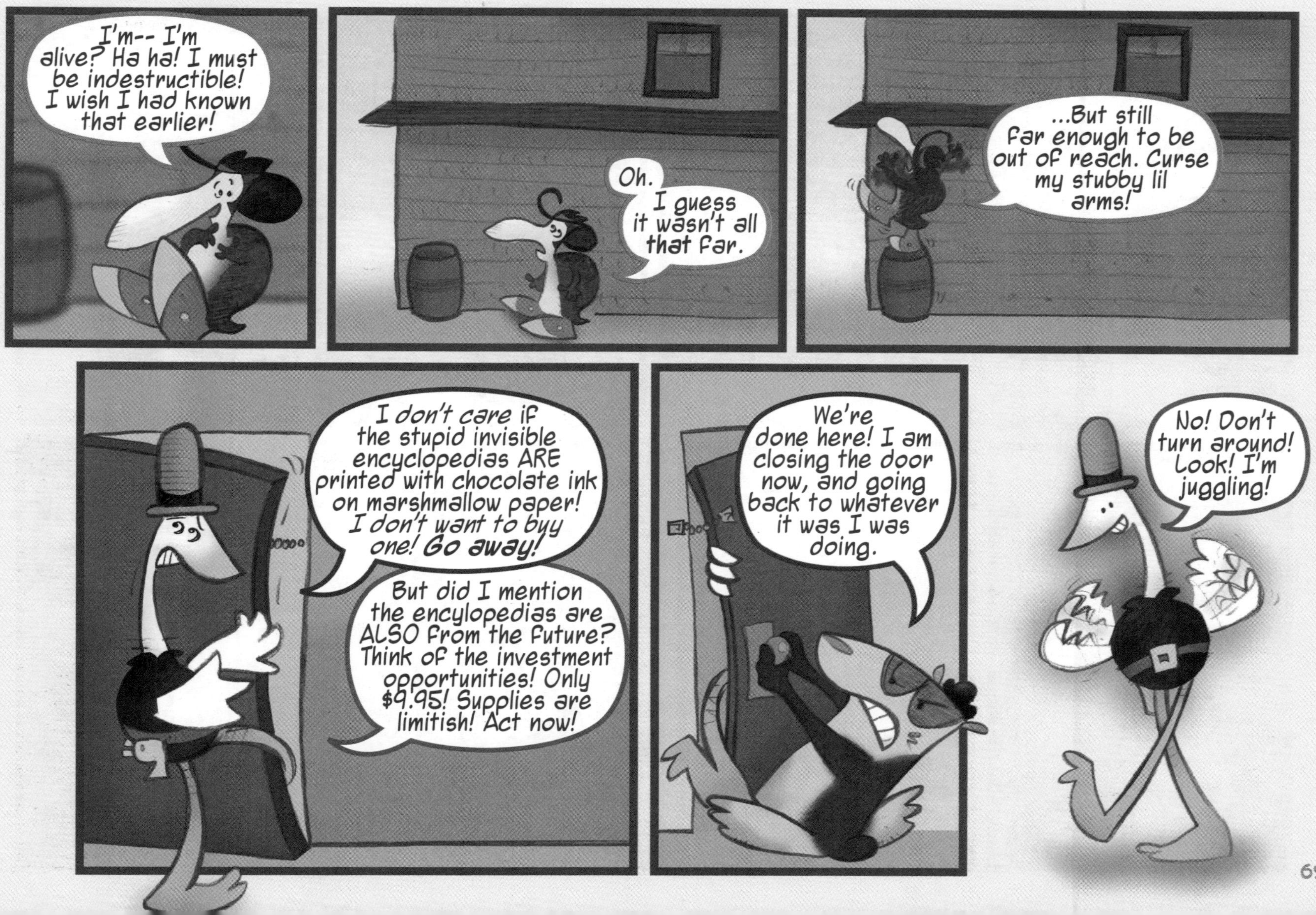
I'm-- I'm alive? Ha ha! I must be indestructible! I wish I had known that earlier!
Oh. I guess it wasn't all that far.
...But still far enough to be out of reach. Curse my stubby lil arms!
I *don't care* if the stupid invisible encyclopedias ARE printed with chocolate ink on marshmallow paper! I *don't want* to buy one! **Go away!**
But did I mention the encylopedias are ALSO from the future? Think of the investment opportunities! Only $9.95! Supplies are limitish! Act now!
We're done here! I am closing the door now, and going back to whatever it was I was doing.
No! Don't turn around! Look! I'm juggling!

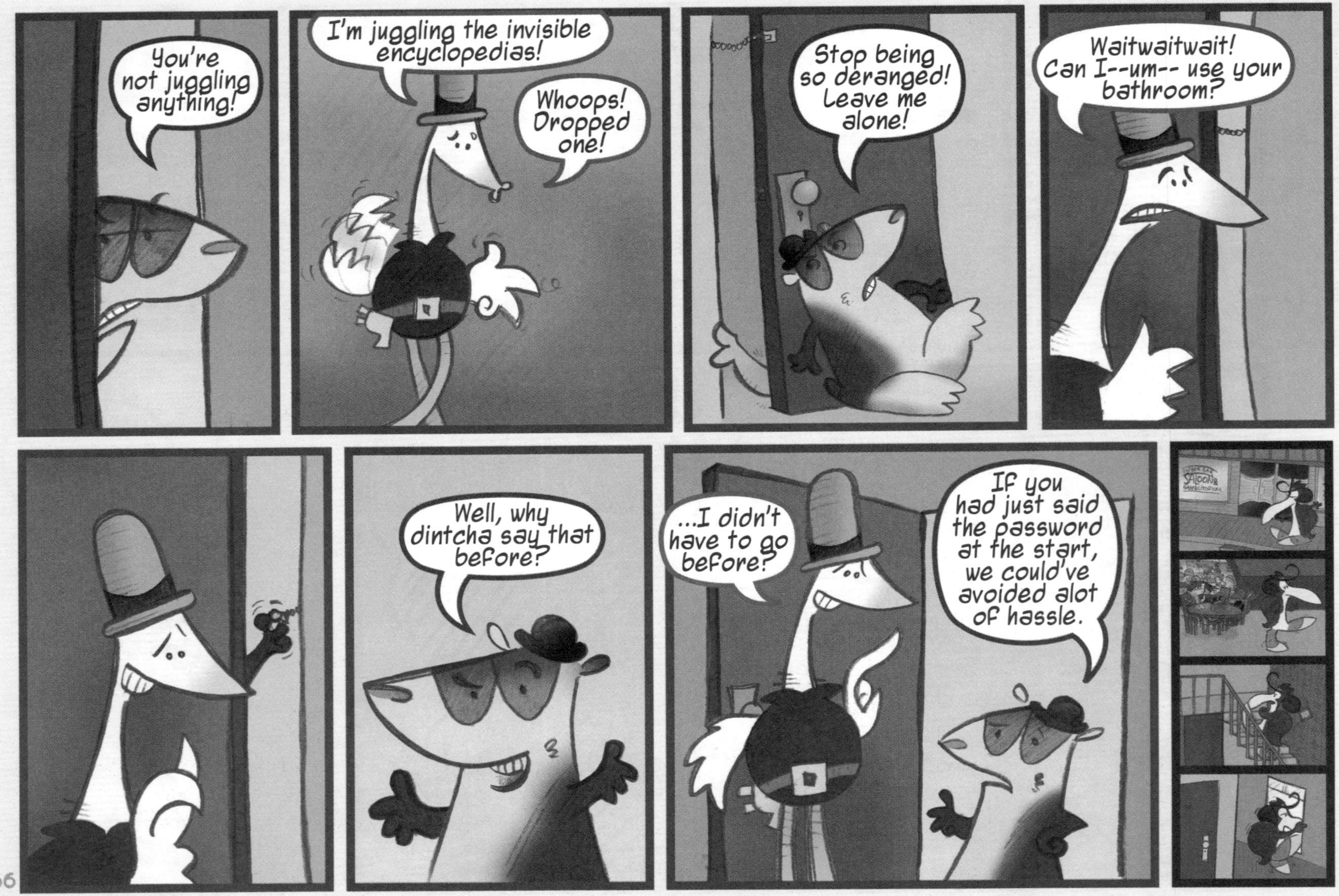
You're not juggling anything!
I'm juggling the invisible encyclopedias!
Whoops! Dropped one!
Stop being so deranged! Leave me alone!
Waitwaitwait! Can I--um-- use your bathroom?
Well, why dintcha say that before?
...I didn't have to go before?
If you had just said the password at the start, we could've avoided alot of hassle.

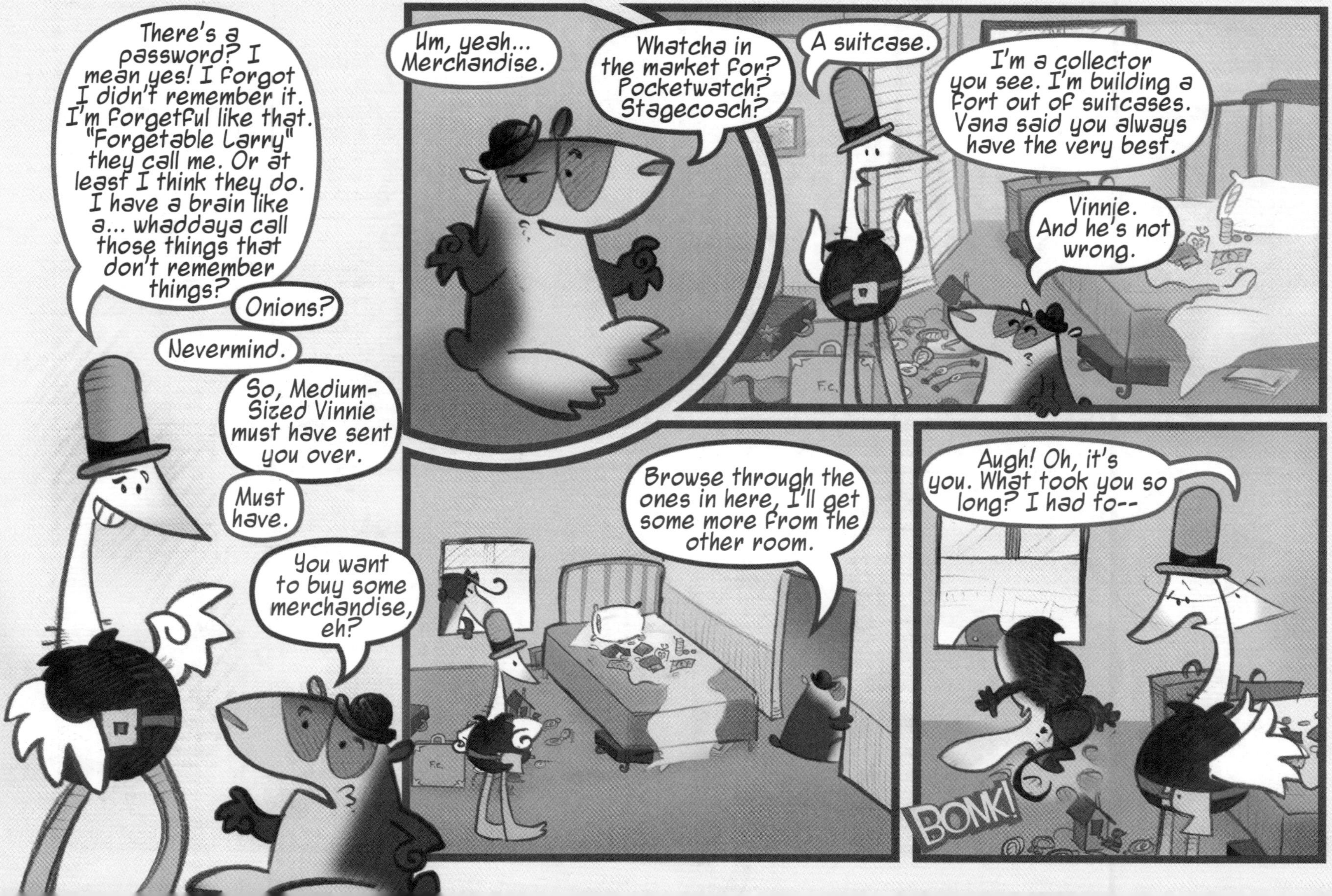

There's a password? I mean yes! I forgot I didn't remember it. I'm forgetful like that. "Forgetable Larry" they call me. Or at least I think they do. I have a brain like a... whaddaya call those things that don't remember things?
Onions?
Nevermind.
So, Medium-Sized Vinnie must have sent you over.
Must have.
You want to buy some merchandise, eh?
Um, yeah... Merchandise.
Whatcha in the market for? Pocketwatch? Stagecoach?
A suitcase.
I'm a collector you see. I'm building a fort out of suitcases. Vana said you always have the very best.
Vinnie. And he's not wrong.
F.C.
Browse through the ones in here, I'll get some more from the other room.
F.C.
Augh! Oh, it's you. What took you so long? I had to--
BONK!

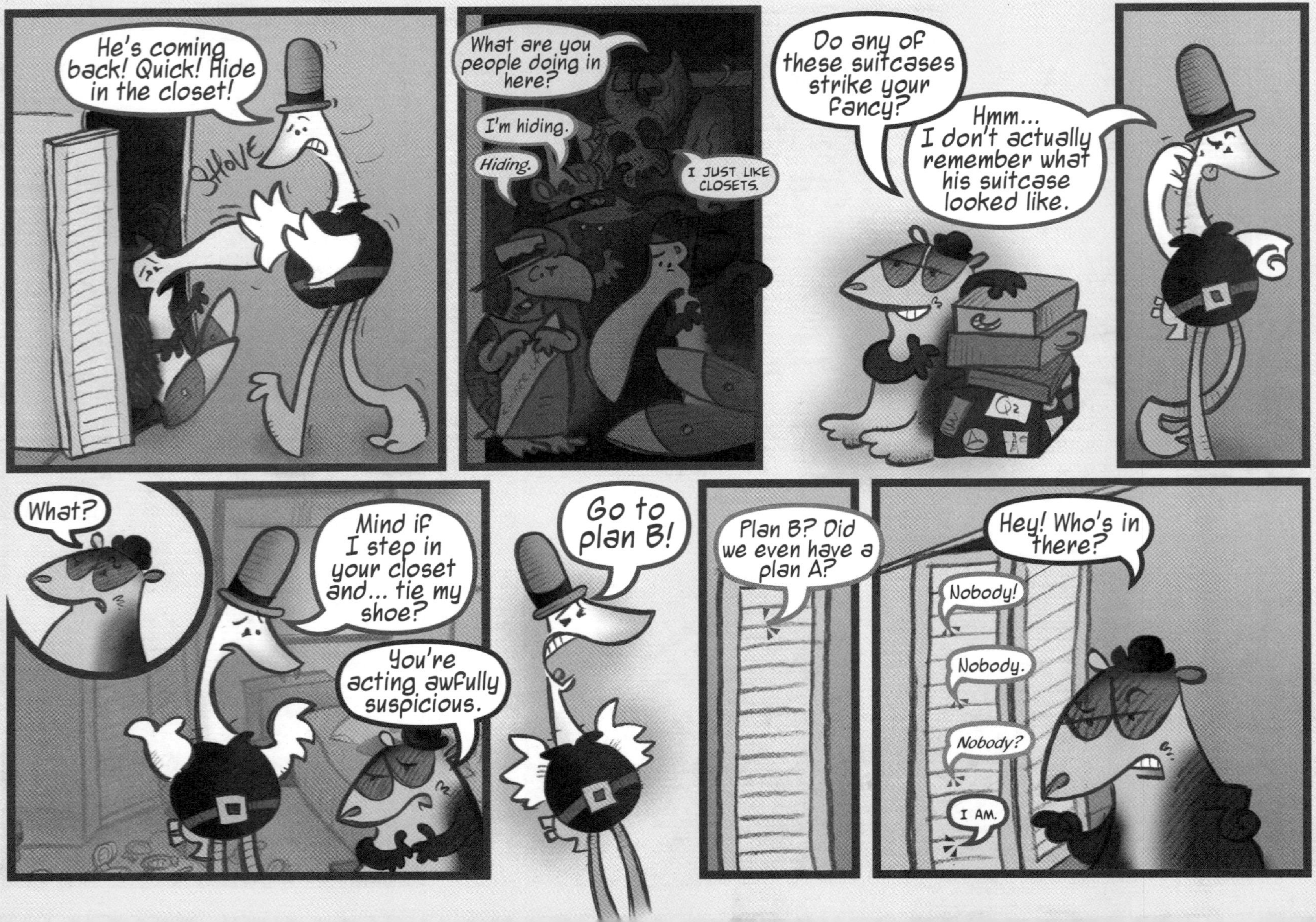
He's coming back! Quick! Hide in the closet!
SHOVE
What are you people doing in here?
I'm hiding.
Hiding.
I JUST LIKE CLOSETS.
Do any of these suitcases strike your fancy?
Hmm... I don't actually remember what his suitcase looked like.
What?
Mind if I step in your closet and... tie my shoe?
You're acting awfully suspicious.
Go to plan B!
Plan B? Did we even have a plan A?
Hey! Who's in there?
Nobody!
Nobody.
Nobody?
I AM.

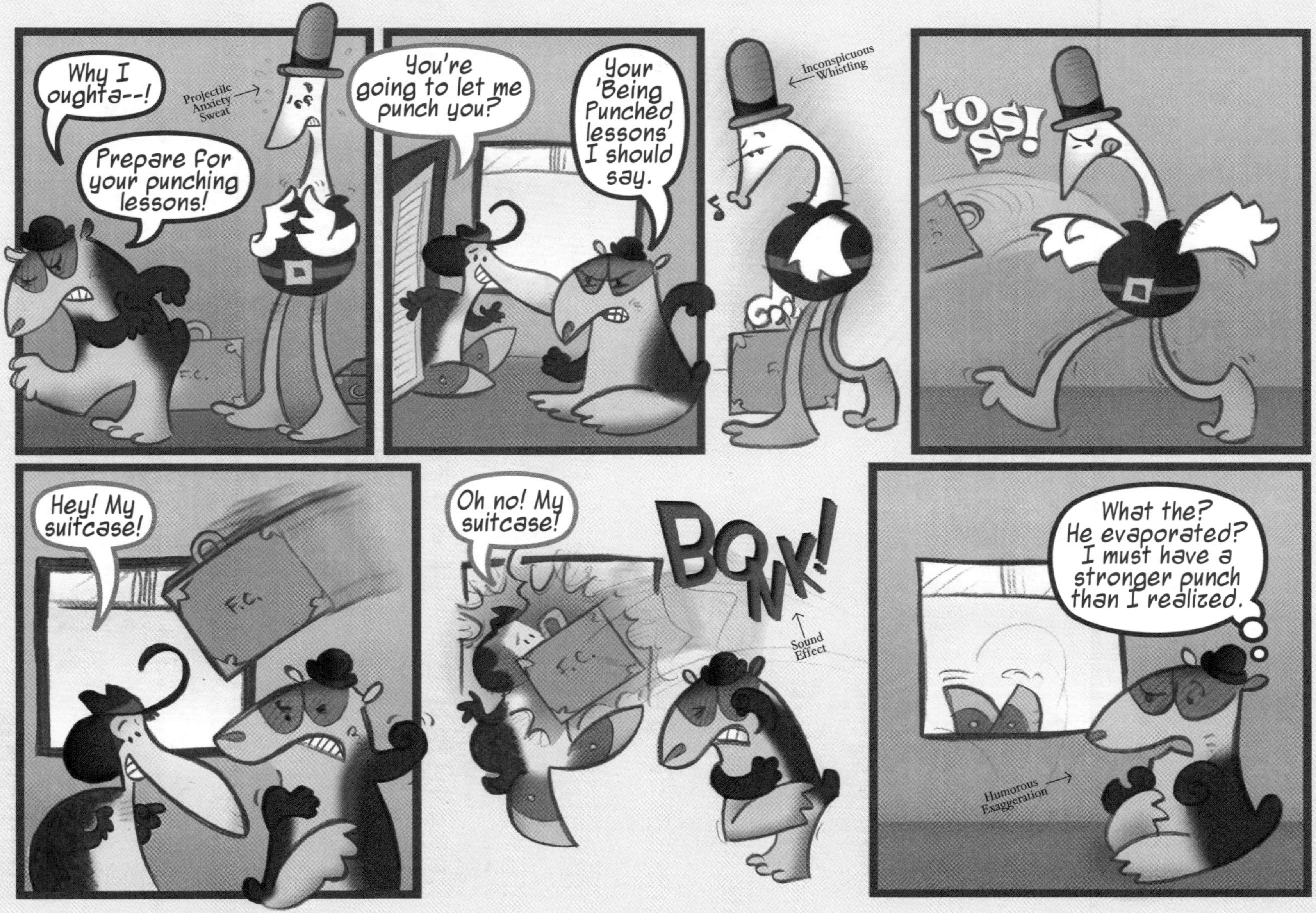
Why I oughta--!
Projectile Anxiety Sweat
Prepare for your punching lessons!
You're going to let me punch you?
Your 'Being Punched lessons' I should say.
Inconspicuous Whistling
F.C.
toss!
Hey! My suitcase!
F.C.
Oh no! My suitcase!
BONK!
Sound Effect
What the? He evaporated? I must have a stronger punch than I realized.
Humorous Exaggeration

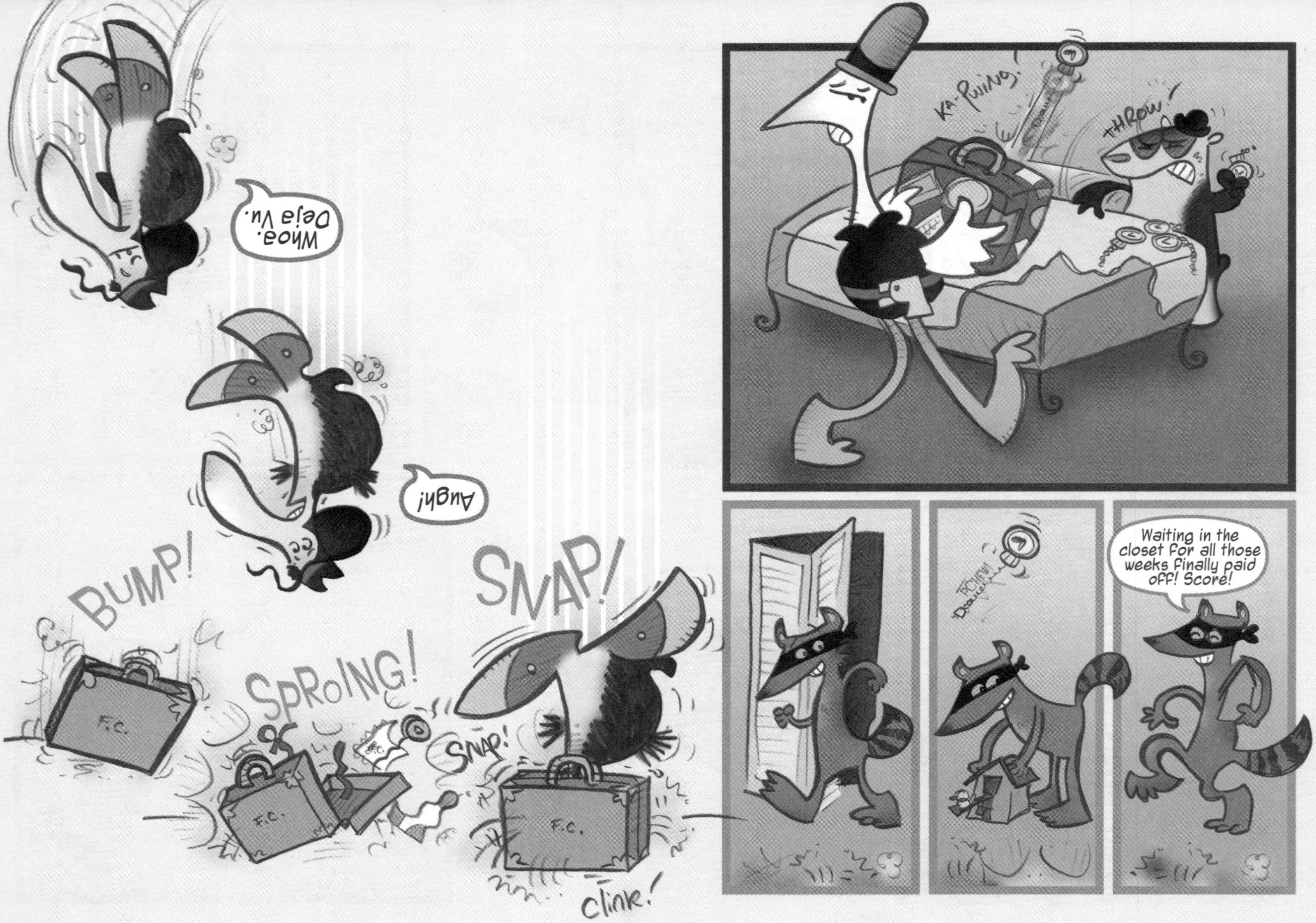
Whoa. Deja Vu.
Augh!
BUMP!
SPROING!
SNAP!
SNAP!
Clink!
KA-PWING!
THROW!
PCHEW!
Waiting in the closet for all those weeks finally paid off! Score!

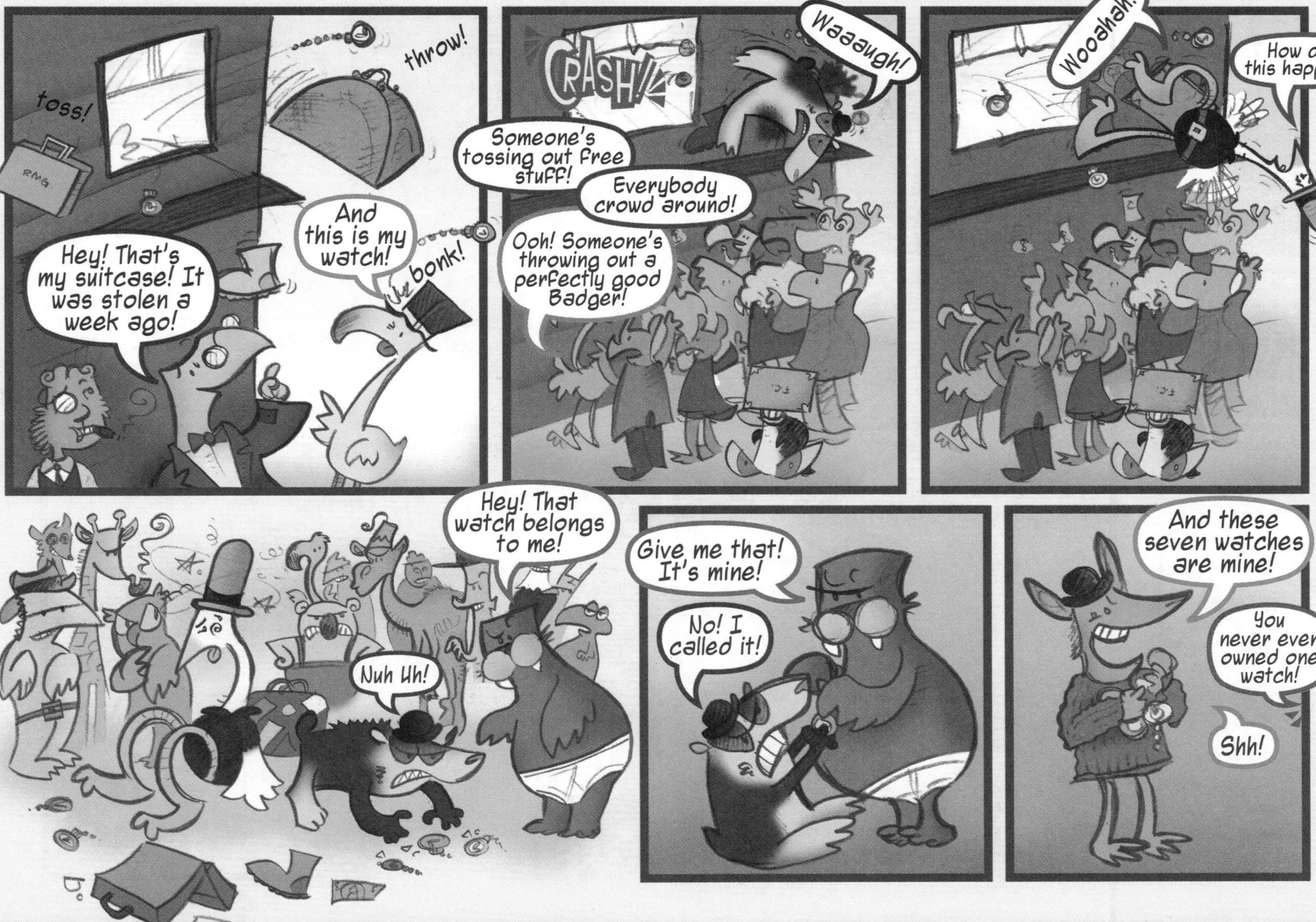
toss!
throw!
RMG
Hey! That's my suitcase! It was stolen a week ago!
And this is my watch!
bonk!
CRASH!
Waaaugh!
Someone's tossing out free stuff!
Everybody crowd around!
Ooh! Someone's throwing out a perfectly good Badger!
Wooahah!
How did this happen?
Hey! That watch belongs to me!
Nuh Uh!
Give me that! It's mine!
No! I called it!
And these seven watches are mine!
You never even owned one watch!
Shh!

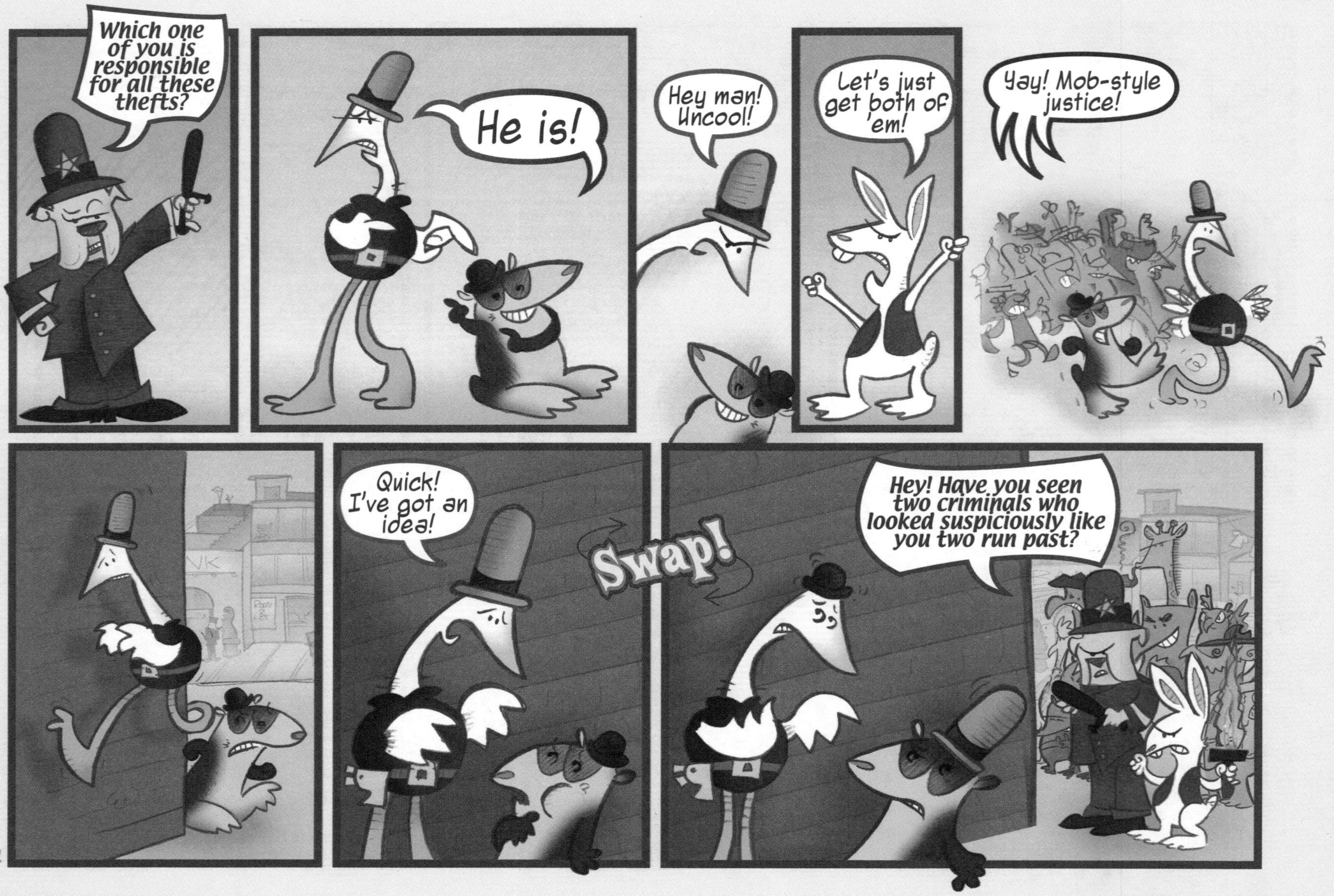
Which one of you is responsible for all these thefts?
He is!
Hey man! Uncool!
Let's just get both of 'em!
Yay! Mob-style justice!
Quick! I've got an idea!
Swap!
Hey! Have you seen two criminals who looked suspiciously like you two run past?

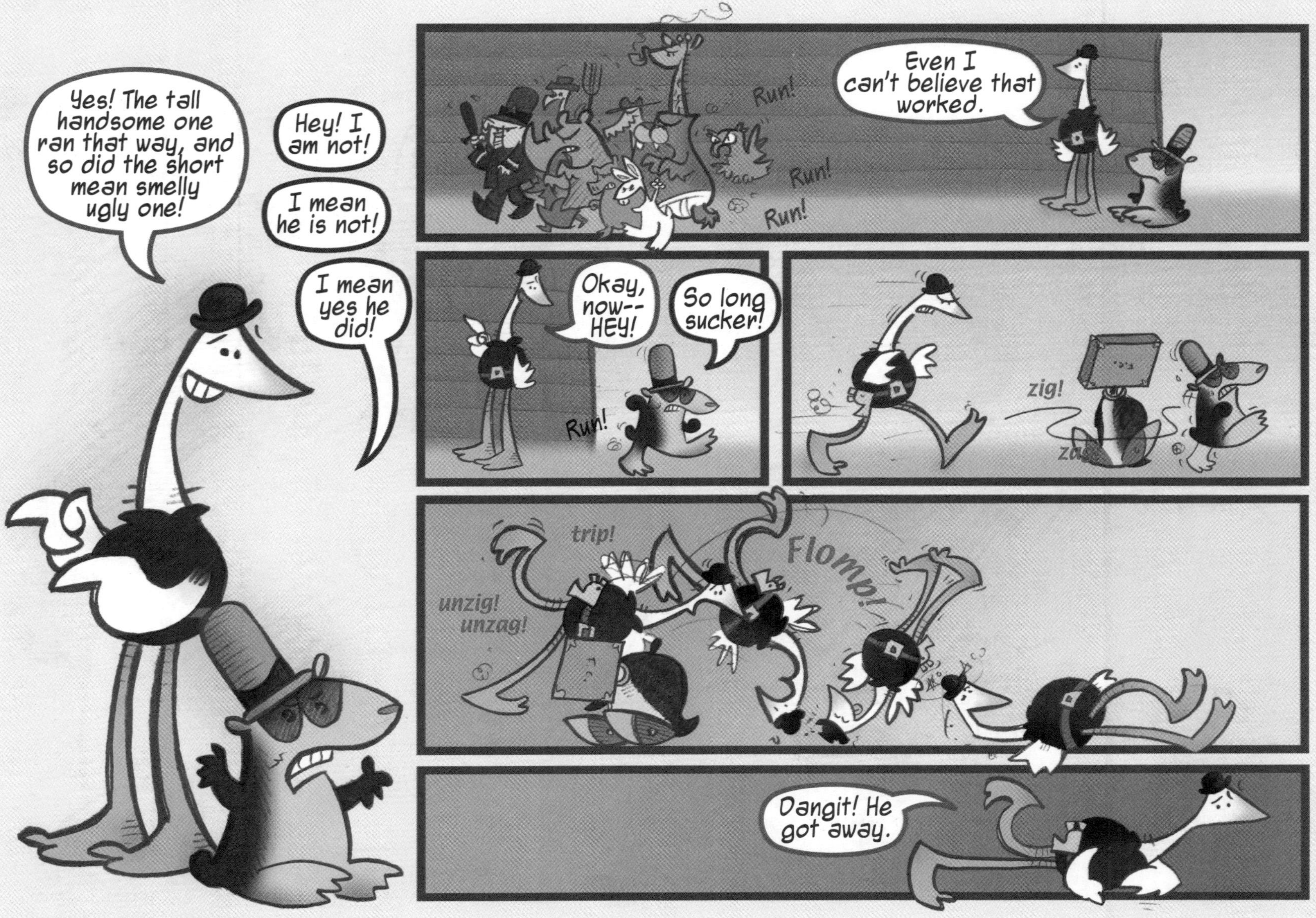

Yes! The tall handsome one ran that way, and so did the short mean smelly ugly one!
Hey! I am not!
I mean he is not!
I mean yes he did!
Run!
Run!
Run!
Even I can't believe that worked.
Okay, now--HEY!
So long sucker!
Run!
zig!
trip!
unzig!
unzag!
Flomp!
Dangit! He got away.

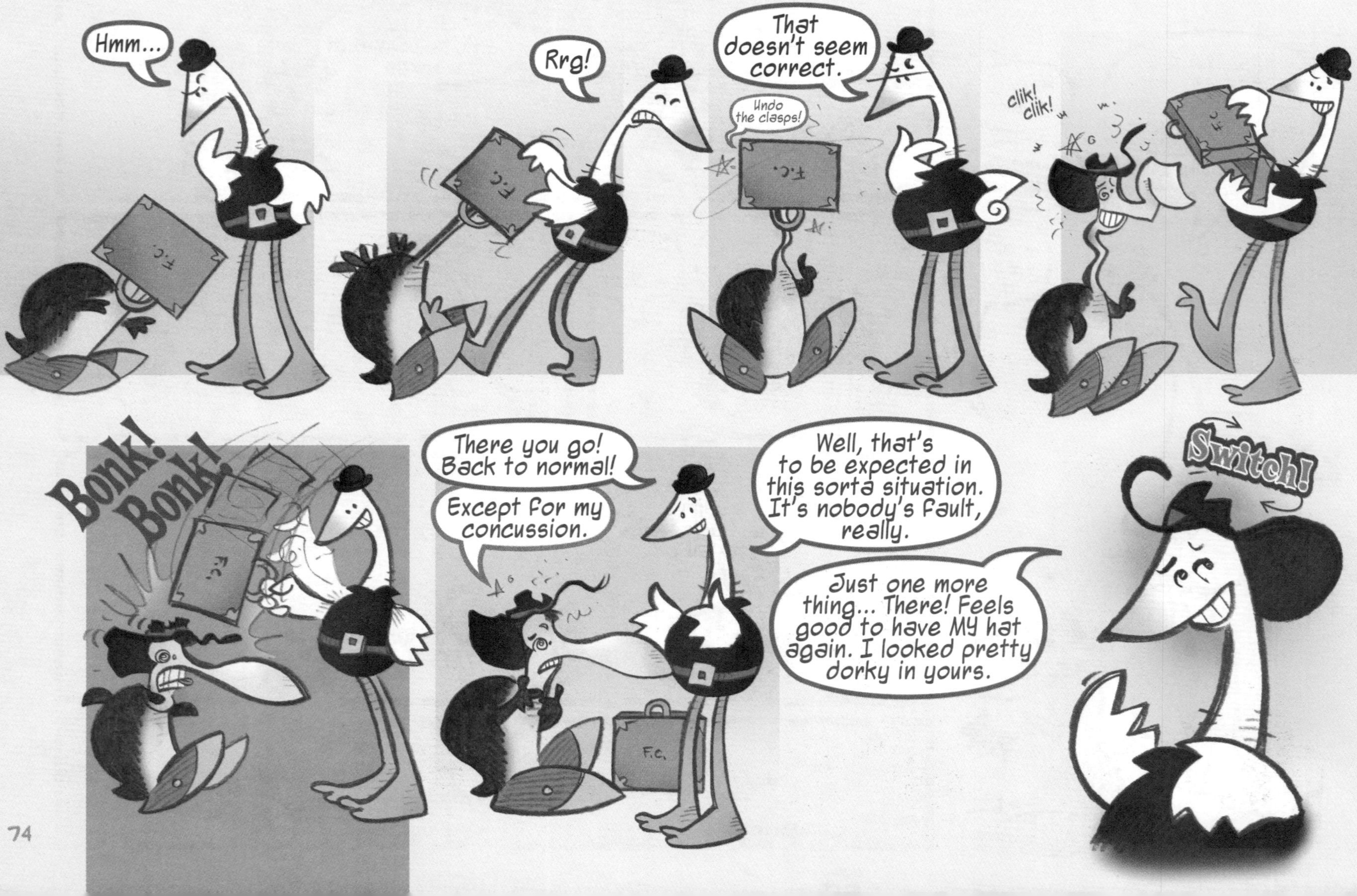
Hmm...
Rrg!
That doesn't seem correct.
Undo the clasps!
clik! clik!
Bonk! Bonk!
There you go! Back to normal!
Except for my concussion.
Well, that's to be expected in this sorta situation. It's nobody's fault, really.
Just one more thing... There! Feels good to have MY hat again. I looked pretty dorky in yours.
Switch!

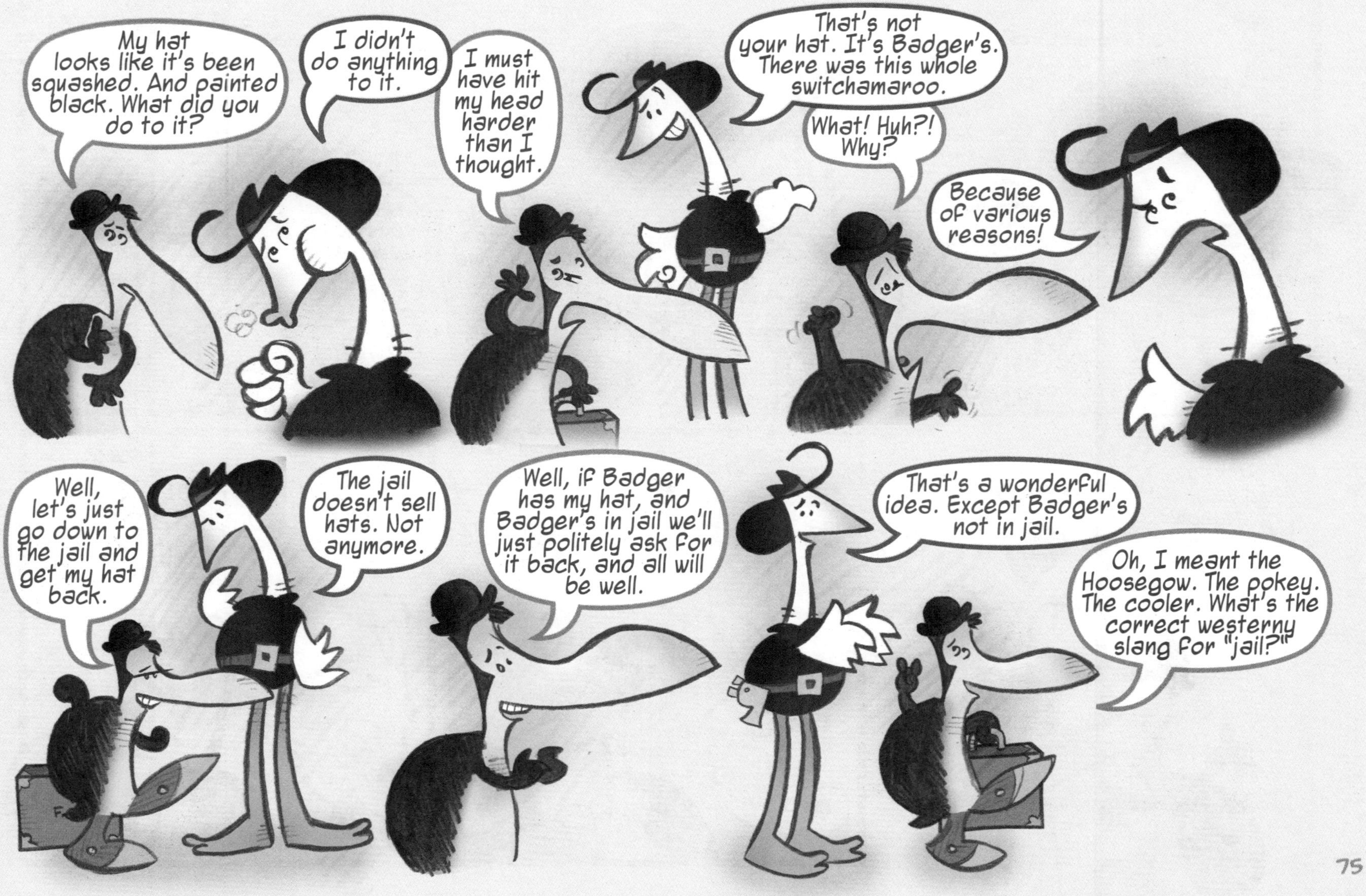
My hat looks like it's been squashed. And painted black. What did you do to it?
I didn't do anything to it.
I must have hit my head harder than I thought.
That's not your hat. It's Badger's. There was this whole switchamaroo.
What! Huh?! Why?
Because of various reasons!
Well, let's just go down to the jail and get my hat back.
The jail doesn't sell hats. Not anymore.
Well, if Badger has my hat, and Badger's in jail we'll just politely ask for it back, and all will be well.
That's a wonderful idea. Except Badger's not in jail.
Oh, I meant the Hoosegow. The pokey. The cooler. What's the correct westerny slang for "jail?"

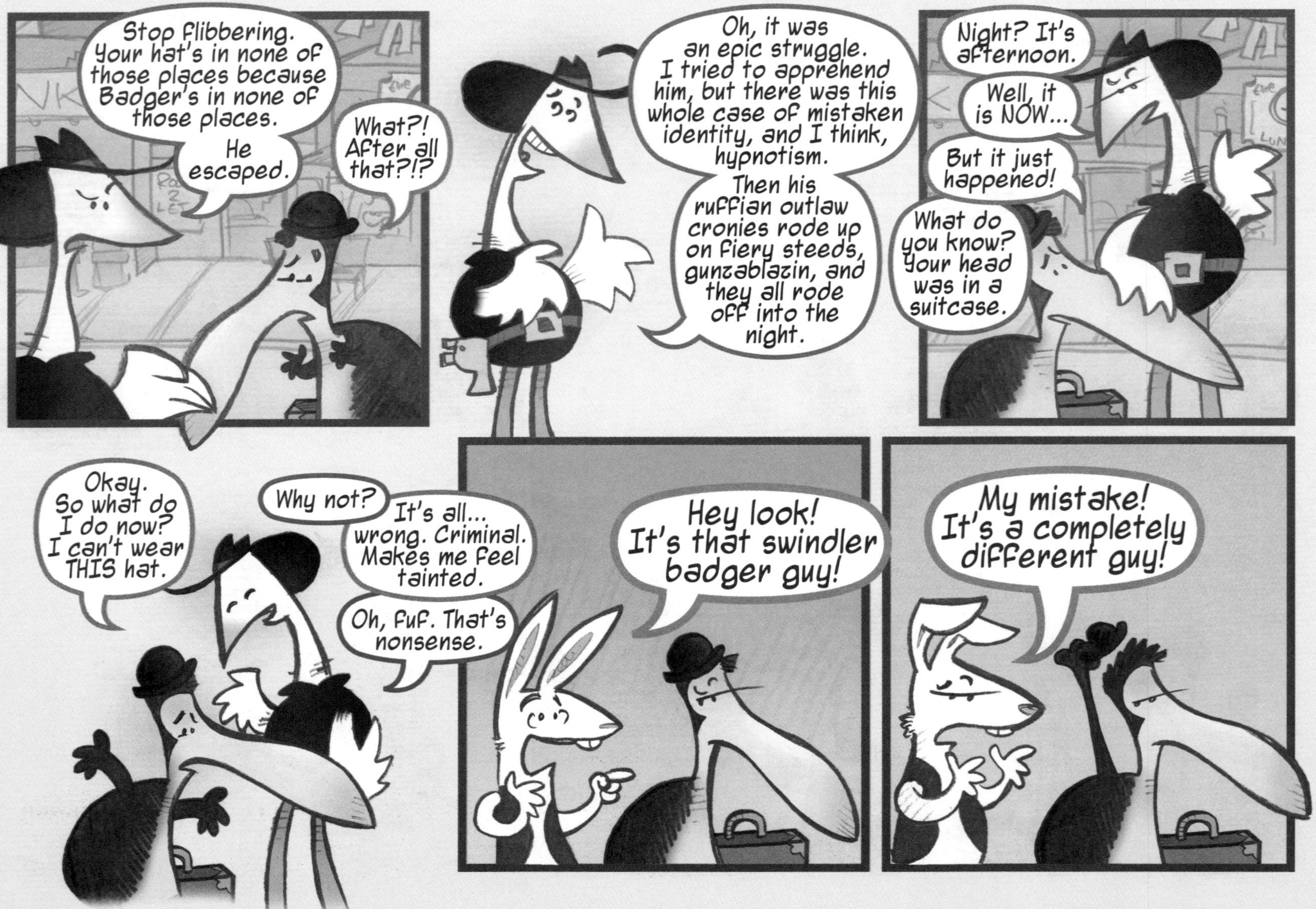
Stop flibbering. Your hat's in none of those places because Badger's in none of those places.
He escaped.
What?! After all that?!?
Oh, it was an epic struggle. I tried to apprehend him, but there was this whole case of mistaken identity, and I think, hypnotism.
Then his ruffian outlaw cronies rode up on fiery steeds, gunzablazin, and they all rode off into the night.
Night? It's afternoon.
Well, it is NOW...
But it just happened!
What do you know? Your head was in a suitcase.
Okay. So what do I do now? I can't wear THIS hat.
Why not?
It's all... wrong. Criminal. Makes me feel tainted.
Oh, fuf. That's nonsense.
Hey look! It's that swindler badger guy!
My mistake! It's a completely different guy!

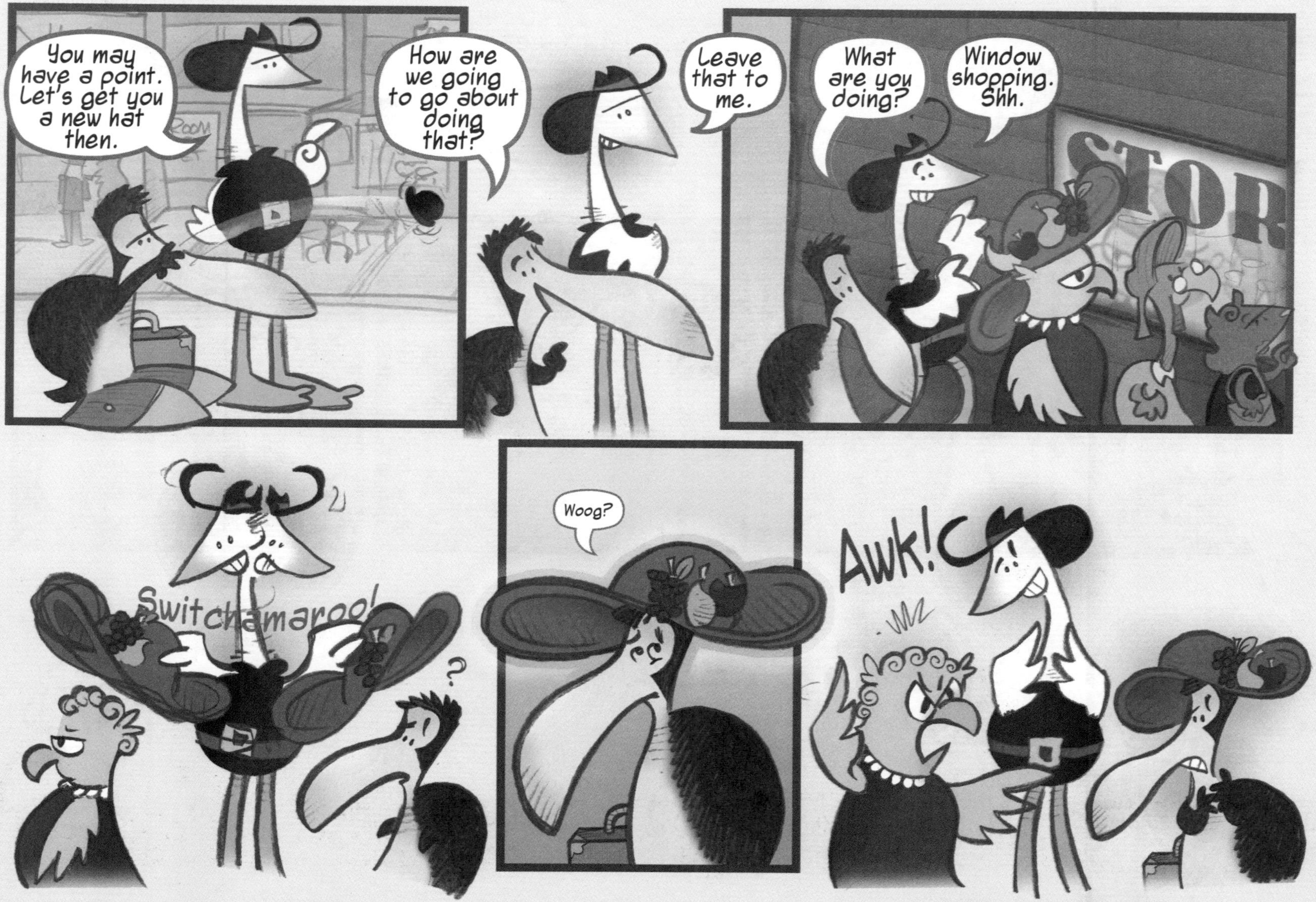

You may have a point. Let's get you a new hat then.
How are we going to go about doing that?
Leave that to me.
What are you doing?
Window shopping. Shh.
STOR
Switchamaroo!
?
Woog?
Awk!

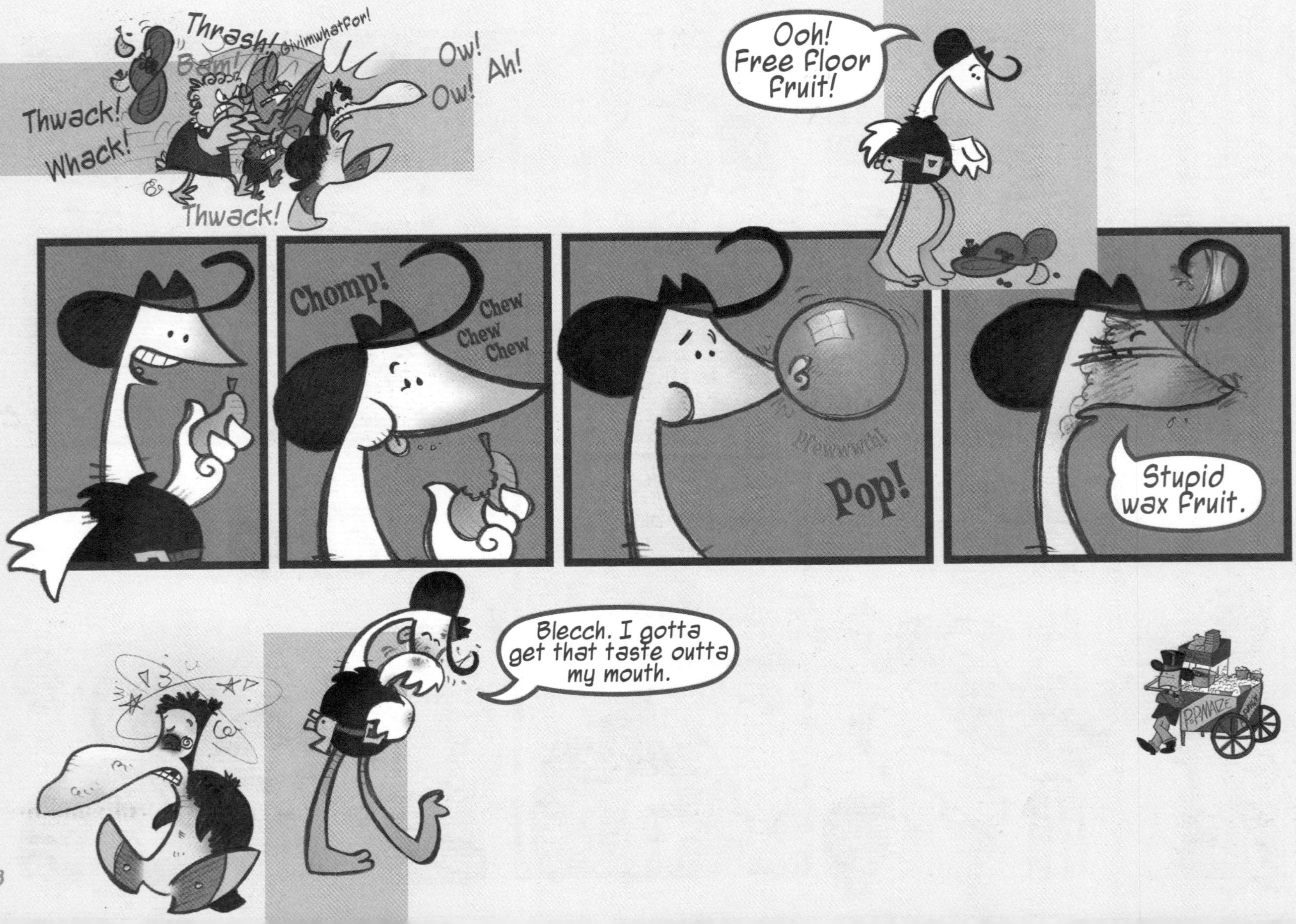
Thrash!
Bam!
Givimwhatfor!
Thwack!
Whack!
Ow!
Ow!
Ah!
Thwack!
Ooh! Free floor fruit!
Chomp!
Chew Chew Chew
Pfewwwth!
Pop!
Stupid wax fruit.
Blecch. I gotta get that taste outta my mouth.
POPMAIZE

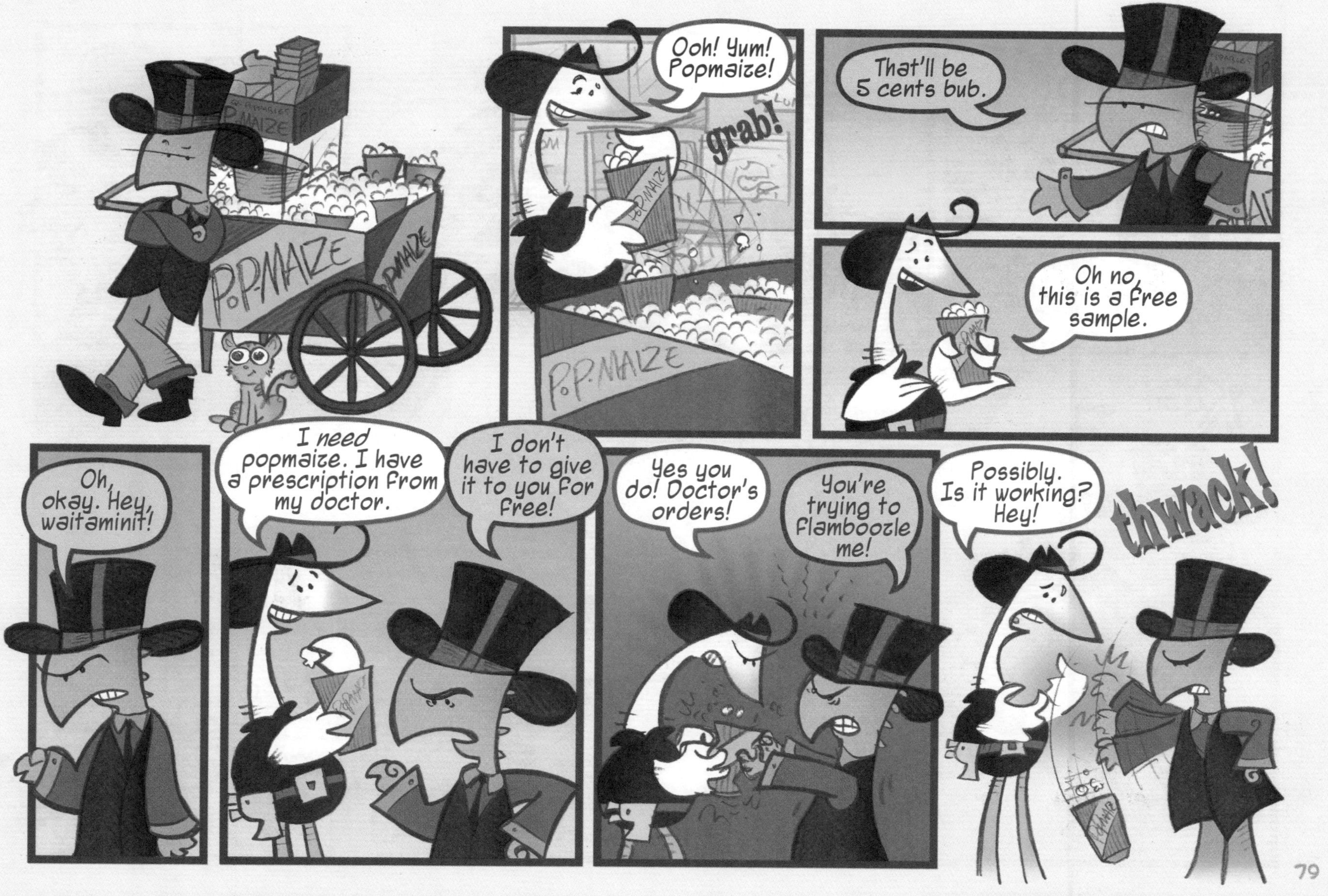
P.O.P. MAIZE
Ooh! Yum! Popmaize!
grab!
That'll be 5 cents bub.
Oh no, this is a free sample.
Oh, okay. Hey, waitaminit!
I need popmaize. I have a prescription from my doctor.
I don't have to give it to you for free!
Yes you do! Doctor's orders!
You're trying to flamboozle me!
Possibly. Is it working? Hey!
thwack!

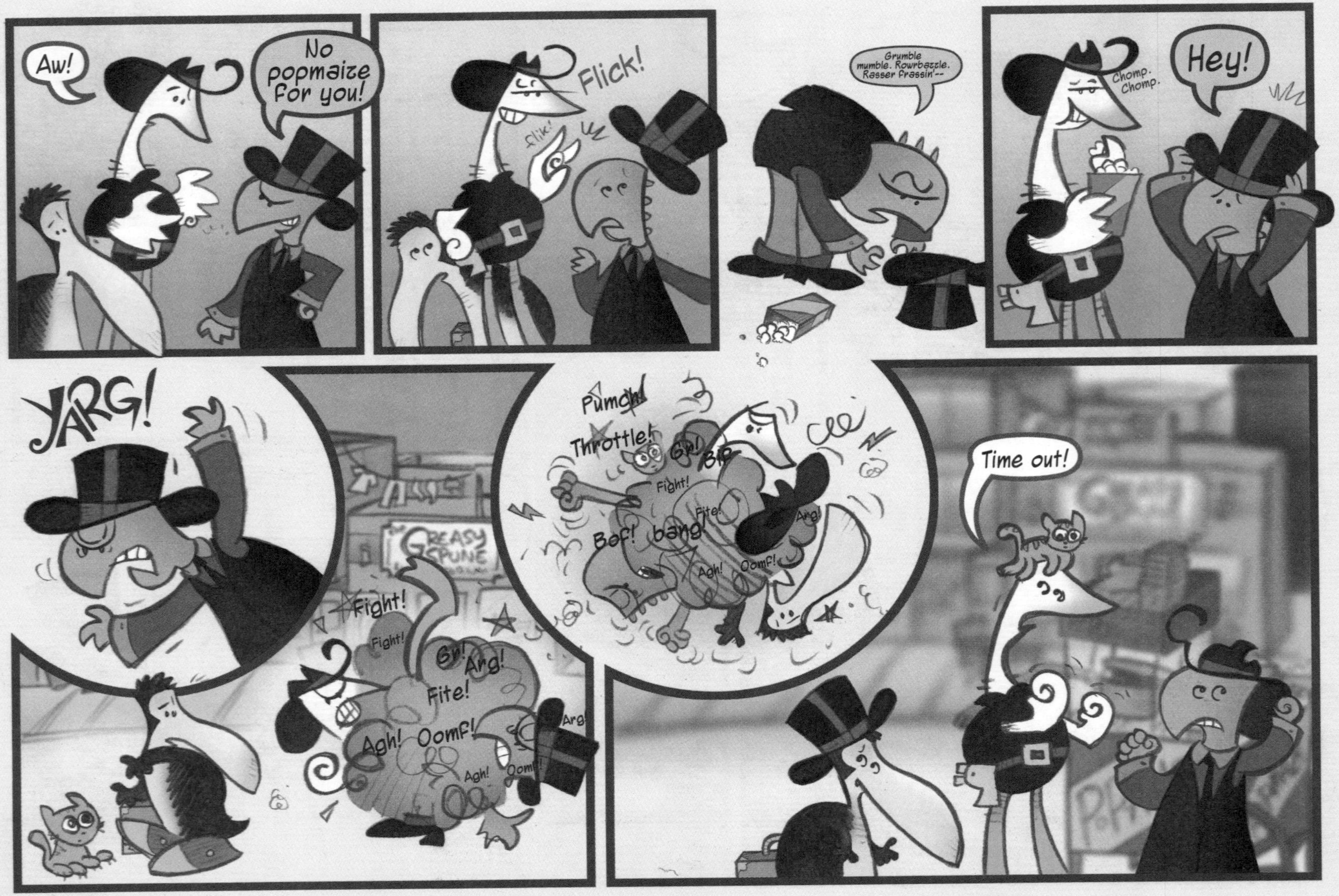
Aw!
No popmaize for you!
Flick!
flik!
Grumble mumble. Rowrbazzle. Rasser frassin'--
Chomp. Chomp.
Hey!
YARG!
THE GREASY SPUNE
Fight!
Fight!
Gr!
Arg!
Fite!
Agh! Oomf!
Agh!
Oomf!
Arg
Pumch!
Throttle!
Gr!
Bip
Fight!
Fite!
Arg!
Bof! bang!
Agh!
Oomf!
Time out!

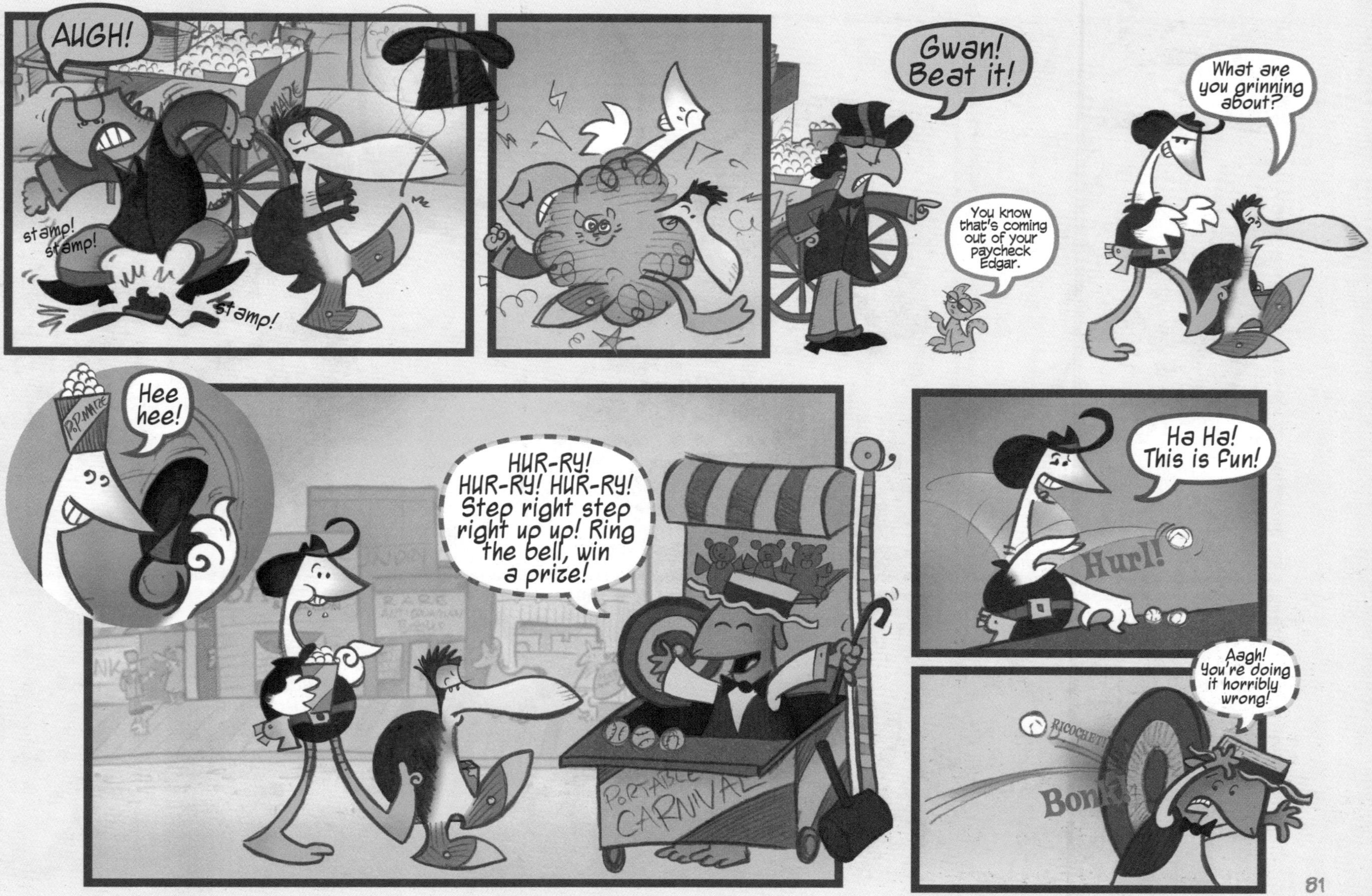
AUGH!
stamp! stamp!
stamp!
Gwan! Beat it!
You know that's coming out of your paycheck Edgar.
What are you grinning about?
POPMAIZE
Hee hee!
HUR-RY! HUR-RY! HUR-RY! Step right step right up up! Ring the bell, win a prize!
PORTABLE CARNIVAL
Ha Ha! This is fun!
Hurl!
Aagh! You're doing it horribly wrong!
RICOCHET
Bonk!

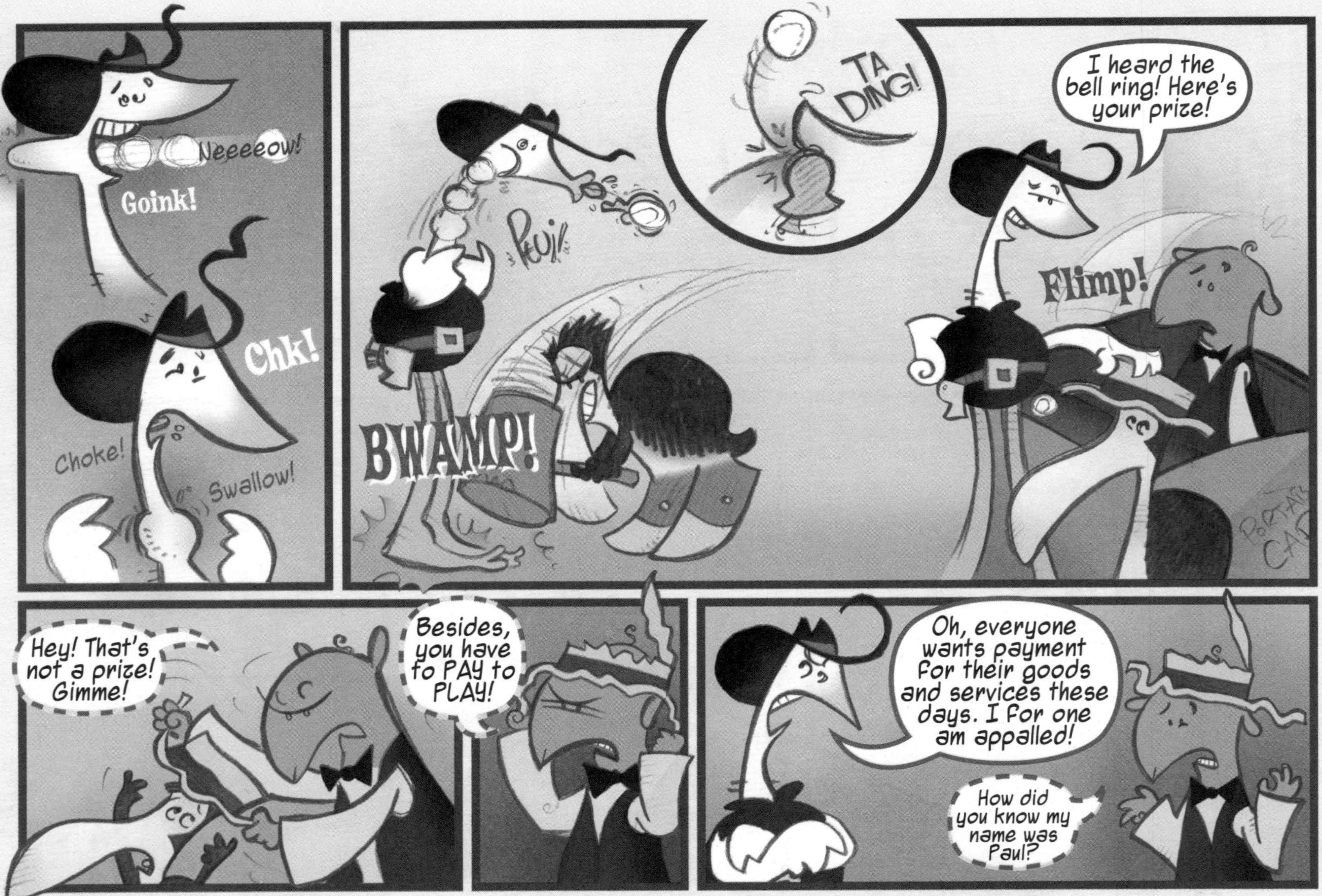
Neeeeow!
Goink!
Chk!
Choke!
Swallow!
Ptui!
BWAMP!
TA DING!
I heard the bell ring! Here's your prize!
Flimp!
Hey! That's not a prize! Gimme!
Besides, you have to PAY to PLAY!
Oh, everyone wants payment for their goods and services these days. I for one am appalled!
How did you know my name was Paul?

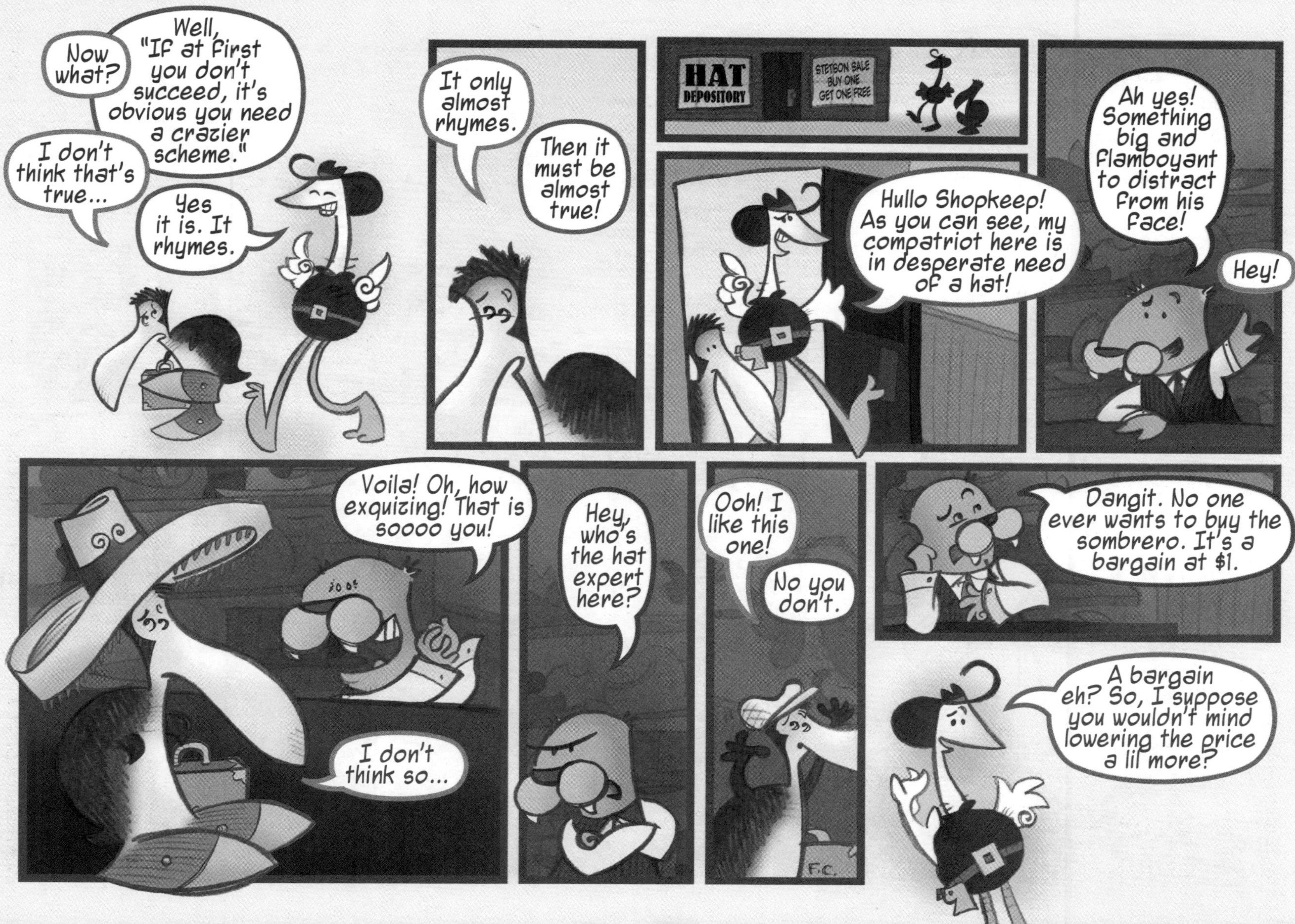
Now what?
Well, "If at first you don't succeed, it's obvious you need a crazier scheme."
I don't think that's true...
Yes it is. It rhymes.
It only almost rhymes.
Then it must be almost true!
HAT DEPOSITORY
STETSON SALE BUY ONE GET ONE FREE
Hullo Shopkeep! As you can see, my compatriot here is in desperate need of a hat!
Ah yes! Something big and flamboyant to distract from his face!
Hey!
Voila! Oh, how exquizing! That is soooo you!
I don't think so...
Hey, who's the hat expert here?
Ooh! I like this one!
No you don't.
F.C.
Dangit. No one ever wants to buy the sombrero. It's a bargain at $1.
A bargain eh? So, I suppose you wouldn't mind lowering the price a lil more?

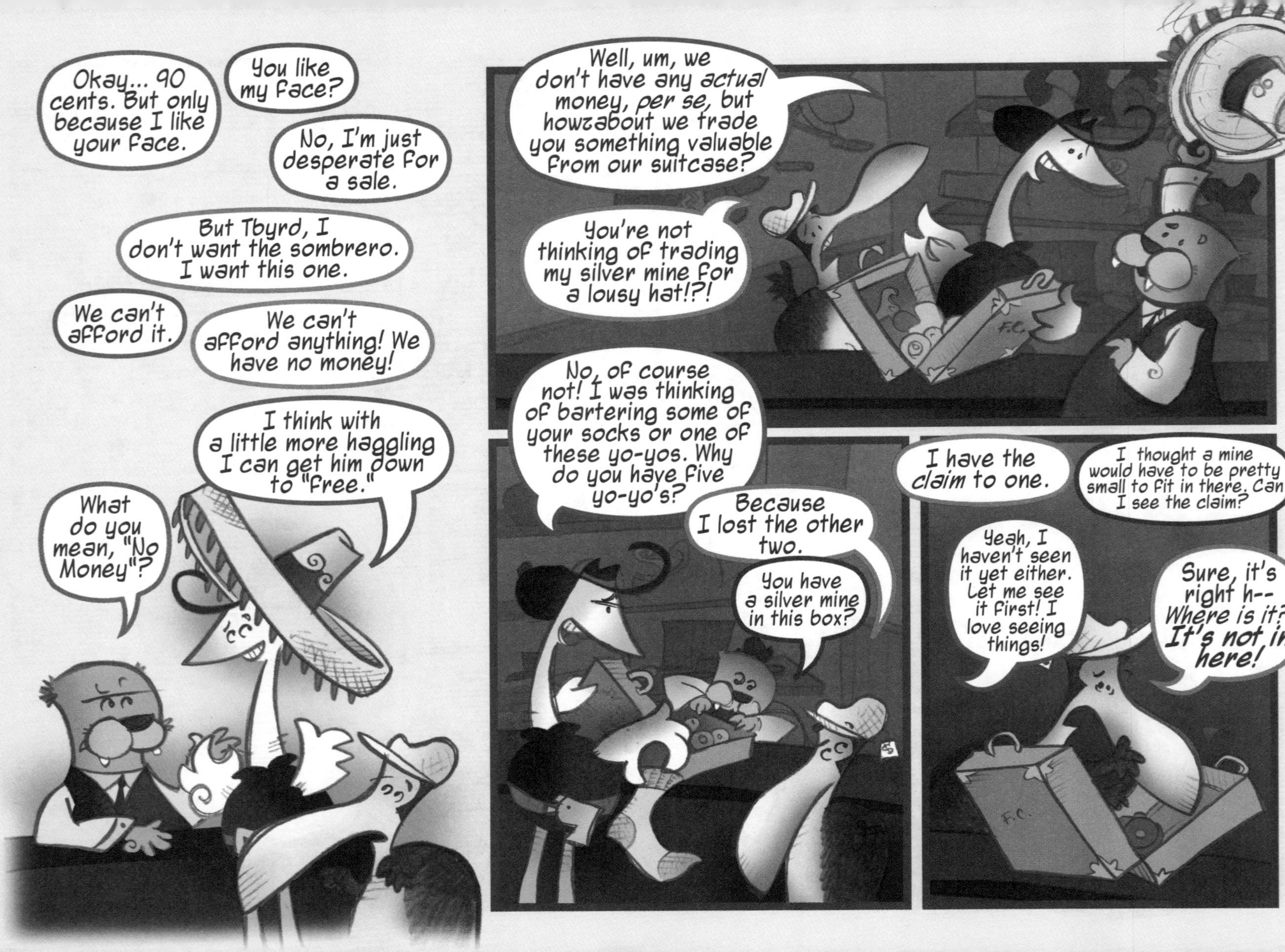
Okay... 90 cents. But only because I like your face.
You like my face?
No, I'm just desperate for a sale.
But Tbyrd, I don't want the sombrero. I want this one.
We can't afford it.
We can't afford anything! We have no money!
I think with a little more haggling I can get him down to "free."
What do you mean, "No Money"?
Well, um, we don't have any *actual* money, *per se*, but howzabout we trade you something valuable from our suitcase?
You're not thinking of trading my silver mine for a lousy hat!?!
No, of course not! I was thinking of bartering some of your socks or one of these yo-yos. Why do you have five yo-yo's?
Because I lost the other two.
You have a silver mine in this box?
I have the *claim* to one.
I thought a mine would have to be pretty small to fit in there. Can I see the claim?
Yeah, I haven't seen it yet either. Let me see it first! I love seeing things!
Sure, it's right h-- Where is it? ***It's not in here!***

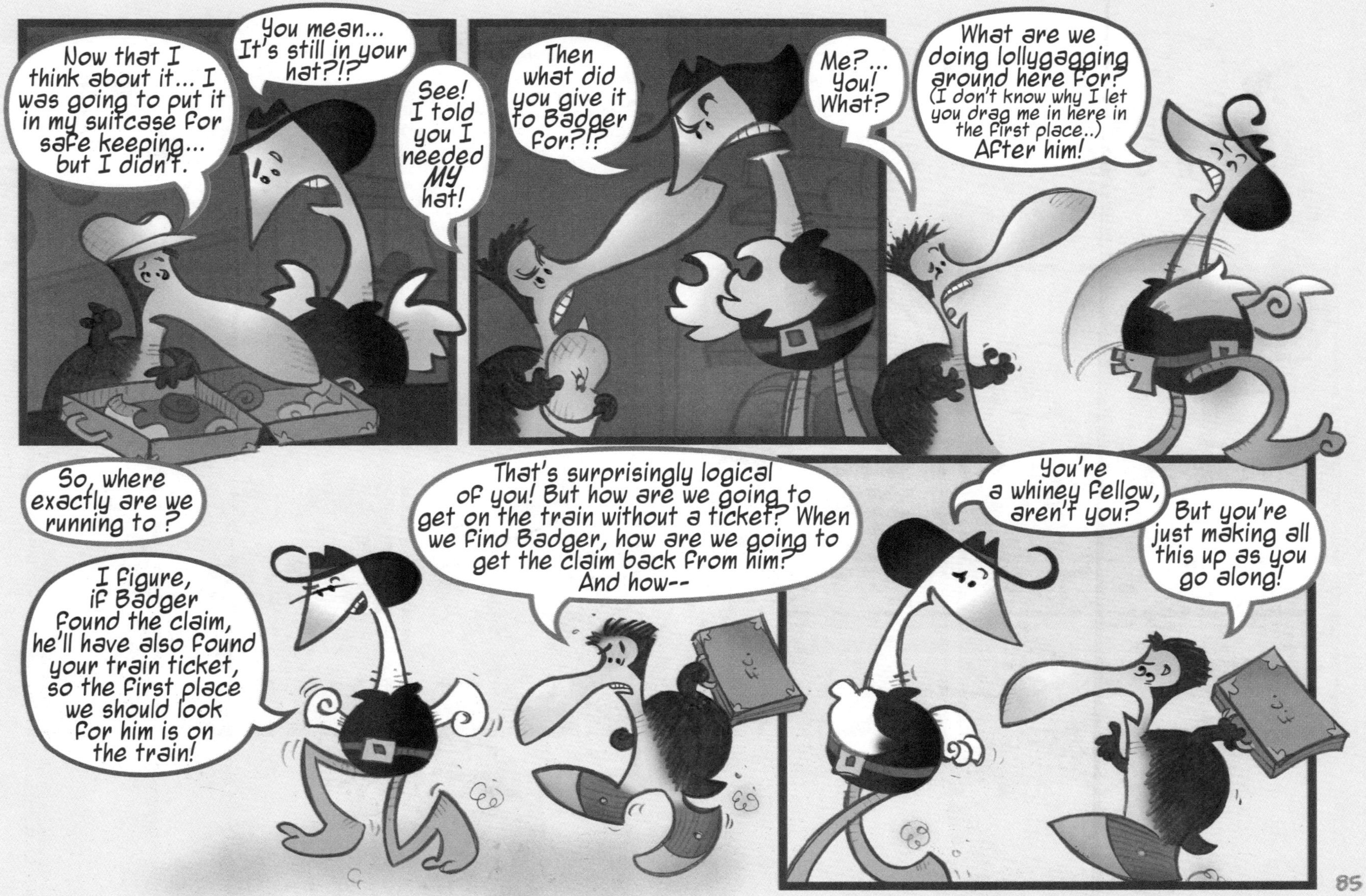
Now that I think about it... I was going to put it in my suitcase for safe keeping... but I didn't.
You mean... It's still in your hat?!?
See! I told you I needed MY hat!
Then what did you give it to Badger for?!?
Me?... You! What?
What are we doing lollygagging around here for? (I don't know why I let you drag me in here in the first place..) After him!
So, where exactly are we running to ?
I figure, if Badger found the claim, he'll have also found your train ticket, so the first place we should look for him is on the train!
That's surprisingly logical of you! But how are we going to get on the train without a ticket? When we find Badger, how are we going to get the claim back from him? And how--
You're a whiney fellow, aren't you?
But you're just making all this up as you go along!

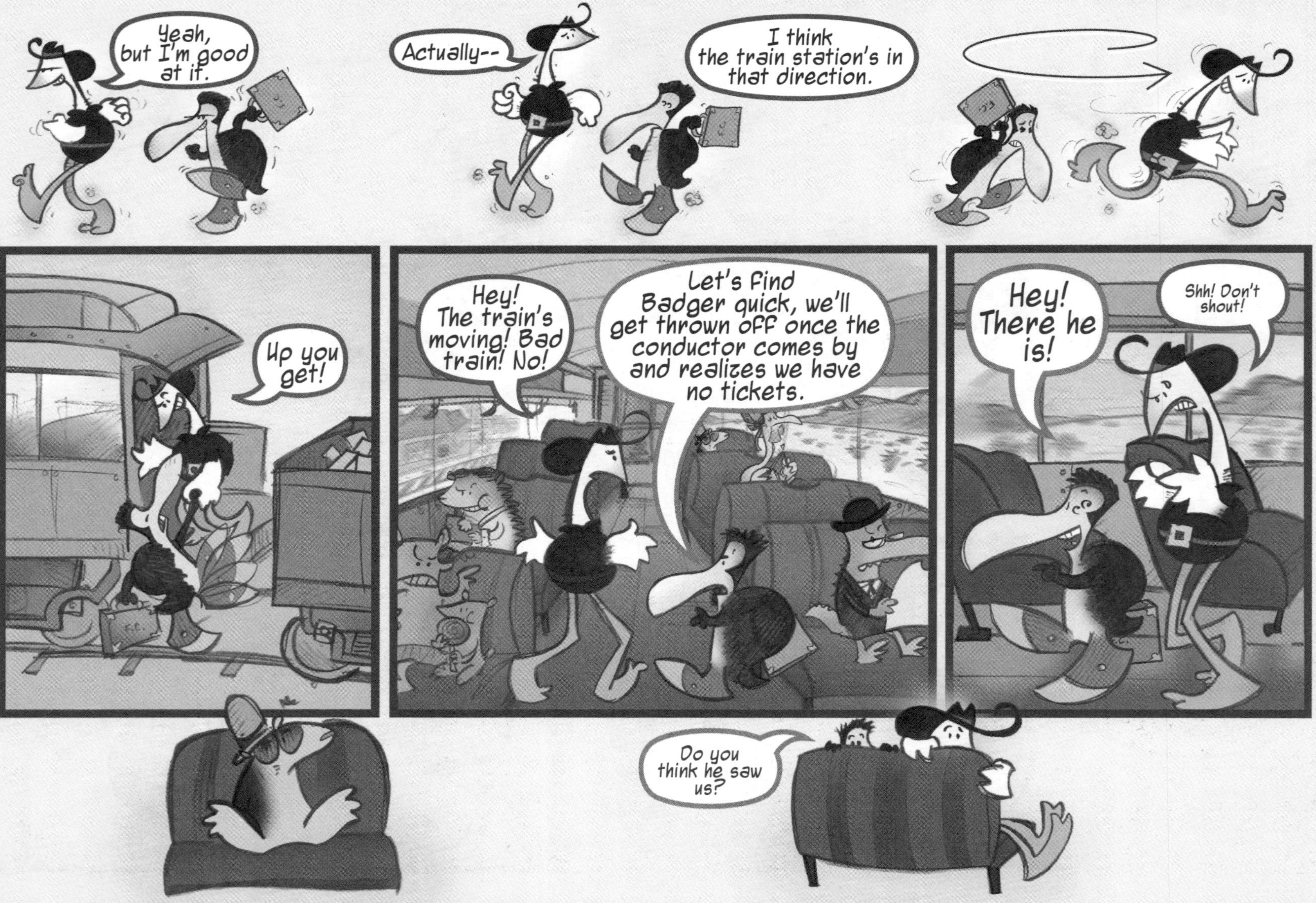

Yeah, but I'm good at it.
Actually--
I think the train station's in that direction.
Up you get!
Hey! The train's moving! Bad train! No!
Let's find Badger quick, we'll get thrown off once the conductor comes by and realizes we have no tickets.
Hey! There he is!
Shh! Don't shout!
Do you think he saw us?

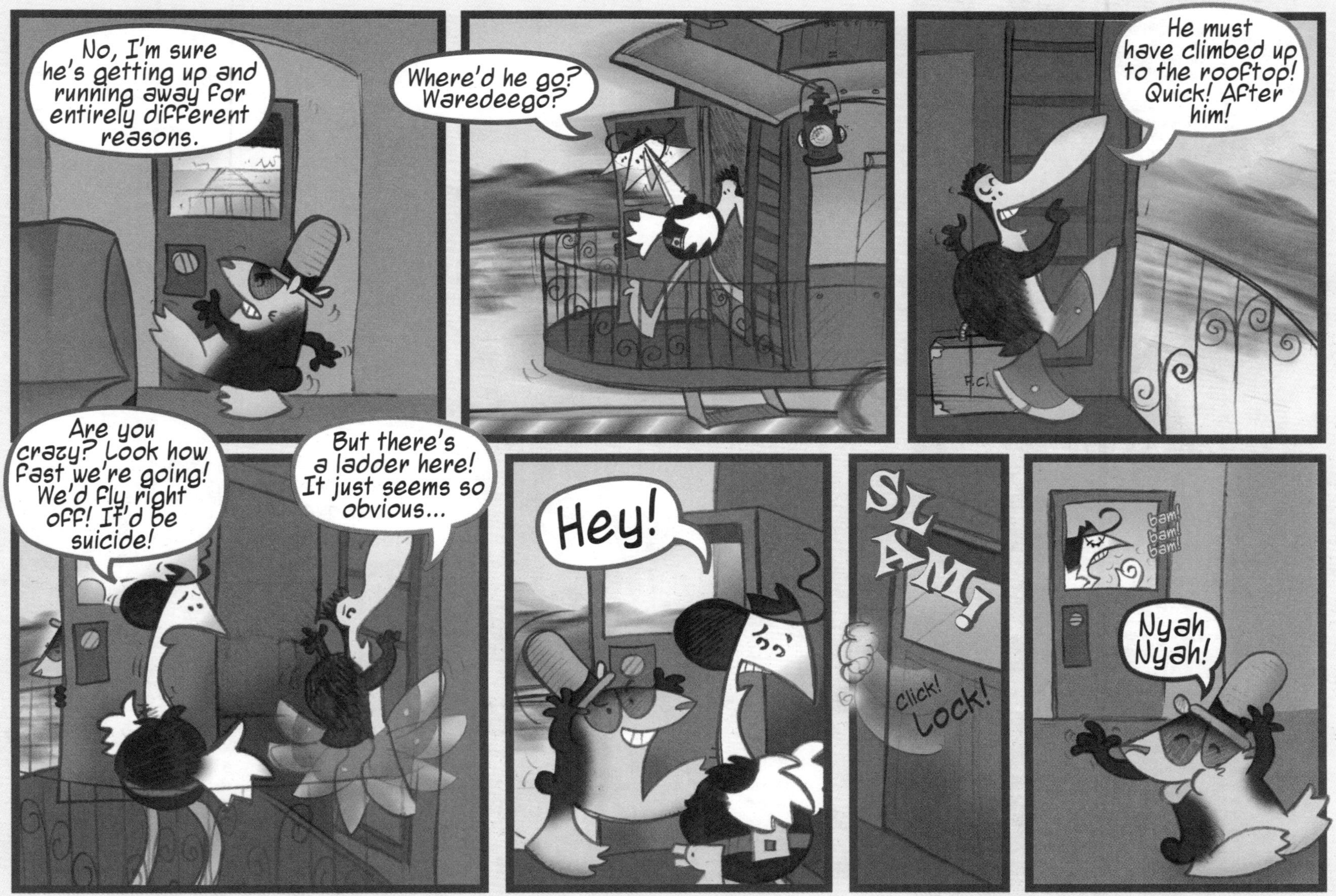

No, I'm sure he's getting up and running away for entirely different reasons.
Where'd he go? Waredeego?
He must have climbed up to the rooftop! Quick! After him!
Are you crazy? Look how fast we're going! We'd fly right off! It'd be suicide!
But there's a ladder here! It just seems so obvious...
Hey!
SLAM!
Click!
Lock!
bam! bam! bam!
Nyah Nyah!

chapter 5

Several Cramped and Windy Hours Later...

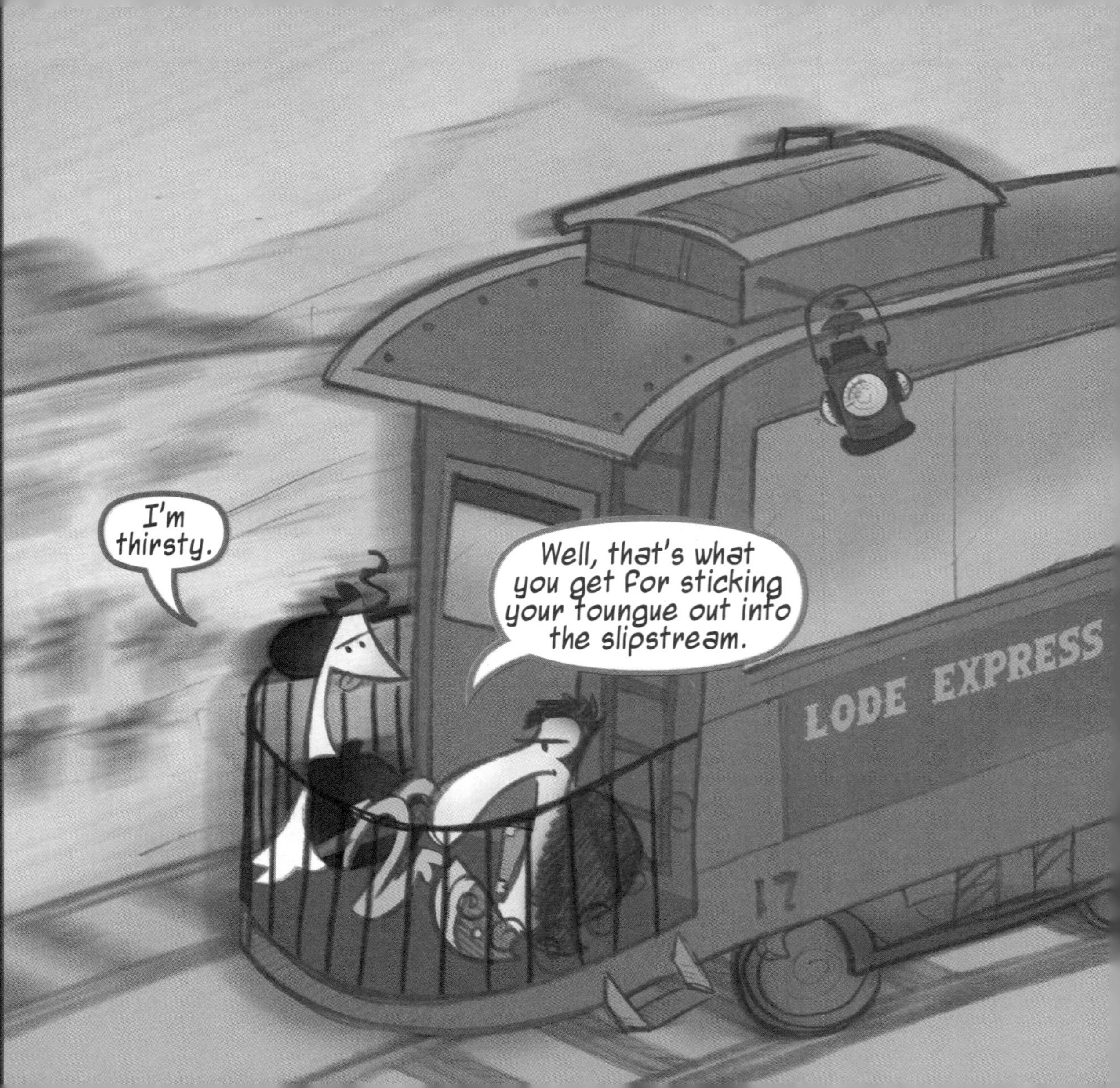
I'm thirsty.
Well, that's what you get for sticking your toungue out into the slipstream.
LODE EXPRESS
17

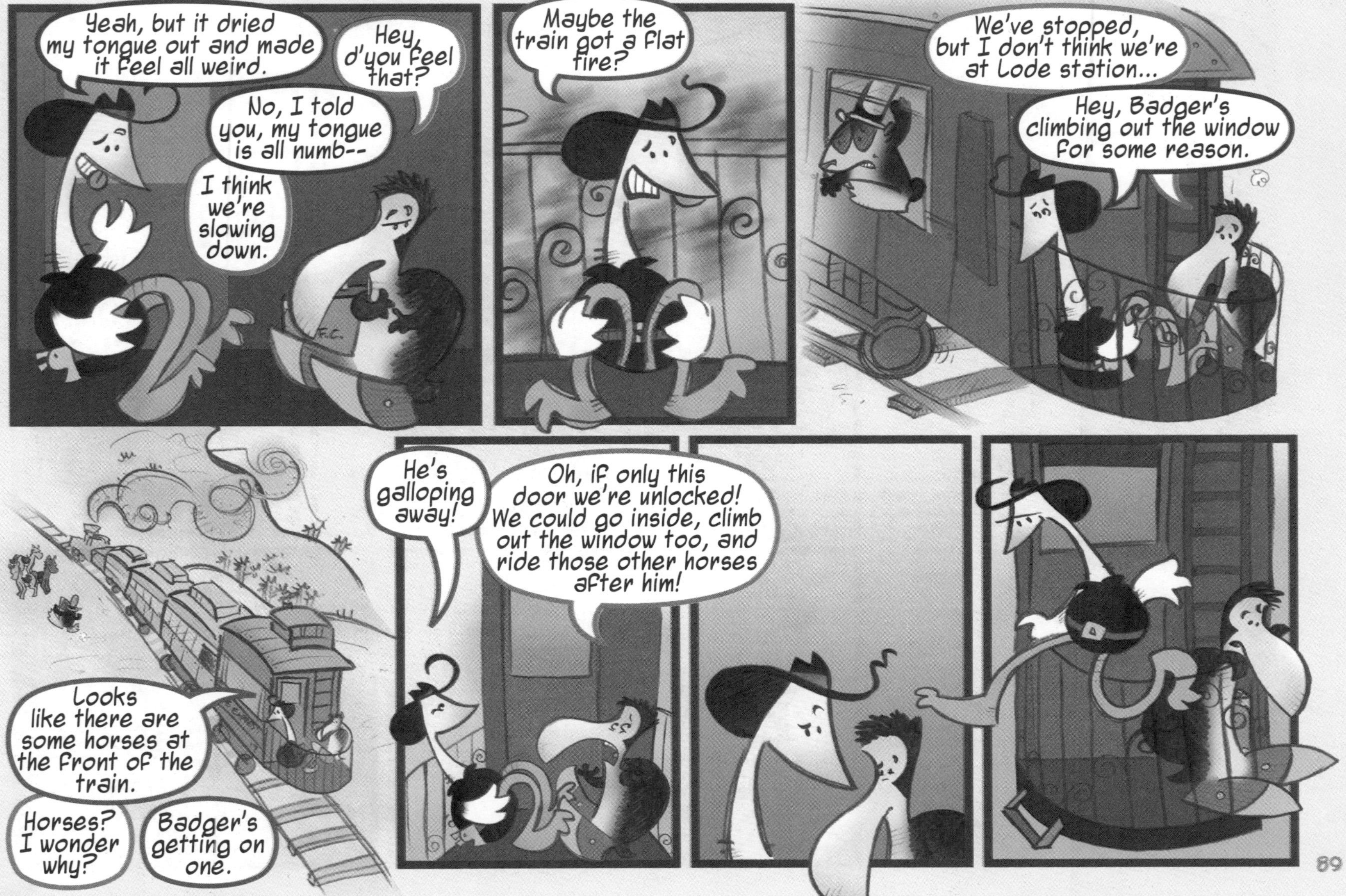
Yeah, but it dried my tongue out and made it feel all weird.
Hey, d'you feel that?
No, I told you, my tongue is all numb--
I think we're slowing down.
Maybe the train got a flat tire?
We've stopped, but I don't think we're at Lode station...
Hey, Badger's climbing out the window for some reason.
Looks like there are some horses at the front of the train.
Horses? I wonder why?
Badger's getting on one.
He's galloping away!
Oh, if only this door we're unlocked! We could go inside, climb out the window too, and ride those other horses after him!

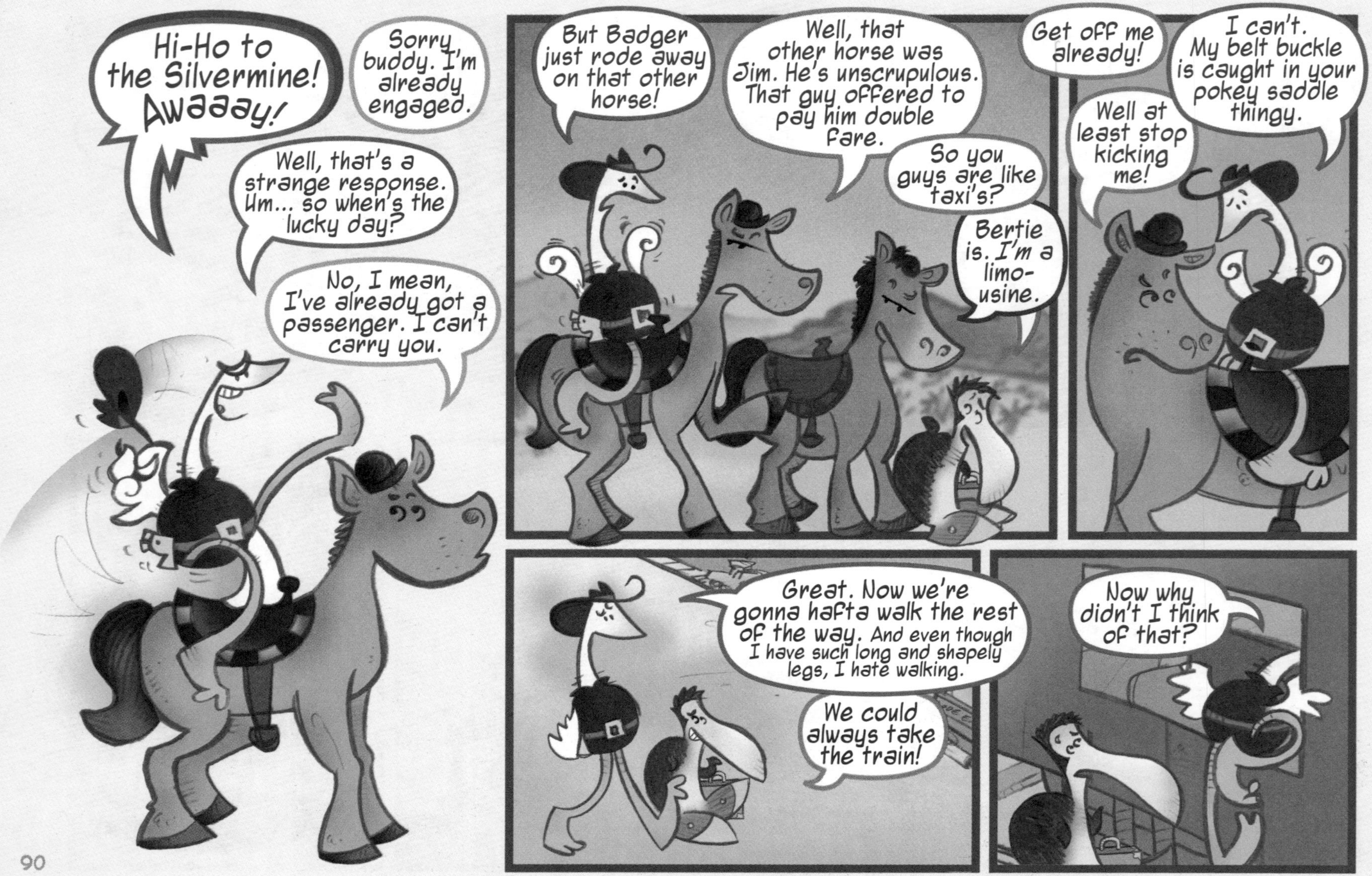
Hi-Ho to the Silvermine! Awaaay!
Sorry buddy. I'm already engaged.
Well, that's a strange response. Um... so when's the lucky day?
No, I mean, I've already got a passenger. I can't carry you.
But Badger just rode away on that other horse!
Well, that other horse was Jim. He's unscrupulous. That guy offered to pay him double fare.
So you guys are like taxi's?
Bertie is. *I'm* a limo-usine.
Get off me already!
I can't. My belt buckle is caught in your pokey saddle thingy.
Well at least stop kicking me!
Great. Now we're gonna hafta walk the rest of the way. And even though I have such long and shapely legs, I hate walking.
We could always take the train!
Now why didn't I think of that?

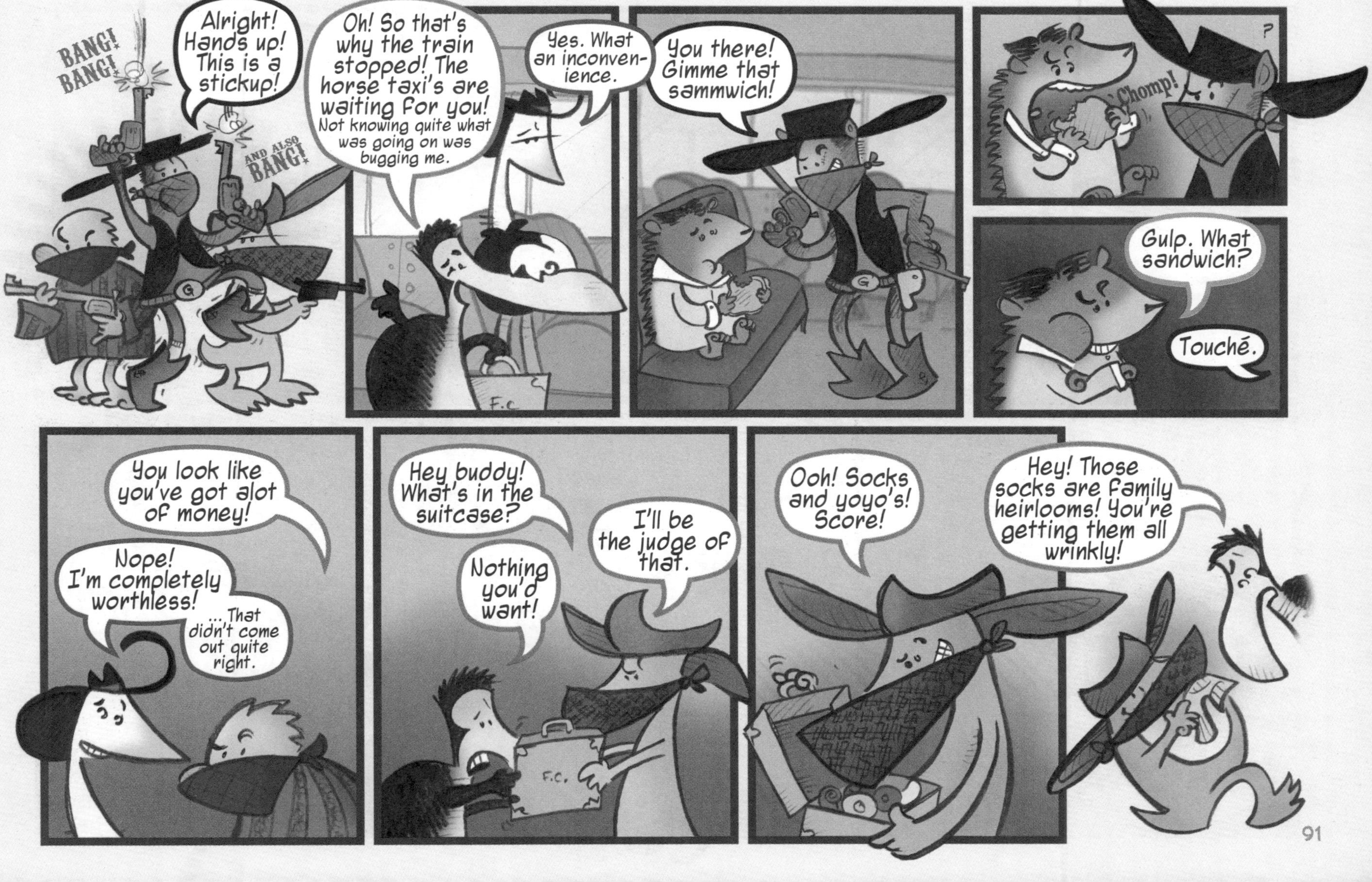
BANG! BANG!
Alright! Hands up! This is a stickup!
AND ALSO BANG!
Oh! So that's why the train stopped! The horse taxi's are waiting for you!
Not knowing quite what was going on was bugging me.
Yes. What an inconvenience.
F.C.
You there! Gimme that sammwich!
Chomp!
?
Gulp. What sandwich?
Touché.
You look like you've got alot of money!
Nope! I'm completely worthless!
...That didn't come out quite right.
Hey buddy! What's in the suitcase?
Nothing you'd want!
I'll be the judge of that.
F.C.
Ooh! Socks and yoyo's! Score!
Hey! Those socks are family heirlooms! You're getting them all wrinkly!

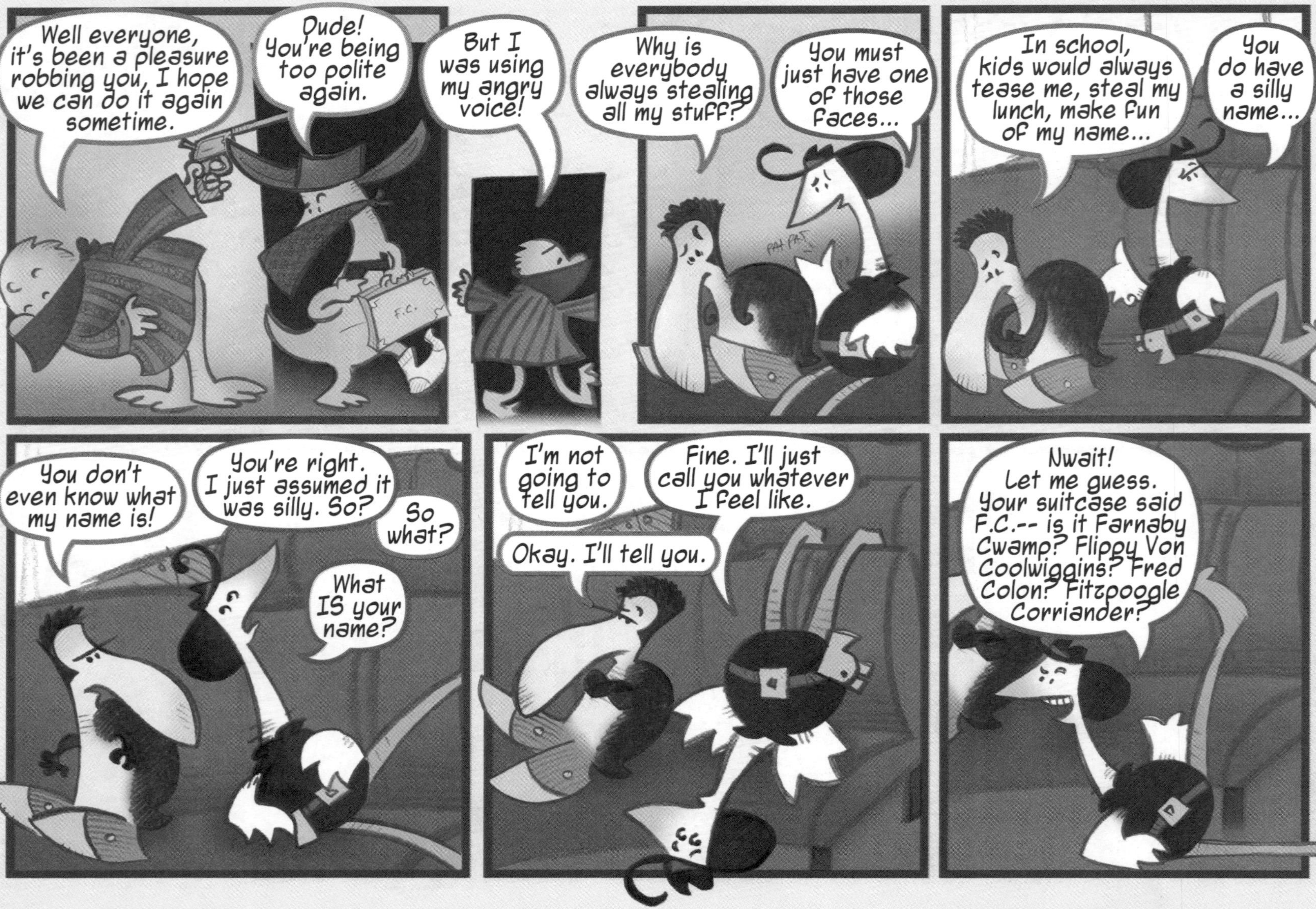
Well everyone, it's been a pleasure robbing you, I hope we can do it again sometime.
Dude! You're being too polite again.
F.C.
But I was using my angry voice!
Why is everybody always stealing all my stuff?
You must just have one of those faces...
PAT PAT
In school, kids would always tease me, steal my lunch, make fun of my name...
You do have a silly name...
You don't even know what my name is!
You're right. I just assumed it was silly. So?
So what?
What IS your name?
I'm not going to tell you.
Fine. I'll just call you whatever I feel like.
Okay. I'll tell you.
Nwait! Let me guess. Your suitcase said F.C.-- is it Farnaby Cwamp? Flippy Von Coolwiggins? Fred Colon? Fitzpoogle Corriander?

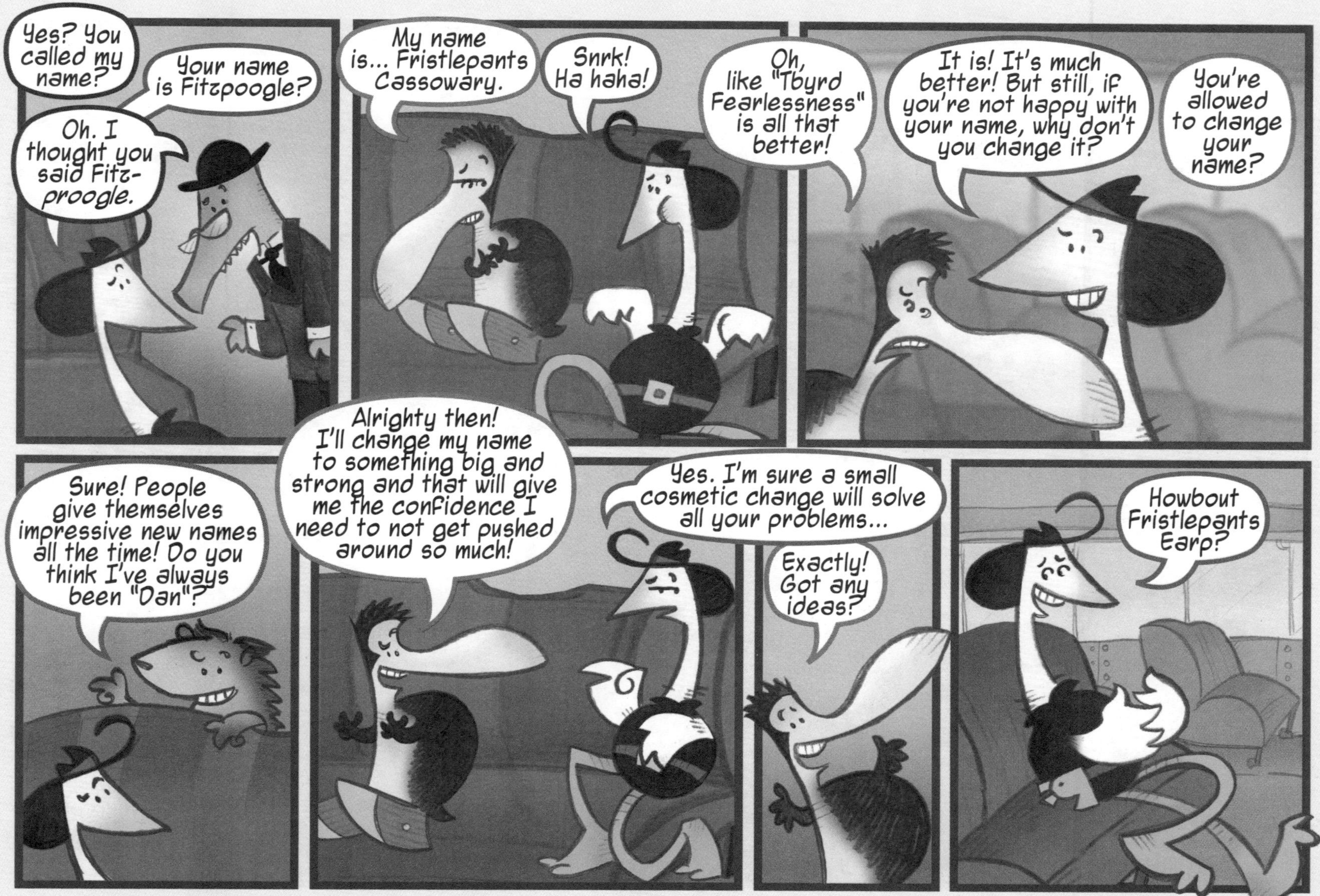
Yes? You called my name?
Your name is Fitzpoogle?
Oh. I thought you said Fitz-proogle.
My name is... Fristlepants Cassowary.
Snrk! Ha haha!
Oh, like "Tbyrd Fearlessness" is all that better!
It is! It's much better! But still, if you're not happy with your name, why don't you change it?
You're allowed to change your name?
Sure! People give themselves impressive new names all the time! Do you think I've always been "Dan"?
Alrighty then! I'll change my name to something big and strong and that will give me the confidence I need to not get pushed around so much!
Yes. I'm sure a small cosmetic change will solve all your problems...
Exactly! Got any ideas?
Howbout Fristlepants Earp?

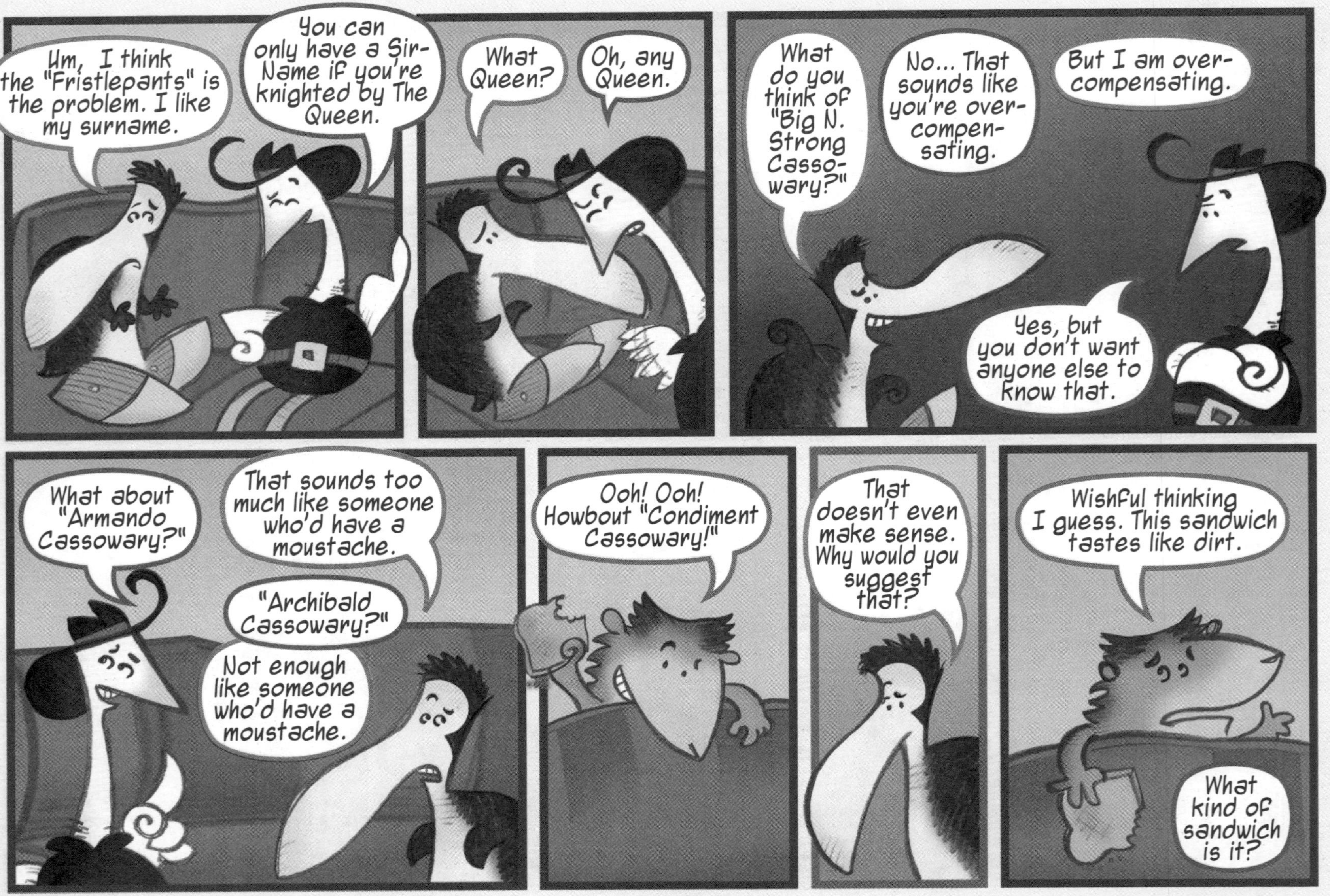
Um, I think the "Fristlepants" is the problem. I like my surname.
You can only have a Sir-Name if you're knighted by The Queen.
What Queen?
Oh, any Queen.
What do you think of "Big N. Strong Cassowary?"
No... That sounds like you're over-compensating.
But I am over-compensating.
Yes, but you don't want anyone else to know that.
What about "Armando Cassowary?"
That sounds too much like someone who'd have a moustache.
"Archibald Cassowary?"
Not enough like someone who'd have a moustache.
Ooh! Ooh! Howbout "Condiment Cassowary!"
That doesn't even make sense. Why would you suggest that?
Wishful thinking I guess. This sandwich tastes like dirt.
What kind of sandwich is it?

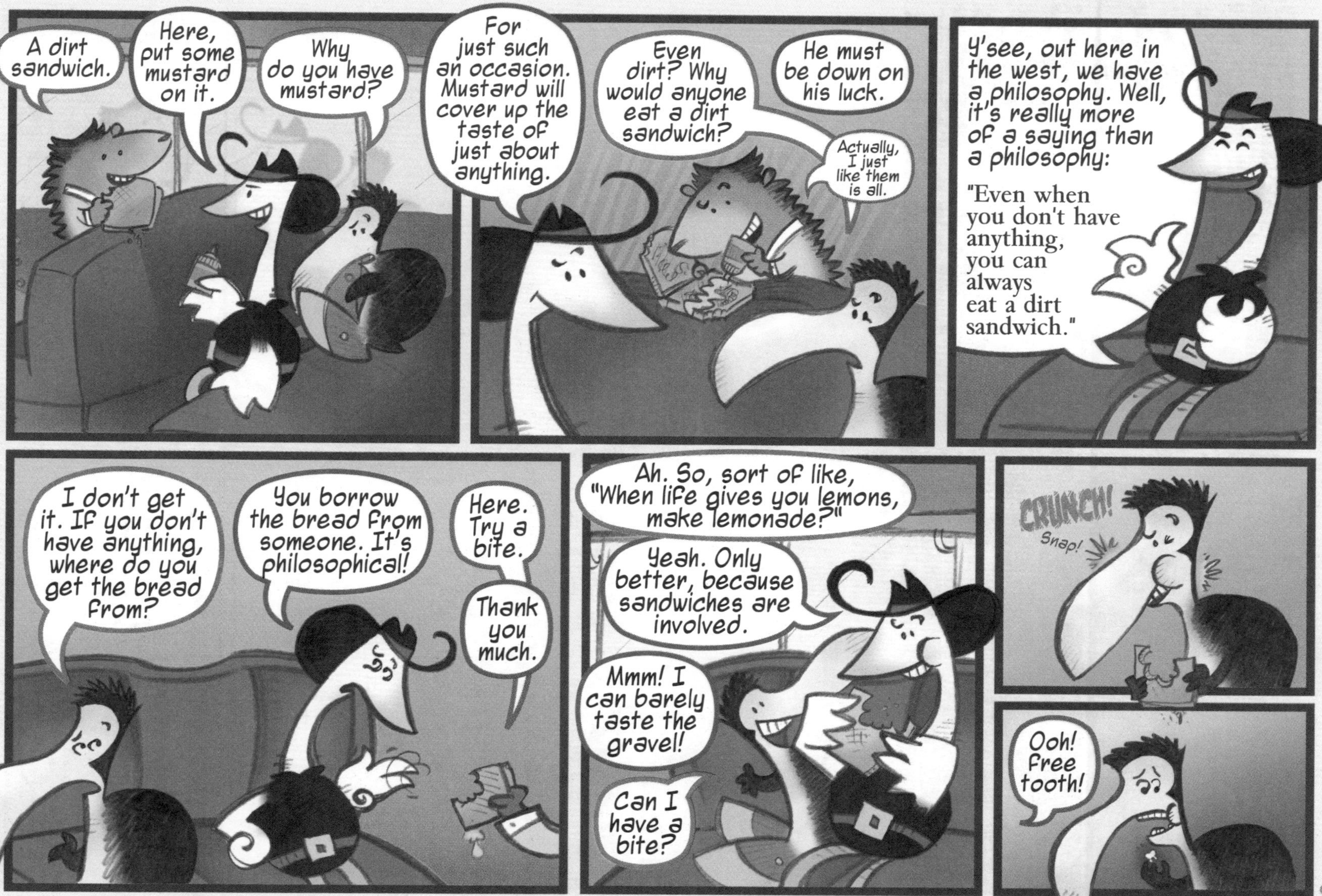
A dirt sandwich.
Here, put some mustard on it.
Why do you have mustard?
For just such an occasion. Mustard will cover up the taste of just about anything.
Even dirt? Why would anyone eat a dirt sandwich?
He must be down on his luck.
Actually, I just like them is all.
Y'see, out here in the west, we have a philosophy. Well, it's really more of a saying than a philosophy:
"Even when you don't have anything, you can always eat a dirt sandwich."
I don't get it. If you don't have anything, where do you get the bread from?
You borrow the bread from someone. It's philosophical!
Here. Try a bite.
Thank you much.
Ah. So, sort of like, "When life gives you lemons, make lemonade?"
Yeah. Only better, because sandwiches are involved.
Mmm! I can barely taste the gravel!
Can I have a bite?
CRUNCH!
Snap!
Ooh! Free tooth!

chapter 6

The Big Dramatic Conclusion and Whatnot.

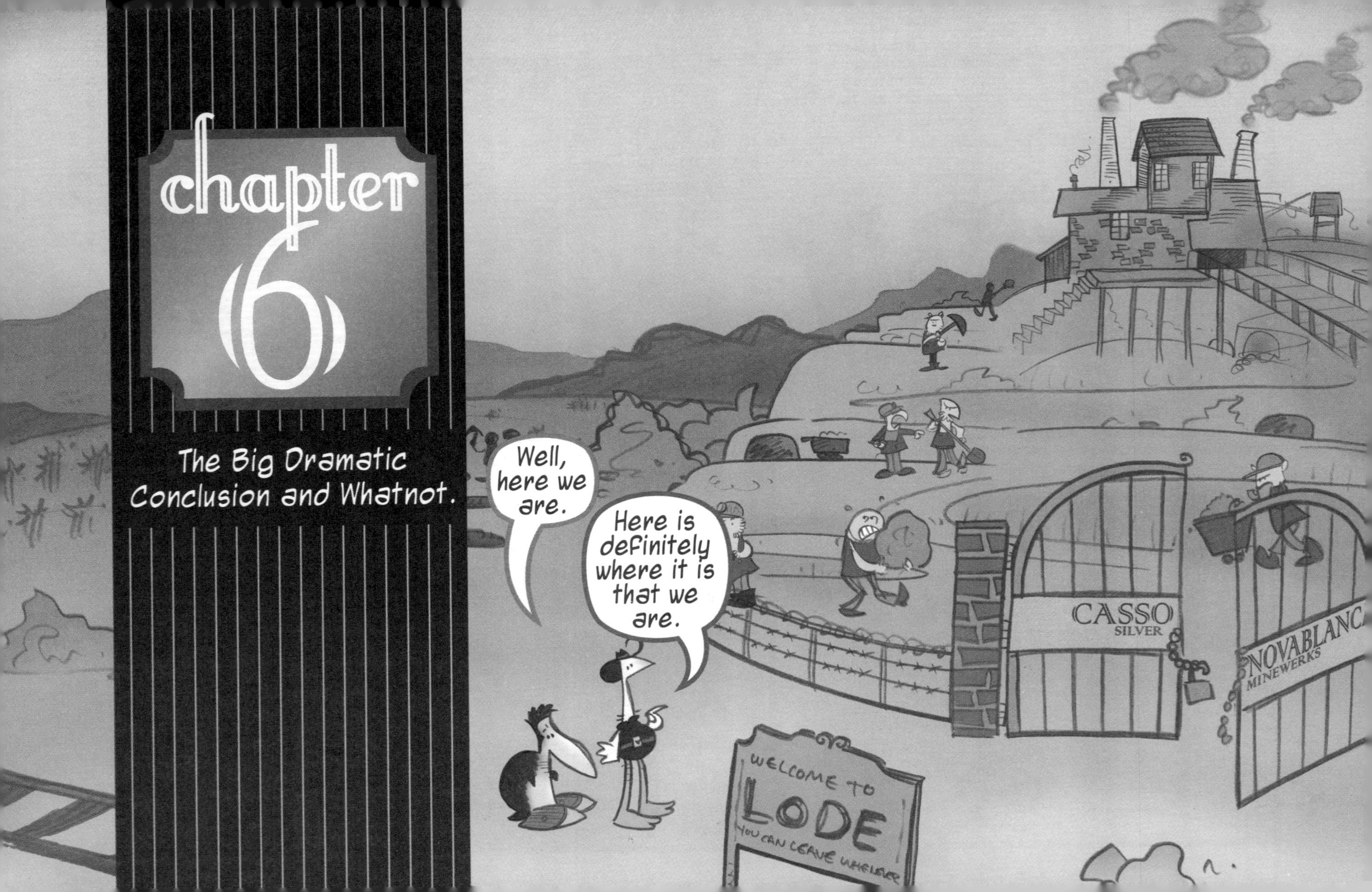

Well, here we are.
Here is definitely where it is that we are.
CASSO SILVER
NOVABLANCA MINEWERKS
WELCOME TO LODE
YOU CAN LEAVE WHENEVER

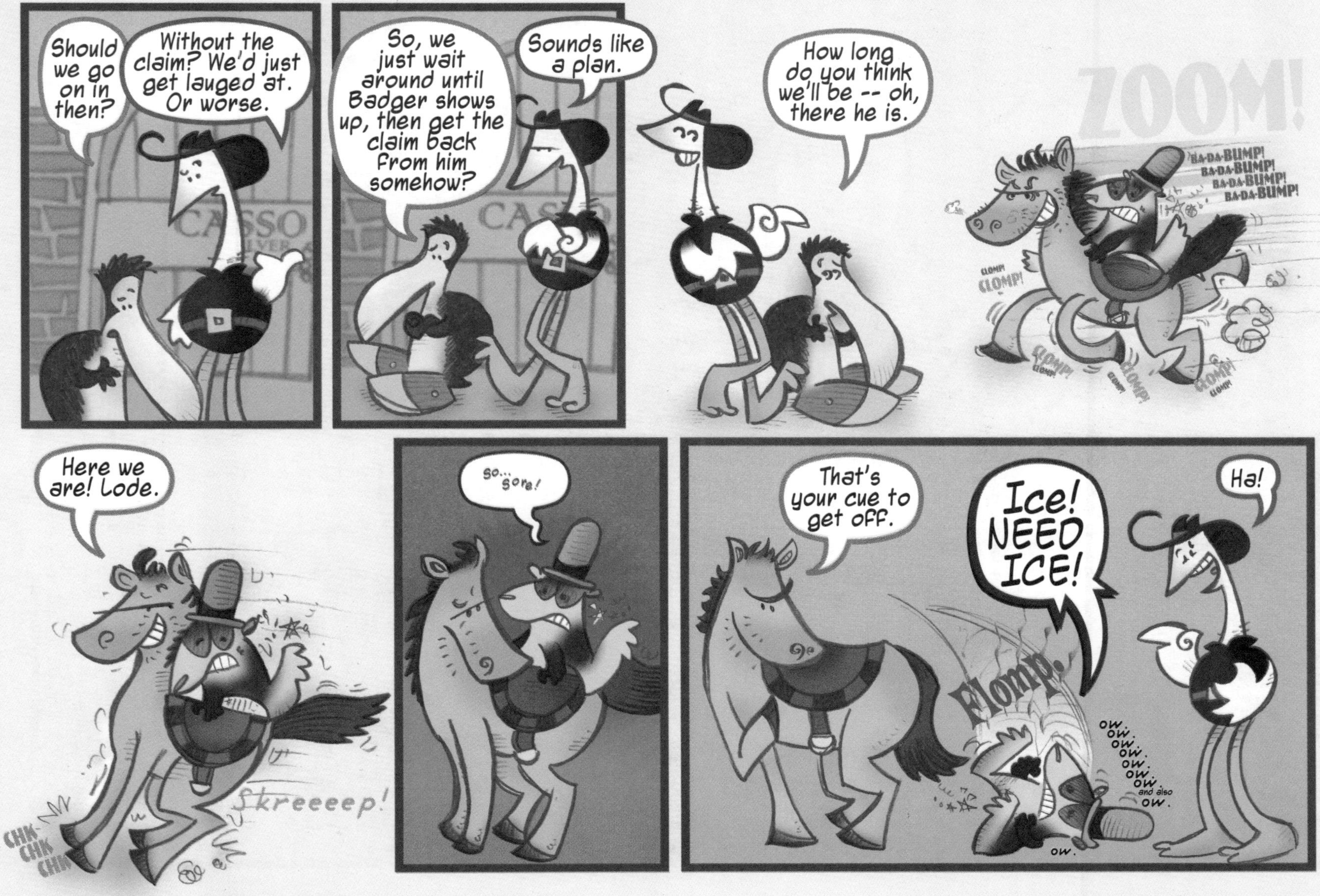

Should we go on in then?
Without the claim? We'd just get lauged at. Or worse.
So, we just wait around until Badger shows up, then get the claim back from him somehow?
Sounds like a plan.
How long do you think we'll be -- oh, there he is.
ZOOM!
BA-DA-BUMP! BA-DA-BUMP! BA-DA-BUMP! BA-DA-BUMP!
CLOMP! CLOMP!
CLOMP! CLOMP!
CLOMP! CLOMP!
CLOMP! CLOMP!
Here we are! Lode.
Skreeeeep!
CHK CHK CHK
so... sore!
That's your cue to get off.
Ice! NEED ICE!
Ha!
Flomp.
ow. ow. ow. ow. ow. ow. ow. and also ow.
ow.

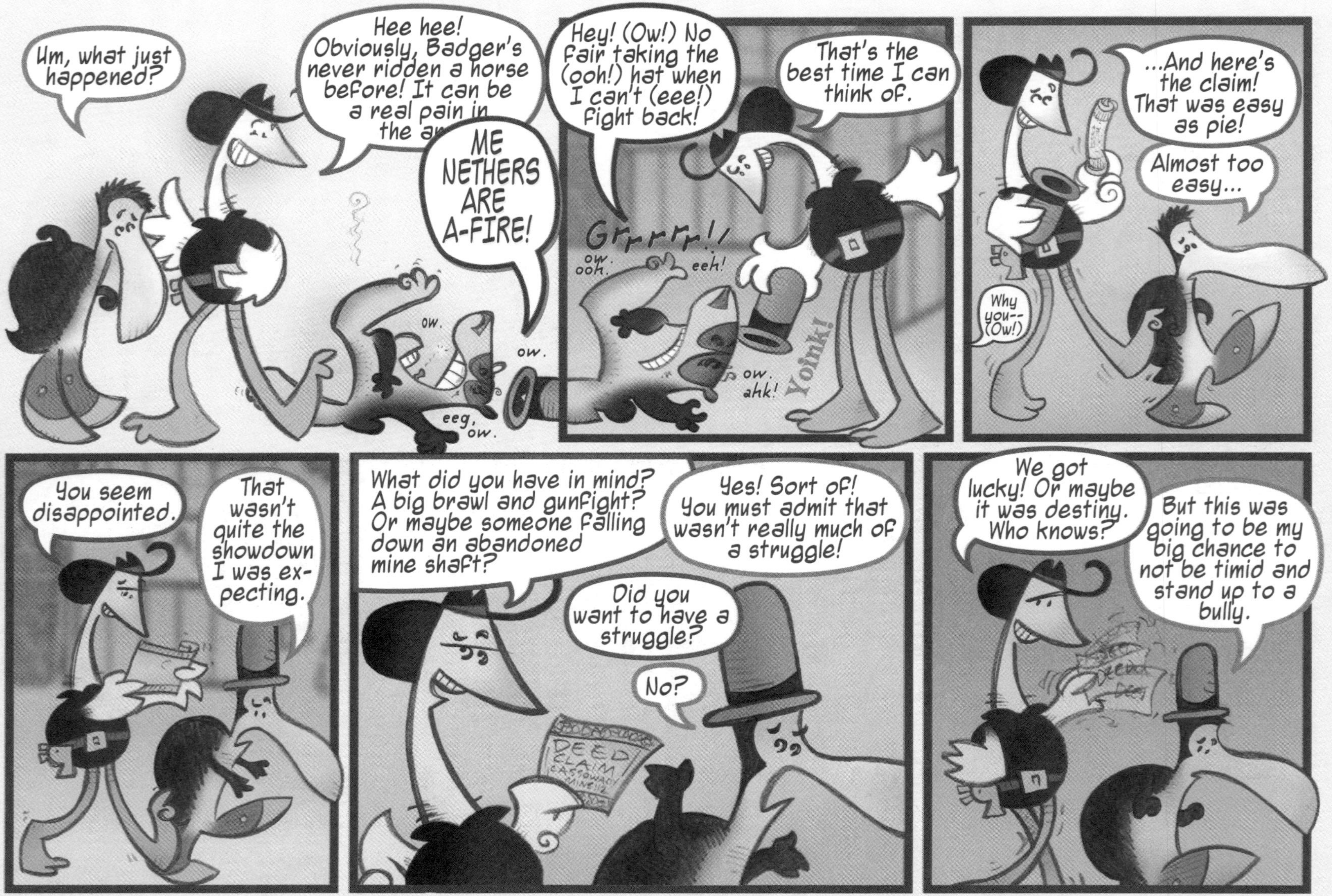
Um, what just happened?
Hee hee! Obviously, Badger's never ridden a horse before! It can be a real pain in the an
ME NETHERS ARE A-FIRE!
ow.
ow.
eeg, ow.
Hey! (Ow!) No fair taking the (ooh!) hat when I can't (eee!) fight back!
That's the best time I can think of.
Grrrrrr!!
ow. ooh.
eeh!
ow. ahk!
Yoink!
...And here's the claim! That was easy as pie!
Almost too easy...
Why you-- (Ow!)
You seem disappointed.
That wasn't quite the showdown I was expecting.
What did you have in mind? A big brawl and gunfight? Or maybe someone falling down an abandoned mine shaft?
Yes! Sort of! You must admit that wasn't really much of a struggle!
Did you want to have a struggle?
No?
DEED
CLAIM
CASSOWARY MINE #2
We got lucky! Or maybe it was destiny. Who knows?
But this was going to be my big chance to not be timid and stand up to a bully.

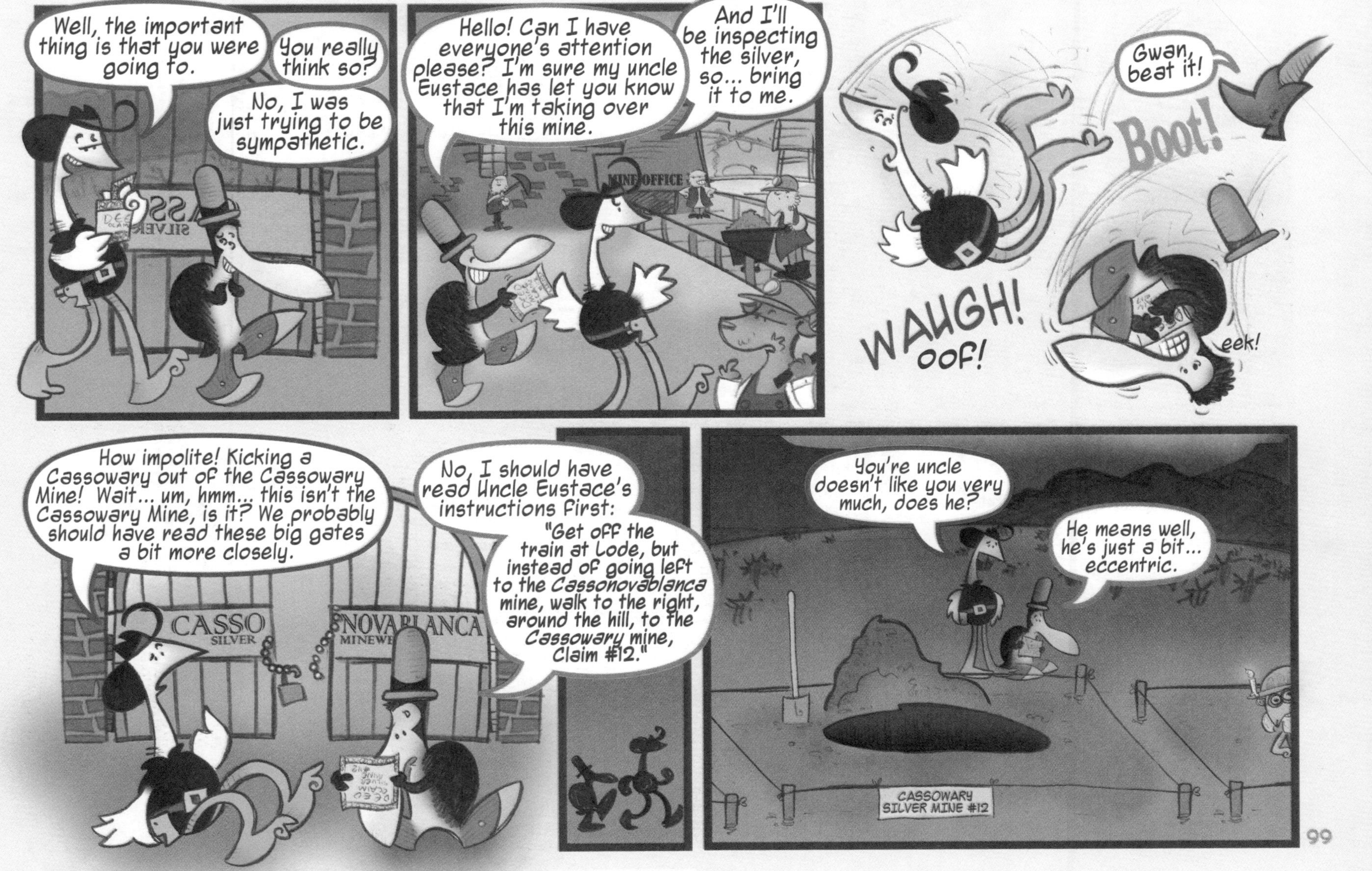

Well, the important thing is that you were going to.
You really think so?
No, I was just trying to be sympathetic.
Hello! Can I have everyone's attention please? I'm sure my uncle Eustace has let you know that I'm taking over this mine.
And I'll be inspecting the silver, so... bring it to me.
MINE OFFICE
Gwan, beat it!
Boot!
WAUGH!
OOF!
eek!
How impolite! Kicking a Cassowary out of the Cassowary Mine! Wait... um, hmm... this isn't the Cassowary Mine, is it? We probably should have read these big gates a bit more closely.
CASSO SILVER
No, I should have read Uncle Eustace's instructions first:
"Get off the train at Lode, but instead of going left to the Cassonovablanca mine, walk to the right, around the hill, to the Cassowary mine, Claim #12."
You're uncle doesn't like you very much, does he?
He means well, he's just a bit... eccentric.
CASSOWARY SILVER MINE #12

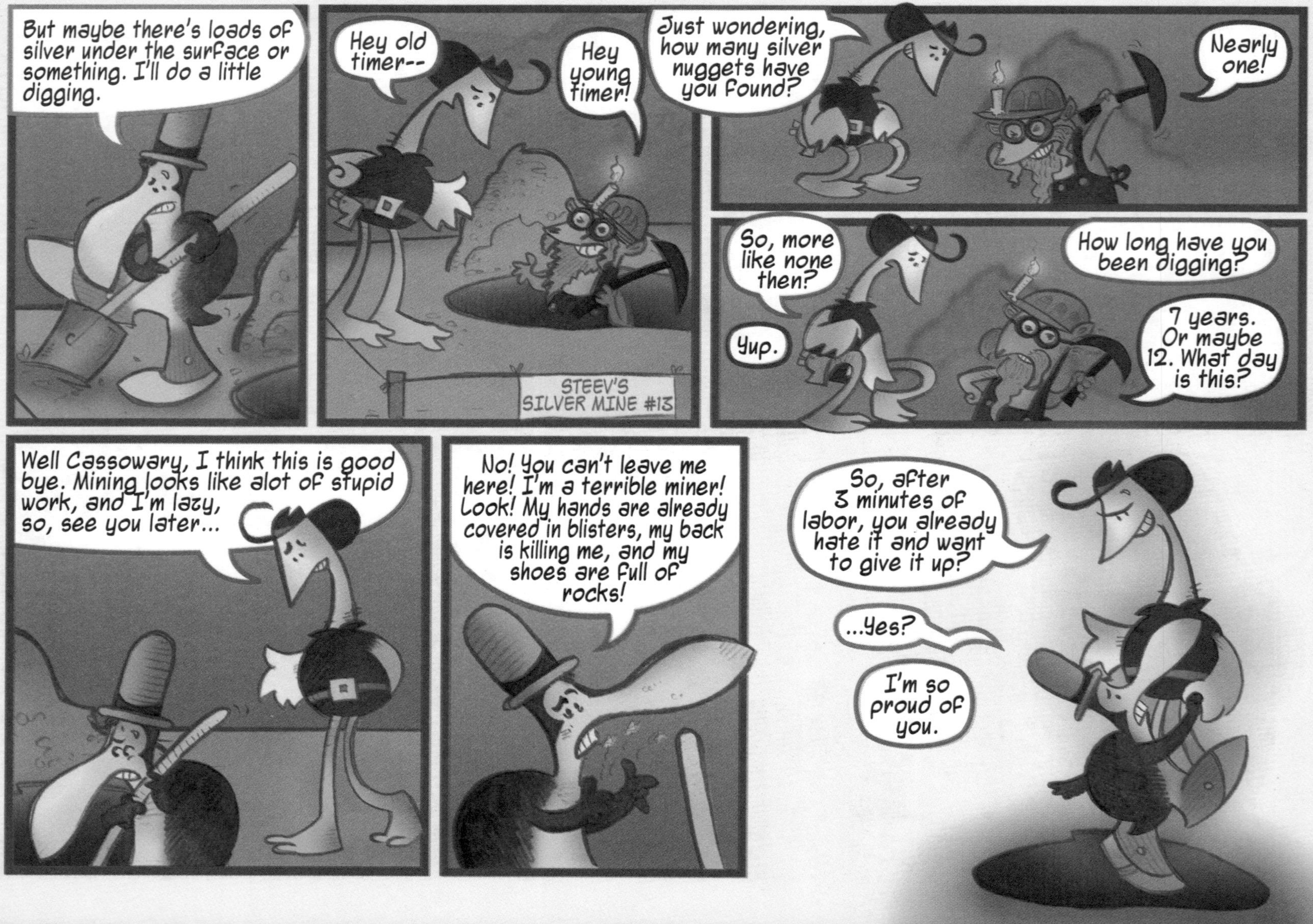
But maybe there's loads of silver under the surface or something. I'll do a little digging.
Hey old timer--
Hey young timer!
Just wondering, how many silver nuggets have you found?
Nearly one!
STEEV'S SILVER MINE #13
So, more like none then?
Yup.
How long have you been digging?
7 years. Or maybe 12. What day is this?
Well Cassowary, I think this is good bye. Mining looks like alot of stupid work, and I'm lazy, so, see you later...
No! You can't leave me here! I'm a terrible miner! Look! My hands are already covered in blisters, my back is killing me, and my shoes are full of rocks!
So, after 3 minutes of labor, you already hate it and want to give it up?
...Yes?
I'm so proud of you.

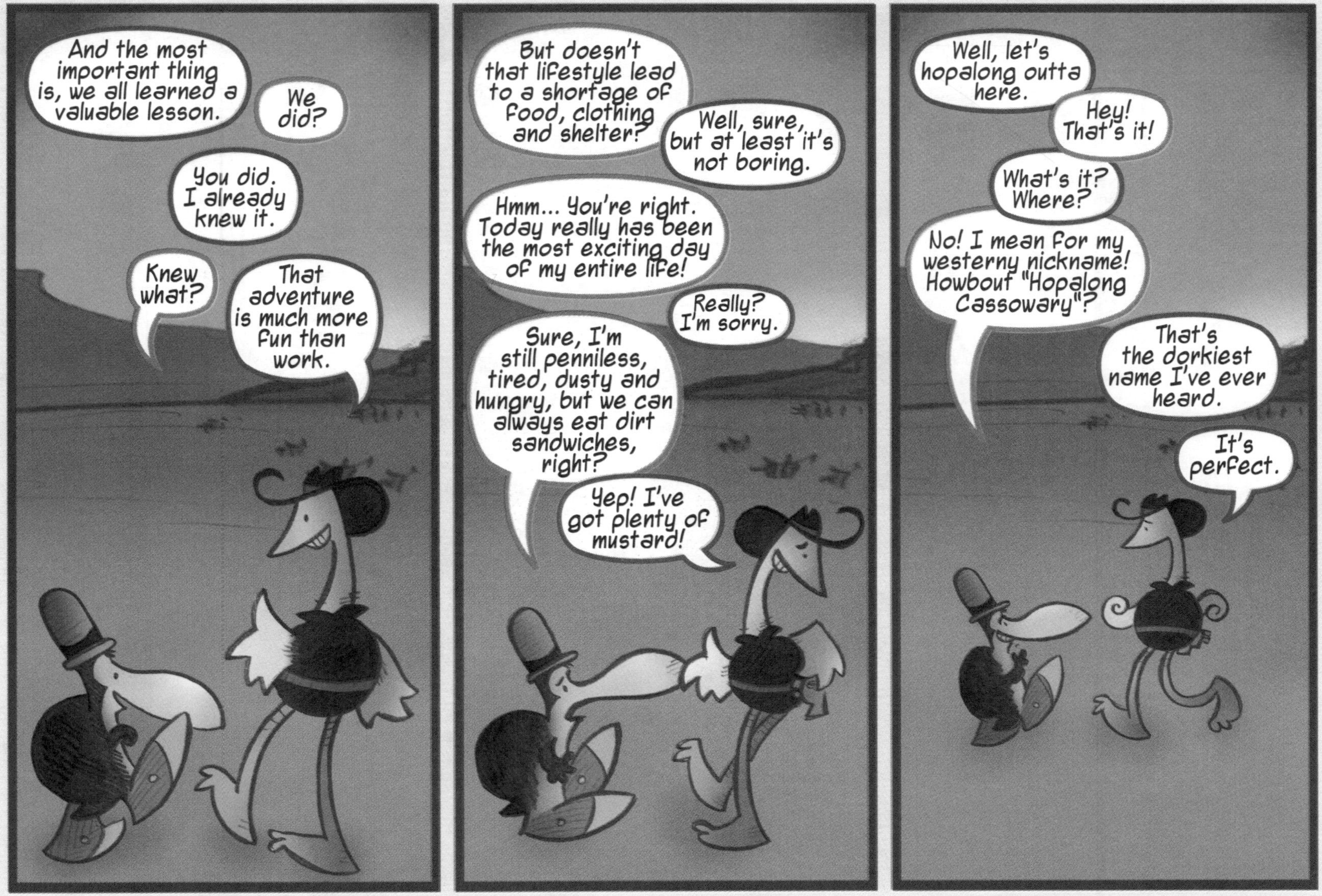
And the most important thing is, we all learned a valuable lesson.
We did?
You did. I already knew it.
Knew what?
That adventure is much more fun than work.
But doesn't that lifestyle lead to a shortage of food, clothing and shelter?
Well, sure, but at least it's not boring.
Hmm... You're right. Today really has been the most exciting day of my entire life!
Really? I'm sorry.
Sure, I'm still penniless, tired, dusty and hungry, but we can always eat dirt sandwiches, right?
Yep! I've got plenty of mustard!
Well, let's hopalong outta here.
Hey! That's it!
What's it? Where?
No! I mean for my westerny nickname! Howbout "Hopalong Cassowary"?
That's the dorkiest name I've ever heard.
It's perfect.

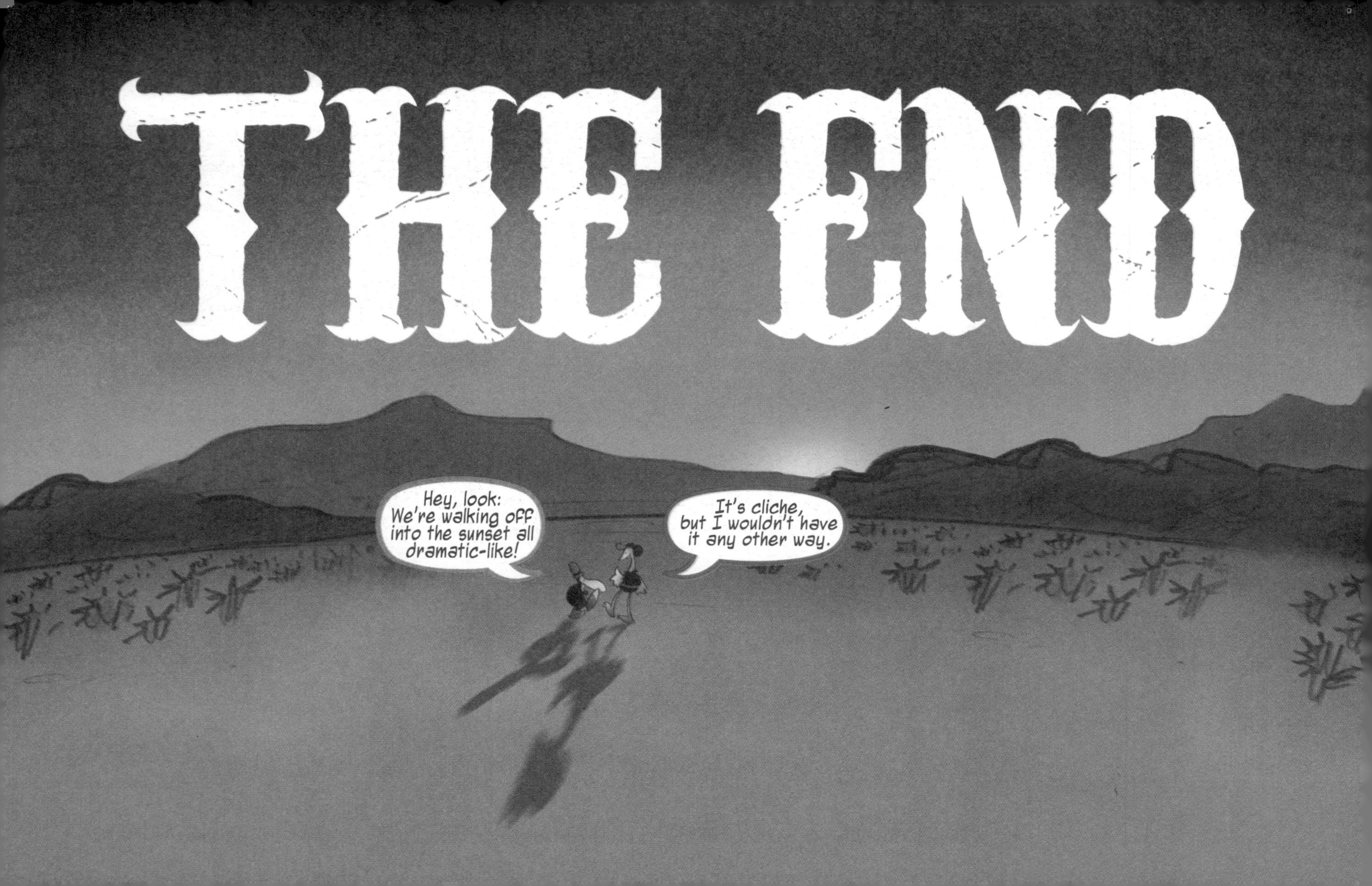
THE END
Hey, look: We're walking off into the sunset all dramatic-like!
It's cliche, but I wouldn't have it any other way.

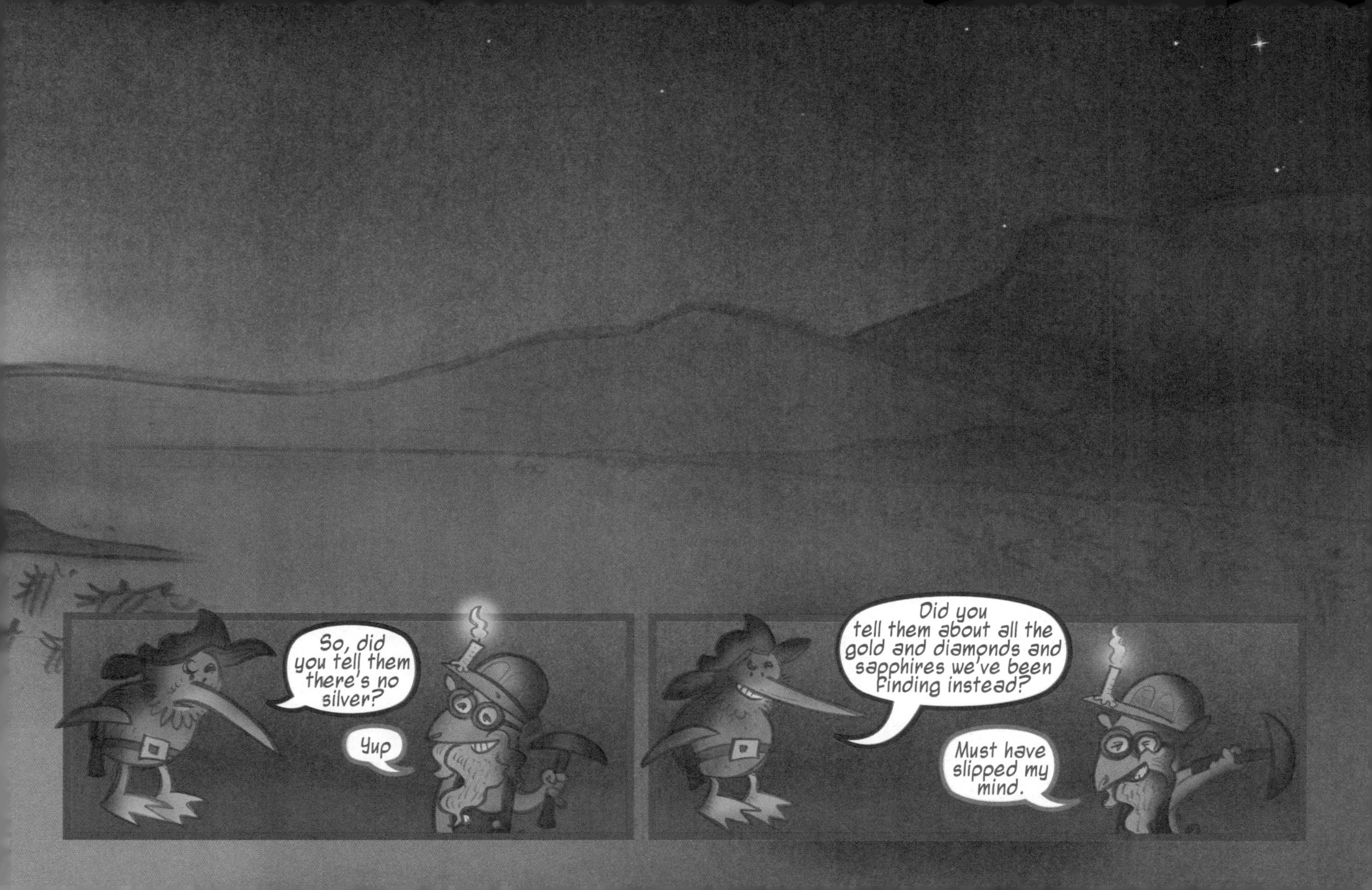
So, did you tell them there's no silver?
Yup
Did you tell them about all the gold and diamonds and sapphires we've been finding instead?
Must have slipped my mind.

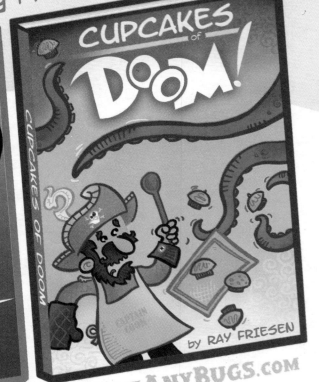